Challenges of the Internet of Things

Digital Tools and Uses Set

coordinated by
Imad Saleh

Volume 7

Challenges of the Internet of Things

Technology, Use, Ethics

Edited by

Imad Saleh
Mehdi Ammi
Samuel Szoniecky

WILEY

First published 2018 in Great Britain and the United States by ISTE Ltd and John Wiley & Sons, Inc.

ISTE Ltd
27-37 St George's Road
London SW19 4EU
UK

www.iste.co.uk

John Wiley & Sons, Inc.
111 River Street
Hoboken, NJ 07030
USA

www.wiley.com

Cet ouvrage a bénéficié d'une aide de l'ANR au titre du programme Investissement d'avenir (ANR-10-LABX-80-01).
Special copy – not for sale, cannot be returned or exchanged.

Library of Congress Control Number: 2018949572

British Library Cataloguing-in-Publication Data
A CIP record for this book is available from the British Library
ISBN 978-1-78630-361-5

Contents

Chapter 4. Enabling Fast-prototyping of Connected Things using the WiNo* Family 77

Adrien VAN DEN BOSSCHE, Réjane DALCÉ and Thierry VAL

Chapter 5. Multi-standard Receiver for Medical IoT Sensor Networks. 105

Tarak ARBI and Benoit GELLER

Chapter 10. Modeling Power to Act for an Ethics of the Internet of Things

Samuel SZONIECKY

Introduction

It is our pleasure to present the book *Challenges of the Internet of Things: Technology, Use and Ethics* which is based on a selection of articles presented in the French Open Science journal *Internet des Objets*, available at: https://www.openscience.fr/Internet-des-objets.

This book examines the problems pertaining to the IoT based on three different approaches: technology, use and ethics. The technology used to produce artifacts (physical objects, infrastructures), programs (algorithmic, software) and data (Big Data, linked data, metadata, ontologies) is the subject of many innovations in the field of the IoT, itself rich and stimulating. Along with this technological boom, the IoT is now used in new fields of application, including transport, administration, housing, maintenance, health, sports and well-being. Being a favored interface with digital ecosystems at the center of social exchanges, the IoT is developing the power to act with both good and bad consequences, thereby making it difficult to assess fair activity[1].

In Chapter 1, "Internet of Things (IoT): Concepts, Issues, Challenges and Perspectives"[2], Imad Saleh presents an in-depth review of the subject based on his article published in 2017 [SAL 17]. The author presents the definitions of connected objects, the Internet of Things and the Internet of Everything (IoE). He then establishes a connection between the IoT and Big Data, and cloud computing and data science. Furthermore, he provides the details of the issues and challenges encountered in the IoT, both at a

---

Introduction written by Imad SALEH, Mehdi AMMI and Samuel SZONIECKY.
1 https://ido2017.sciencesconf.org/.
2 [SAL 17].

technical and a human level in the IoT ecosystem, and presents blockchain and its relationship with the IoT. In conclusion, the author provides an overview of the IoT using a figure for clarification.

In Chapter 2, "Deep Learning Approach of Raw Human Activity Data", Hamdi Amroun, M'Hamed (Hamy) Temkit and Mehdi Ammi offer an approach to recognizing certain physical activities using a network of connected objects. The approach involves the classification of certain human activities: walking up and down the stairs, standing still, sitting and lying down. This study uses a network of connected objects: a smartwatch, a smartphone and a connected remote control. These objects were worn by participants during an uncontrolled experiment (i.e. in an uncontrolled environment). Sensor data from these devices were classified using deep neural networks (DNN) without prior pre-processing of input data (raw data). The authors show how their DNN model provides the best results compared with other conventional models such as Decision Trees (DT) and Support Vector Machines (SVM). The results show that participant activity was classified with an accuracy of more than 98.53% on average.

In Chapter 3, "Study and Development of a Smart Cup for Monitoring Post-Stroke Patients' Activities at Home", Mehdi Ammi, Mehdi Boukallel, Margarita Anastassova, Hamdi Amroun and Maxence Bobin present the existing platforms for post-stroke follow-up and activity recognition. They then introduce the design concept for a "smart cup", which includes collected data and sensory feedback offered to patients. Next, the technical realization of a prototype is described, as well as data processing information including the calculation of the orientation of the cup and its capacity to detect and characterize tremors, followed by a method of analysis. Furthermore, they present planned studies with health professionals and patients. Finally, they conclude with perspectives concerning the smart cup.

In Chapter 4, "Enabling Fast-prototyping of Connected Things using the WiNo* Family", Adrien van den Bossche, Réjane Dalcé and Thierry Val discuss the ability of an open platform to provide fast prototyping of nodes that can be used for connected objects. One of the strategic choices was to place the platform in the open-source ecosystem, from both hardware and software points of view. Their contributions are distinguished from the competition by using components from the Arduino world, the ability to integrate a large number of transceivers and therefore a very large diversity of existing and future physical layers, as well as ergonomics that facilitates the development of protocols and innovation applications.

In Chapter 5, "Multi-standard Receiver for Medical IoT Sensor Networks", Benoit Geller and Tarak Arbi study the rise in the narrow band mode of the IEEE 802.15.6 standard, which provides information about an OFDM receiver (multiple orthogonal subcarriers; see [MIC 01]), which can be used, for example, by a conventional WiFi receiver to serve as a multi-standard receiver.

In Chapter 6, "Ambient Atoms: A Device for Ambient Information Visualization", Sébastien Crouzy, Stan Borkowski and Sabine Coquillart offer a new ambient visualization device known as Ambient Atoms. Ambient Atoms is a simple connected and flexible object which is in the form of a table where information can be symbolically visualized. A sample application of an informative visualization of an apartment is discussed.

In Chapter 7, "New Robust Protocol for IoV Communications", Lylia Alouache, Nga Nguyen, Makhlouf Aliouat and Rachid Chelouah first provide some definitions of vehicular networks, application domains, communication technologies and quality of service (QoS) obstacles in the Internet of Vehicles (IoV). They then present their proposition to detect and circumvent disconnection zones using a new geographic routing protocol based on: (1) the estimation of the contact time between vehicles, (2) the data loads to be transferred and (3) the logs of communication anomalies. The objective is to ensure the availability, reliability and robustness of inter-vehicular communications by taking these three different criteria into account in an algorithm for routing data packets.

In Chapter 8, "Interconnected Virtual Space and Theater: A Research–Creation Project on Theatrical Performance Space in the Network Era", Georges Gagneré, Cédric Plessiet and Rémy Sohier present their experiments based on a cross-examination between theatrical staging specialists and researchers involved in virtual reality, digital art and video games. In the first section, the authors discuss the scenic device upon which their presentation is based. In the second section, they discuss in detail the impact of augmenting the player's game using an avatar, in relation to the scenic constraints encountered on a theatrical stage. In the third section, the authors present the IT aspects of the project by focusing on the exchanges between the various elements of the device and by describing the algorithms that allow for the real-time movement of an actor using capturing devices. Finally, they discuss how the experimental device between a physical actor and an avatar modifies the nature of the collaboration that takes place between the directors, actors and digital artists in terms of the direction of an actor/avatar.

In Chapter 9, "Mobile Telephones and Mobile Health: A Societal Question at Issue in Public Space", Brigitte Juanals discusses elements from the field of Information and Communication Sciences and deals with socio-political challenges and mobile information access systems, including the production and access to online content and services from a portable computer terminal, with particular attention paid to mobile phones (smartphones). He addresses the challenges of the IoT concerning the use of socio-technical systems in mobile health, which has destabilized the traditional organization of health itself.

In Chapter 10, "Modeling of Power to Act for an Ethics of the Internet of Things", Samuel Szoniecky discusses current reflections on ethics and the IoT and opens a democratic debate on the problems they cause, in order to propose a method for modeling the IoT's power of action which aims to evaluate and compare the ethics of these technologies. In order to do this, Szoniecky developed tools to model these connected objects in order to understand their impact on our daily lives. The aim of this research is to propose a simple signage system in order to indicate the ethical position of objects, such as pictograms which inform consumers about the energy quality of household appliances. However, before arriving at the expression of the power to act in this simplified form, the author questions the theoretical and graphic principles of these diagrams as well as their design.

We would like to warmly thank all the authors who contributed to this book as well as our colleagues Jean-Max Noyer, Ioan Roxin, Christophe Kolski and Richard Chbeir for their contribution to the publication of the *Internet des Objets* journal and Khalid Mekouar, President and Pedagogical Director at ESISA (Morocco), and Ibtissam Mekouar for their kindness, availability and support during our conferences in Fez.

Internet of Things (IoT): Concepts, Issues, Challenges and Perspectives

This chapter is an in-depth review of our article published in 2017. We considered some elements to develop concepts based on the IoT. In this chapter, we present: (1) the connected object (CO), (2) a definition of the Internet of Things, (3) steps and technologies in the IoT ecosystem, (4) IoT to the Internet of Everything (IoE), (5) IoT and Big Data, (6) cloud computing applied to Big Data and the IoT, (7) data science and the IoT, (8) issues and challenges of the IoT, (9) opportunities and threats in the IoT ecosystem, (10) security of the IoT, (11) blockchain and the IoT and (12) conclusion, summarizing the perspectives of the IoT.

1.1. Introduction

The Internet in general and the Web in particular have continued to evolve – from the Web of information to the Web of individualized[1] Things – via various connected objects thanks to miniaturization and technological development, which make room for a double approach: being connected and communicating consistently without any constraints as regards space and time so as to meet the demands and needs of users in terms of services, communication and information [ROX 17, THE 13].

Chapter written by Imad SALEH.

1 In 2011, Vlad Trifa coined the concept of the "Web of Things" (WoT) in his thesis as being the integration of connected objects on the Internet as well as on the Web. This concept is based on the coupling of "social, programmable, semantic, physical and real-time webs, many particular facets that the WoT would have" [ROX 17, p. 38]. Vlad Mihai Trifa, "Building blocks for a participatory Web of Things", thesis, Eidgenössische Technische Hochschule (ETH) Zürich, no. 19890, available at: http://e-collection.library.ethz.ch/view/eth:4641.

The Internet is gradually transforming into a HyperNetwork, just like a network consisting of multitudes of connections between artifacts (physical, documentary), actors (biological, algorithmic), scripts and concepts (linked data, metadata, ontologies, folksonomy), called the "Internet of Things (IoT)", connecting billions of people and objects. It has become the most powerful tool ever invented by man to create, modify and share information. This transformation shows the evolution of the Internet: from a computer network to a network of personal computers, then to a nomadic network integrating communication technologies [CHA 12]. Developments in machine-to-machine (M2M) technologies for remote machine control and the first use of IP (Internet Protocol) in the year 2000 on mobile cellular networks have accelerated the evolution from M2M to the IoT [WOO 11].

1.2. The connected object (CO)

Before defining IoT concepts, it is important to define a connected object as being a device whose primary purpose is neither to be a computer system nor to be a Web Access interface. For example, an object such as a coffee machine or a lock was designed without integrating a computer system or Internet connection. Integrating an Internet connection to a CO enriches it in terms of functionality and interaction with its environment. This makes it an *Enriched CO (ECO)*; for example, the integration of an Internet connection to a coffee machine will make it remotely accessible.

A CO can independently interact with the physical world without human intervention. It has several constraints such as memory, bandwidth or energy usage. It must be adapted for a purpose and has some form of intelligence, which is the ability to receive and transmit data with software through embedded sensors [ROX 17]. A CO has value when connected to other objects and software components; for example, a connected watch is only relevant within a health or wellbeing-oriented ecosystem, which goes far beyond knowing the time.

A connected object (CO) has three key elements:

– generated or received, stored or transmitted data;

– algorithms to process this data;

– the ecosystem in which it will react and integrate.

Use properties of a CO [SAL 17] are:

– ergonomics (usability, workability, etc.);

– aestheticism (shapes, colors, sounds, sensations, etc.);

– usage (cultural history, profile, social matrix, etc.);

– metamorphism (adaptability, customization, modulation, etc.).

Some researchers talk of "hyper objects" [MAV 03] as able to pool their resources to perform everyday tasks as they are linked by "invisible links" within the same ecosystem. In this context, researchers such as [WEI 93] have already considered ubiquitous computing to be where *"the most profound technologies are the ones that have become invisible. Those ones which, when tied together, form the fabric of our daily life to the point of becoming inseparable"* [WEI 91, p. 94].

Communication between objects is passed through identifications that are known to each other. An object must have one or more IDs (barcodes) to be recognized by another so as to establish connection. The GS1 system has proposed a technology based on RFID tags[2] that will uniquely associate the logistical information related to an object with a URL. Google has proposed the Physical Web project to uniquely associate a URL with an object[3]. The ubiquity of heterogeneous, mobile and fragile objects in our life poses the problem of trust models adapted to this complex and fragile ecosystem [SZO 17]. Behind these technologies is the fight for norms and standards for the IoT between giant Internet companies because each wishes to impose its technologies.

1.3. Internet of Things: definition

Kevin Ahston[4], the co-founder of MIT's Auto-ID Center, used the term "Internet Of Things" in 1999. The term IoT was first used during a presentation made by Procter & Gamble (P&G). This term conjures up the

---

2 RFID is a barcode-like radio-identification process.

3 https://google.github.io/physical-web/.

4 He participated in the creation of the RFID standard.

world of objects, devices and sensors that are interconnected[5] through the Internet.

The CERP-IoT (Cluster of European Research Projects on the Internet of Things) defines the Internet of Things as: "*a dynamic infrastructure of a global network. This global network has auto-configuration capabilities based on standards and interoperable communication protocols. In this network, physical and virtual objects have identities, physical attributes, virtual personalities, intelligent interfaces, and are integrated into the network in a transparent way*" [SUN 10].

This definition presents the two sides of the IoT: the temporal and spatial sides, which allow people to connect from anywhere at any time through connected objects [CHA 12] (Figure 1.1) (smartphones, tablets, sensors, CCTV cameras, etc.). The Internet of Things must be designed for easy use and secure manipulation to avoid potential threats and risks, while masking the underlying technological complexity.

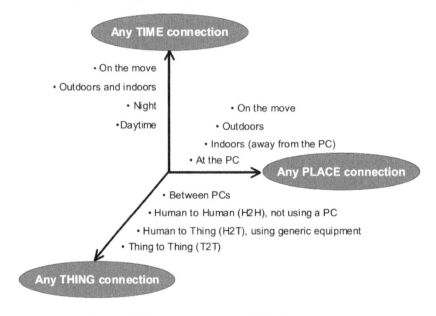

Figure 1.1. *A new dimension for the IoT (source: ITU 2005 [INT 05, taken from [CHA 12])*

5 "That 'Internet of Things' Thing", *RFID Journal*, available at: http://www.rfidjournal. com/articles/view?4986 visited January 2, 2017.

The rapid evolution of this "Internet of Things" shifts the balance between computer and everyday products due to two factors: the generalization of computing resources and the ownership of Web services by users [THE 13].

1.3.1. *Applications*

IoT applications are now practically affecting our day-to-day life such as:

– health and telemonitoring systems to help people;

– connected agriculture to optimize the use of water;

– connected vehicles to help optimize urban traffic management;

– connected appliances to help optimize the consumption and distribution of electrical energy;

– digital arts;

– connected watches for wellbeing and sport.

These examples of applications show that the IoT is integrated into our daily lives and improves people's quality of life [BOU 17a, BOU 17b, NOY 17, AMR 17, GAG 17, CRO 17]. It gives rise to a new market by creating new jobs and trades. It also helps businesses grow, and gives impetus to competitiveness. According to the GSMA [GSM 18], the IoT is a huge growing industry at all hardware and software levels that is expected to provide mobile operators with a comfortable income of about \$1200 billion by 2020.

1.4. Steps and technologies in the IoT ecosystem

COs are at the heart of the IoT, but it is necessary to connect all of these objects and enable them to exchange information and interact within the same network. The setting up of the IoT goes through the following steps: identification, sensors setup, object interconnection, integration and network connection. Table 1.1 presents possible steps and protocols [ROX 17].

Identify	Capture	Connect	Integrate	Network
Enabling the identification of each connected element.	Implementing devices that bring the real and virtual worlds closer. The objects basic functions (the temperature sensor for a thermometer, for example).	Establishing a connection between the objects so they can communicate and exchange data.	Using a communication means of connecting objects to the virtual world.	Linking objects and their data to the computing world via a network (the Internet, for example).
IPv4, IPv6	MEMS, RF MEMS, NEMS	SigFox, LoRa	RFID, NFC, Bluetooth, Bluetooth LE, ZigBee, WiFi, cellular networks	CoAP, MQTT, AllJoyn, REST HTTP

Table 1.1. *Steps and technologies to set up the IoT [ROX 17, p. 73]*

1.4.1. *IoT architecture*

Given the rapid development of the IoT, it became necessary to have a reference architecture that would standardize systems design and promote interoperability[6] and communication between the different IoT ecosystems (Figure 1.2 presents the IoT/M2M value chain). For example, an object with the X mark will have to send information to a Y platform via the Z network. Interoperability can be seen from two standpoints, either "closed" within large ecosystems that share the same standards, or "native", based on more global standards, for example, the v1 of the Internet with IP or HTTP.

---

6 See Frédéric Charles' articles in the journal Zdnet (in French): http://www.zdnet.fr/blogs/ green-si/iot-sortir-de-l-internet-des-silos-39855298.htm.

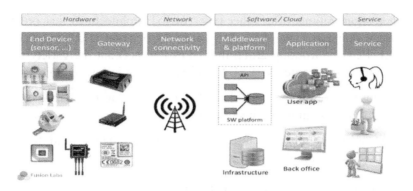

Figure 1.2. *Stéphane Monteil's presentation (January 2016)[7]*

In March 2015, the Internet Architecture Board (IAB)[8] issued the RFC[9] 7452. It proposed four common interaction patterns between IoT actors[10] [see ROX 17, p. 64]:

– *Communication between objects:* this model is based on wireless communication between two objects. Information is transmitted through the integration of wireless communication technology such as ZigBee or Bluetooth.

– *Communication from objects to the cloud:* in this model, data collected by sensors are transmitted to service platforms via a network.

– *Communication from objects to a gateway:* this model is based on an intermediary that links the sensors and applications in the cloud.

– *From objects to back-end data sharing[11]:* the purpose of this model is to share data between service providers. It is based on the "programmable web" concept. Manufacturers are implementing an API that allows aggregated data to be used by other manufacturers [ROX 17].

7 "Microsoft Azure IoT Services, architectures, demos", available at: https://www.fusionlabs. fr/language/fr/livres-blancs/.
8 IAB's goal is to ensure Internet development. The organization is divided into working groups, "task forces", including the Internet Engineering Task Force (IETF).
9 Requests For Comments (RFC) are a numbered series of official documents describing the technical aspects of the Internet or different computer hardware.
10 "RFC 7452 – Architectural Considerations in Smart Object Networking", available at: https://tools.ietf.org/html/rfc7452, visited June 11, 2017.
11 The term "back-end" refers to the non-visible part of a software. These are algorithms and other computer processes.

Other organizations offer other types of IoT architectures that prioritize application contexts. The IEEE Standards Association (IEEE-SA) created the IEEE P2413[12] working group that takes into account the variety of IoT application domain contexts. IEEE P2413 has set the following objectives:

– propose a reference model that takes into account relationships, interactions and common architectural elements for various domains;

– develop a reference architecture that is accountable and take into account all areas of applications [ROX 17].

IEEE P2413 proposes a three-level model[13]:

– *Applications*: this concerns applications and services offered to customers.

– *Cloud computing*: this concerns the service platforms for which data is intended. This level makes it possible to establish a link between sensors and platform networks as well as data processing software [ROX 17].

– *Sensor networks*: the lowest level corresponds to sensors and the communication between them (machine-to-machine). This is a network of sensors which generates data and subsequently supplies service offerings [ROX 17].

This model is called "cloud-centric"[14] because it is largely based on the cloud. The IEEE considers cloud computing as a central element for the development of the IoT.

Other companies like the American company Cisco, have proposed layered architectures. In October 2013, Jim Green presented "Building the Internet of Things", the model envisaged by his company for the IoT. It is composed of seven layers (Figure 1.3).

---

12 "P2413 – Standard for an Architectural Framework for the Internet of Things (IoT)", IEEE SA, available at: https://standards.ieee.org/develop/project/2413.html, accessed June 11, 2017.
13 See Ioan Roxin and Aymeric Bouchereau, "Introduction to the Technologies of the ecosystem of the Internet of Things", in Nasreddine Bouhaï and Imad Saleh (ed.), *Internet of Things: Evolutions and Innovations*, ISTE Ltd, London and John Wiley & Sons, New York, 2017.
14 "Cloud-centric" refers to a concept centered on cloud computing.

IoT World Forum Reference Model

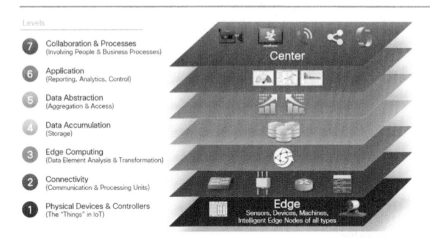

Levels

7 Collaboration & Processes
(Involving People & Business Processes)

6 Application
(Reporting, Analytics, Control)

5 Data Abstraction
(Aggregation & Access)

4 Data Accumulation
(Storage)

3 Edge Computing
(Data Element Analysis & Transformation)

2 Connectivity
(Communication & Processing Units)

1 Physical Devices & Controllers
(The "Things" in IoT)

Center

Edge
Sensors, Devices, Machines,
Intelligent Edge Nodes of all types

Figure 1.3. *The different layers of the Internet of Things (according to Cisco[15])*

These models show companies' enthusiasm for open and interoperable IoT ecosystem developments to be accepted by market participants. Despite these architectures, much is still to be done to propose a global reference model that takes into account the specificities of the IoT.

1.5. From the IoT to the Internet of Everything (IoE)

According to Cisco[16] [CIS 13], the convergence between the networks of people, processes, data and objects, and the IoT is moving toward the Internet of Everything (IoE) (see Figure 1.4). It is a multidimensional Internet that combines the fields of the IoT and Big Data [INS 15].

---

15 "Building the Internet of Things | An IoT Reference Model", http://fr.slideshare.net/Cisco/building-the-internet-of-things-an-iot-reference-model.
16 http://www.cisco.com/c/dam/en_us/solutions/industries/docs/gov/everything-for-cities.pdf.

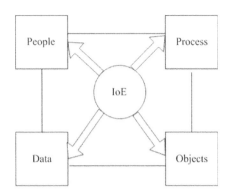

Figure 1.4. *Internet of Everything (IoE)*

"*People:* Connect people in a more relevant way and with more value.

Process: Provide the right information to the right person (or machine) at the right time.

Data: Rely on data to bring out the most useful information for decision-making.

Objects: Physical devices and objects connected to the Internet for intelligent decision-making". (Source: [CIS 13], taken from [INS 15]).

The IoE presents a broader vision of the IoT as the network is distributed and decentralized. It is equipped with artificial intelligence at all levels to better protect networks and allow the user to have personalized data, which helps in decision-making. This is a marketing idea of the IoE.

1.6. IoT and Big Data

Big Data[17] is a huge volume of digital data generated by Internet users, connected objects and so on. Big Data is at the heart of IoT development. Without this data, COs remain as physical devices unconnected to the real

---

17 According to the archives of the digital library of the Association for Computing Machinery (ACM), the term "Big Data" appeared in October 1997, in scientific articles dealing with technological challenges with the aim of visualizing "large data sets" [ROX 17, p. 48].

world. Big Data is a global concept which refers to six variables (6Vs) [ROX 17, p. 48]:

– *volume*: this relates to the volume of generated data;

– *variety*: this relates to data types, namely raw, semi-structured or unstructured data, coming from several sources such as the Web, connected objects and networks;

– *speed or velocity*: this relates to the frequency of generated, captured and shared data;

– *veracity*: this relates to the reliability and credibility of collected data;

– *value*: this relates to the advantages derived from the use of Big Data;

– *visualization*: this relates to the restitution of information, so that it is comprehensible and interpretable in spite of its volume, structure, source and constant evolution [ROX 17].

Today, we know where, when and who produces structured data or not (Big Data). These clarifications make *"the success of Twitter which, in addition to the textual content of the message, encapsulates spatio-temporal information and by crossing with the profile of the author, adds information on a particular social network"* [SZO 12]. This poses significant epistemological and methodological problems [BOY 12, RIE 12] with regard to the multiplication of "micro-interpretations" of data and their representation [SZO 12].

These data play an important role in the economic development of companies. The analyses of "digital traces" left by the use of the Internet allow us to personalize the service suitably for the user's profile and location. Data produced by connected objects can provide information about user habits, skills or relationships. Digital companies have already understood the importance of controlling user traces and increasing their number. Some companies offer to control this data and identify objects. This raises ethical and authenticity issues for the user of produced data. In this context, the more objects possess intelligent algorithms to perceive and act, the more they become autonomous and increase problems related to private life. It is therefore important to develop technologies to allow objects to have *auto-immunity* against malicious codes or unauthorized penetrations to prevent data propagation or erroneous codes. Data can be located and stored in a centralized or globalized database, in databases distributed using cloud computing technologies.

Some data may or may not be useful, but the major challenge lies in contextualizing this data to make sense of it, so as to create value for users and businesses. Data transmitted by the IoT are raw and unprocessed materials, which are useful when they are combined and processed to form meaningful information. It is necessary to filter data for their utility knowing that data may be useful for some processes but not for others. The role of intelligent algorithms can be a solution to filter the relevance of data. Nevertheless, it is difficult to systematically transform this huge data into information and subsequently into knowledge that can be used in everyday life. One approach consists of semantically enriching these data through ontologies to facilitate their reuse and to allow the implementation of reasoning mechanisms [SEY 15]. Moreover, if knowledge is complemented by experiments, data will be transformed into knowledge and will enrich the abilities of the IoT ecosystem (Figure 1.5). Data generated or produced by the IoT raises questions regarding their owners and the right to them.

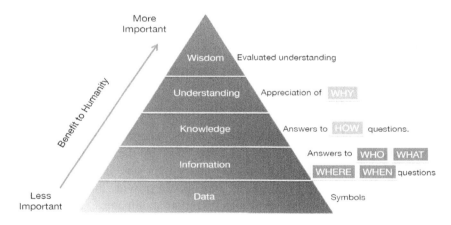

Figure 1.5. *Slide 11, taken from the presentation of Bob Gill, P.Eng., FEC, smIEEE, November 29, 2016. For a color version of this figure, see www.iste.co.uk/saleh/challenges.zip*

1.7. Cloud computing applied to Big Data and the IoT

Cloud computing platforms will store, retrieve and analyze data from remote servers. *"Cloud computing applied to Big Data and the IoT allows the centralization of data and processing power. Cognitive analysis and automatic learning techniques [machine learning] are among the 'tools' that exploit large volumes of data"* [ROX 17, p. 49]. Research in the cognitive field and the improvement of learning techniques necessarily contribute to the development of the IoT and the best exploitation of data generated by objects. [ROX 17, p. 49]

1.8. Data science and the IoT

Data science is a science capable of providing a necessary foundation for Big Data [PIN 17, p. 132]. It makes data permanently generated by the visual and interpretable IoT.

It is based on techniques such as *data mining, machine learning, visual analytics, cloud computing, parallel computing and information retrieval* [PIN 17, CIT 18]. Data science deals with data processing and the visualization process in all areas based on the constant flow of data such as transportation, insurance and health [PIN 17].

Data science precisely defines the current forms of analytical visualization [PIN 17]. Data visualization is a fundamental step in identifying models, trends and relationships between data using Big Data. Visualization allows the emergence of the field of study called *visual analytics*, which is based on *"the use and interactive visual analysis of large and complex data (dataset)"* [PIN 17]. It *"represents the analytical process and requires a high degree of monitoring and human–machine interaction"* [PIN 17, p. 132]. Data science makes it possible to discover new algorithms for data visualization [CHE 15].

Figure 1.6 summarizes the relationship between the technologies described below and the IoT [NOY 17].

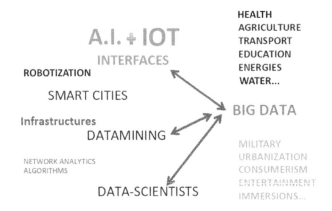

Figure 1.6. *Taken from Jean-Max Noyer's article [NOY 17]*

1.9. Stakes and challenges of the IoT

The IoT affects all areas of the co-construction of knowledge, from the management of companies and administrations through to educational and hyper-urban technologies. It transforms our localized relationship into a globalized relationship by transcending geographical boundaries [SAL 12, SAL 14]. These technological, societal and human transformations raise many questions about societal and economic change, as well as research, creativity and innovation. It is important to think of building new instruments for a technical future at the service of human development.

1.9.1. *Technological challenges*

The IoT is at the center of all modern technological developments, where the issue of interfaces and protocols in a major strategic situation is raised. "*All information, be it textual, sound or visual [and also input gesture] is in constant interaction with all the others, it becomes reticular*"[18]. The IoT transforms the Internet into a globalized HyperNetwork with all its points of forming as many information nodes as possible without borders [SAL 12, SAL 14].

---

18 Jean-Pierre Balpe, available at: http://hyperfiction.blogs.liberation.fr/2007/10/25/des-hypertextes/, visited January 10, 2018.

Challenges in terms of computer programming are immense. New methods of design, development, debugging and maintenance must be set up. From innovative symbolic languages, future computer scientists will transform simple code lines into autonomous agents that are capable of existing in the complexity of ubiquitous and distributed systems, to adapt to users' demands in order to recommend new uses or even accompany them in the evolution of their modes of existence.

A major challenge for the IoT at the technical and functional level is to manage technological heterogeneity and standards of objects coupled with multitudes of application needs and uses in terms of security services. It should be noted that these needs can evolve over time depending on the context and taste. In fact, how do we ensure individual authentication of several million heterogeneous objects, equipped with heterogeneous communication technologies, across multiple administrative domains? [VER 11]. This raises managerial issues and the security of objects in a heterogeneous environment at the physical and logical level. "*In fact, the Internet of Things is a complex system in which people interact with a technological ecosystem based on smart objects and through complex processes. The interaction of these four components of the IoT (people, smart objects, technological ecosystem, processes) are giving rise to a systemic dimension to the security of the IoT*" [CHA 12, p. 54]. Therefore, tensions on the security of the IoT are created during the interaction of smart objects with its environment. These tensions (*trust, responsibility, identification and autoimmunity*) are characterized by a cognitive and systemic dimension induced by the growing autonomy of objects [CHA 12].

1.9.2. *Societal challenges*

The challenge for the future will be to respond as creatively as possible to anthropological concerns, climate regime shifts, biodiversity, industrial implications and energy transition, bio-political involvement as well as ethics of accessibility, cultural diversity and redefinitions of the notion of "personal data". However, questions are also raised concerning the dissemination of intellectual technologies as counterpowers in a centric data society, by proposing models of analysis, conceptual frameworks equal to what is advanced, design methods and rules of usage recognized by all users and by new collective intelligence of usage.

1.9.3. *Environmental challenges*

The constantly increasing number of connected objects has consequences on the environment. It can be translated from the increase in electronic waste and their recycling, on the one hand, and energy consumption, on the other hand. This is a major challenge that is attracting more and more governments to study the impact of connected objects on global warming and their impact on populations. For example, the European Union[19] has set a 2020 target to reduce CO_2 emissions by 20% and improve energy efficiency by 20% in order to attain 20% renewable energy. It is therefore necessary that, before manufacturing COs, companies study their service lifespan and usefulness for users in order to reduce the production of unnecessary objects and unnecessary energy consumption.

1.9.4. *Confidence in the IoT*

Thus, the degree of confidence in the IoT and its acceptance are prerequisites for the implementation of adequate measures for personal data protection and private life. As a matter of fact, it is important to provide all user requirements and data security when designing IoT elements [EUR 09]. There are solutions based on cryptography or pre-distribution key management that could accommodate object resource constraints [CHA 12]. Nevertheless, questions are raised about the robustness of such solutions to an IoT that potentially comprises millions of objects.

1.9.5. *Challenges for businesses*

The IoT is constantly growing: "the invisible memory" of the web is based on the traces left by users registered in databases and analyzed by means of statistical and other methods. We feel that it is important that public or private actors seize the opportunity of the evolution of the IoT and this memory to propose unique approaches for the wellbeing of humanity.

– For businesses, it is important to understand user behavior and consumer trends in order to provide tailored services and products.

---

19 Website: https://ec.europa.eu/clima/policies/strategies/2020_fr, visited February 4, 2018.

– Political actors can follow company trends in order to adjust their methods of organization and values, while adapting their programs and their mode of operation.

1.9.6. *Challenges for researchers*

– Researchers in humanities and social sciences (HSS) have "total" fantastic observation means that aim "to revolutionize classical methodologies by eliminating the division between micro and macro, between qualitative and quantitative" [RIE 10].

– Researchers in other sciences (computer science, mathematics, etc.) have a quantity of data to test the reliability, speed and invention of algorithms.

– Researchers in MMI have data and tools that allow them to imagine and create aesthetic and understandable artifacts to visualize data, which is received almost continuously [PIN 17].

"The quantity and wealth of data would suggest that we can move, through a kind of 'zoom', from the whole to the individual and from average to idiosyncrasy" [RIE 10]. The processing and analysis of digital traces and data produced by the IoT are changing both the ways in which researchers produce and communicate knowledge, and the organization of research, its economy as well as its role in society [RIE 10].

The IoT raises a number of epistemological and sociotechnical problems: freedom–control, authority–independence, associativity–uniqueness, automatism–control, actions–interactions, contextualization–decontextualization, adaptivity–integrity, etc. We must now learn to *"think of the mobile, the vague, the uncertain, the near and the distant"*[20].

1.10. Opportunities and threats in the IoT ecosystem

We can notice that applications and services developed around the IoT are likely to improve daily life, by optimizing and automating certain activities. On the other hand, some IoT-related questions arise on the usage

20 Jean-Pierre Balpe, "Des hypertextes à l'hypermonde", available at: http://nt2.uqam.ca/fr/ actualites/des-hypertextes-l'hypermonde, accessed December 6, 2016.

and control of information to prevent hacking, user-abusive surveillance, etc. In Table 1.2, we summarize the opportunities and threats which IoT developments pose at the technical, human and socio-economic levels.

Opportunities	Threats
Fast-growing market	Difficult market access for small companies
Reduction of the cost of technologies	Physical frailty of objects
Competitiveness that fosters innovation	Influence on decision-making to guide innovation
Technological development (Ipv6, miniaturization)	Lack of norms and standards
Increased connection speed	Technological fracture
Improvement of daily life	Political and social manipulation
Connection everywhere without constraints of space and time	Abusive surveillance Environmental impact
Permanent flow of data	Security, protection and data control

Table 1.2. *Opportunities and threats*

1.11. IoT security

Given the emergence of IoT technologies in all areas of everyday life, questions about IoT security are bound to arise. It must be considered from three complementary angles: *technological, human and systemic* [CHA 12]:

– *Technology protection* concerns data security, communications and infrastructure networks as well as their functionality.

– The protection of individuals concerns the protection of the private lives of users ("privacy") to avoid disputes that are likely to be caused by the IoT.

– *"The protection of interconnected systems hosting IoT objects will concern the protection of objects themselves delivered to these systems and the processes they control"* [CHA 12, p. 62].

Yacine Challal [CHA 12] analyzed existing research and the needs of the IoT in terms of security and he concluded that potential developments can be seen around three areas: in the short, medium and long term. In Table 1.3, he illustrates these three areas and summarizes the scientific and technological barriers behind each of them.

Systemic and cognitive approach to IoT security	– Trust models for "object storage" – Autoimmunity of objects – Identification – Responsibility
IT security **Omnipresent mobile**	– Privacy and user-centric security according to the context – Adaptive management of profiles and security policies – Security sharing in the mobile network
Safety of miniaturized embedded networks	– Effective cryptography for embedded computing – Effective and scalable key management – Authentication and effective management of credentials – Secure protection for LLN environments
IoT security	– Technology protection – Protection of individuals – Systems protection

Table 1.3. *Three major projects for security and privacy in the IoT ([CHA 12, p. 63]; we have only modified the presentation)*

1.12. Blockchain and the IoT

1.12.1. *Definition*

Blockchain is a technology developed for the Bitcoin cryptocurrency by Satoshi Nakamoto (pseudonym) in 2008 [NAK 08]. Blockchain France has defined blockchain as *"an information storage and transmission technology, which is transparent, secure, and operates without a central control body. By extension, a blockchain is a database that contains the history of all transactions made between its users since its creation. This database is secure and distributed: it is directly shared by its different users, allowing everyone to check the validity of the chain*[21]*"*.

Blockchain[22] is a distributed registry system where transaction logging is done across multiple nodes in a peer-to-peer (P2P) network.

"Commotion" (http://commotionwireless.net/) and "Blockchain" variations are of decentralized systems. The aim is to break away from the central body by putting in place devices that work independently of a central entity. Moreover, there are political problems that go with it as part of a society of hyper-control[23].

1.12.2. *Operation*

"Any public blockchain must operate with a programmable currency or token[24]*"*, Bitcoin being an example. Bitcoin users, who know each other by exchanging public keys, generate and distribute transactions on the network to transfer money. These transactions are grouped together in a block by users. When a block is filled, it is added to the blockchain after a mining process. To mine a block, network nodes, called "minors", try to solve a cryptographic problem called "Proof-of-Work (PoW)". *"Once the block is validated, it is time-stamped and added to the Blockchain*[25]*"*. At this point,

---

21 Taken from the Blockchain website: https://blockchainfrance.net/decouvrir-la-blockchain/c-est-quoi-la-blockchain/, visited January 30, 2018.
22 See Ahmed Banafa's blog, available at: https://ahmedbanafa.blogspot.com/ (accessed January 30, 2018), for more information.
23 Serge Abiteboul, "S'affranchir de l'autorité centrale avec la blockchain", *La Recherche*, November 2017.
24 Also from the Blockchain website, visited January 30, 2018.
25 Also from the Blockchain website, visited January 30, 2018.

the transaction is visible to the receiver as well as to the entire network (Figure 1.7).

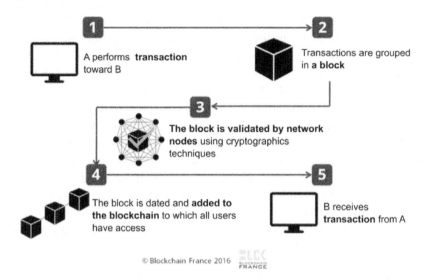

Figure 1.7. *Taken from the company website: https://blockchainfrance.net/ decouvrir-la-blockchain/c-est-quoi-la-blockchain/ (we respected the original figure but the explanations have been translated from French to English)*

In the context of the Internet of Things and because of the interconnection of heterogeneous systems that generate a large volume of personal data, our digital company faces a number of challenges (see below). Given the functioning of distributed blockchain and its consensus mechanisms that reconcile divergent interests and distributed trust through the removal of the single trusted third party, it can offer answers to certain challenges.

However, as stated by Dorri *et al.* [DOR 16], adapting this technology to the IoT is not an easy task. In fact, the mining process requires high computing capacity while the majority of IoT devices have limited resources. Moreover, this process takes time, whereas in most IoT applications, low latency is desirable. In addition, blockchains become difficult to use as the number of nodes in the network increases, while IoT networks should contain a large number of nodes. Finally, the underlying protocols of blockchains create significant indirect traffic which may pose problems for some IoT devices with limited bandwidth [DOR 16].

1.12.3. *Applications*

In this context, many researchers have studied the use and adaptation of blockchain in the IoT. Among them is Mettler [MET 16] who illustrates the use of this technology in the field of health, be it for public health management, medical research based on patients' personal data or for quality assurance in the production of drugs. Moreover, Dorri *et al.* [DOR 17] presented an adaptation of blockchain for the case of smart homes. By grouping devices into clusters and adding local blockchains, they show that it is possible to reduce the load on the network while ensuring the security of user data and the protection of their private lives. Finally, in an article [CHR 16], Christidis *et al.* expose the use of blockchain technology for smart contracts. These smart contracts are *"stand-alone programs that automatically execute the terms and conditions of a contract, without requiring human intervention once started*[26]*"*. Smart contracts can be interesting for the IoT because they allow the automation of long processes, while ensuring their verifiability.

The integration of blockchain into the IoT will lead to significant transformations in several sectors, leading to new models that will require us to reconsider how existing systems and processes are implemented. Blockchain can also be a means of ensuring the security of user data as well as the protection of private life, thus allowing for greater adoption of the IoT[27].

1.13. Conclusion

In a world that is "hyper-connected" through connected objects where users are both transmitters and receivers of data, the IoT opens new fields to explore for the information and communication sciences to, on the one hand, study societal challenges of these new technological and digital transformations, and on the other hand, analyze whether connected objects meet the needs of users who are increasingly demanding in terms of service, communication and information. The IoT must be approached from two

---

26 Also taken from the Blackchain website, visited January 30, 2018.
27 This section was written in January 2018, in collaboration with Amri Toumia, a PhD student.

angles: on the one hand, the industrial and technological reality of connected objects, such as business management, e-administration, e-government and gestures (pedometer, gaze direction, GPS, etc.); and on the other hand, the impacts of connected objects in everyday life, for example on health, housing, cars, insurance, etc.

Figure 1.8 illustrates, according to us, the future developments of the IoT.

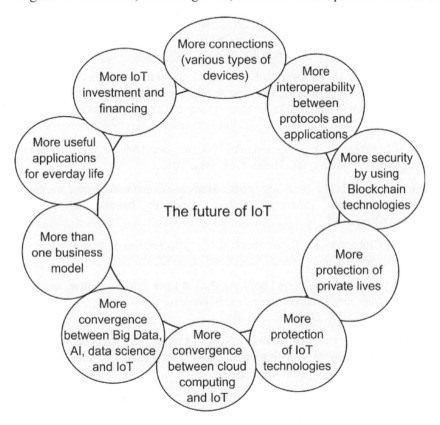

Figure 1.8. *The future of the IoT*

1.14. References

[AMR 17] AMROUM H., TEMKIT M'H., AMMI H. *et al.*, "Apprentissage en profondeur des données brutes de l'activité humaine", *Internet of Things*, vol. 2, no. 2, ISTE OpenScience, 2017.

[BOU 17a] BOUHAÏ N., SALEH I. (eds), *Internet of Things: Evolutions and Innovations*, ISTE Ltd, London and John Wiley & Sons, New York, 2017.

[BOU 17b] BOUHAÏ N., "The IoT: intrusive or indispensable objects?", in BOUHAÏ N., SALEH I. (eds), *Internet of Things: Evolutions and Innovations*, ISTE Ltd, London and John Wiley & Sons, New York, 2017.

[BOY 12] BOYD D., CTAWFORD K., "Critical question for big data", *Information, Communication & Society*, available at: https://people.cs.kuleuven.be/~bettina.be rendt/teaching/ViennaDH15/boyd_crawford_2012.pdf (accessed February 2, 2017), 2012.

[CHA 12] CHALLAL Y., "Sécurité de l'Internet des Objets : vers une approche cognitive et systémique", Thesis, UTC, June 2012.

[CHE 15] CHEN L.M., SU Z., JIANG B., *Mathematical Problems in Data Science: Theoretical and Practical Methods*, Springer International Publishing, Amsterdam, 2015.

[CHR 16] CHRISTIDIS K., DEVETSIKIOTIS M., "Blockchains and smart contracts for the Internet of Things", *IEEE Access*, vol. 4, pp. 2292–2303, 2016.

[CIT 18] CITY UNIVERSITY OF LONDON, MsC in Data Science Course, available at: https://www.city.ac.uk/courses/postgraduate/data-science-msc (accessed on February 6, 2017), 2018.

[CRO 17] CROUZY S., BORKOWSKI S., COQUILLART S., "Ambient Atoms : un périphérique pour la visualisation ambiante d'informations", *Internet of Things*, vol. 2, no. 2, ISTE OpenScience, 2017.

[DOR 16] DORRI A., KANHERE S.S., JURDAK R., "Blockchain in Internet of Things: challenges and solutions", *arXiv*, eprint arXiv:1608.05187, August 2016.

[DOR 17] DORRI A., KANHERE S.S., JURDAK R. *et al.*, "Blockchain for IoT security and privacy: the case study of a smart home", *IEEE International Conference on Pervasive Computing and Communications Workshops*, March 2017.

[EUR 09] EUROPEAN ECONOMIC AND SOCIAL COMMITTEE, Internet of Things – an action plan for Europe, 2009.

[GAG 17] GAGNERÉ G., PLESSIET C., SOHIER R., "Espace virtuel interconnecté et Théâtre. Une recherche-création sur l'espace de jeu théâtral à l'ère du réseau", *Internet of Things*, vol. 2, no. 2, ISTE OpenScience, 2017.

[GSM 18] GSMA, available at: https://www.gsma.com/, 2018.

[INT 05] INTERNATIONAL TELECOMMUNICATION UNION, "Ubiquitous Network Societies: their impact on the telecommunication industry", *ITU Workshop on Ubiquitous Network Societies*, April 2005.

[MAV 03] MAVROMMATI I., KAMEAS A., "The evolution of objects into hyper-objects: will it be mostly harmless?", *Personal and Ubiquitous Computing*, vol. 7, nos 3–4, pp. 176–181, available at: http://dx.doi.org/10.1007/s00779-003-0223-1, 2003.

[MET 16] METTLER M., "Blockchain technology in healthcare: the revolution starts here", *IEEE 18th International Conference on e-Health Networking, Applications and Services (Healthcom)*, pp. 1–3, 2016.

[MIT 13] MITCHELL S., VILLA N., STEWART-WEEKS M. *et al.*, *The Internet of Everything for Cities*, Cisco, 2013.

[INS 15] INSTITUT MONTAIGNE, Big data et objets connectés – faire de la France un champion de la révolution numérique, Report, April 2015.

[NAK 08] NAKAMOTO S., Bitcoin: a peer-to-peer electronic cash system, 2008.

[NOY 17] NOYER J.-M., "L'Internet des Objets, l'Internet of Everything : quelques remarques sur l'intensification du plissement numérique du monde", *Internet of Things*, vol. 1, no. 1, ISTE OpenScience, 2017.

[PIN 17] PINTOA A.L., GONZALES-AGUILAR A., DUTRA M.L. *et al.*, "The visualization of information of the Internet of Things", in BOUHAÏ N., SALEH I. (eds), *Internet of Things: Evolutions and Innovations*, ISTE Ltd, London and John Wiley & Sons, New York, 2017.

[RIE 10] RIEDER B., "Pratiques informationnelles et analyse des traces numériques : de la représentation à l'intervention", *Etudes de communication*, no. 35, pp. 91–104, available at: https://edc.revues.org/2249 (accessed on February 3, 2017), 2010.

[RIE 12] RIEDER B., RÖHLE T., "Digital methods: five challenges", in BERRY D.M. (ed.), *Understanding Digital Humanities*, Palgrave Macmillan, Houndmills, 2012.

[ROX 17] ROXIN I., BOUCHEREAU A., "The ecosystem of the Internet of Things", in BOUHAÏ N., SALEH I. (eds), *Internet of Things: Evolutions and Innovations*, ISTE Ltd, London and John Wiley & Sons, New York, 2017.

[SAL 12] SALEH I., HACHOUR H., "Le numérique comme catalyseur épistémologique", *Revue Française des Sciences de l'Information et de la Communication*, no. 1, available at : http://rfsic.revues.org/168, 2012.

[SAL 14] SALEH I., HACHOUR H., BOUHAÏ N., *Les frontières numériques*, L'Harmattan, 2014.

[SAL 17] SALEH I., "Les enjeux et les défis de l'Internet des Objets (IdO)", *Internet of Things*, vol. 1, no. 1, ISTE OpenScience, 2017.

[SEY 15] SEYDOUX N., BEN ALAYA M., HERNANDEZ N. *et al.*, "Sémantique et Internet des objets : d'un état de l'art à une ontologie modulaire", *26es Journées francophones d'Ingénierie des Connaissances*, Rennes, available at: https://hal.archives-ouvertes.fr/IC-2015/hal-01166052 (accessed on March 3, 2017), June 2015.

[SUN 10] SUNDMAEKER H., GUILLEMIN P., FRIESS P. *et al.* (eds), *Vision and Challenges for Realising the Internet of Things*, Cluster of European Research Projects on the Internet of Things, 2010.

[SZO 12] SZONIECKY S., Evaluation et conception d'un langage symbolique pour l'intelligence collective, vers un langage allégorique pour le Web, Thesis, University of Paris 8, December 2012.

[SZO 17] SZONIECKY S., SAFIN S., "Modélisation éthique de l'Internet des Objets", *Internet of Things*, vol. 2, ISTE OpenScience, 2017.

[THE 13] THEBAULT P., La conception à l'ère de l'Internet des Objets : modèles et principes pour le design de produits aux fonctions augmentées par des applications, Thesis, ParisTech, 2013.

[VER 11] VERMESAN O., FRIESS P., GUILLEMIN P. *et al.*, "Internet of Things Strategic Research Roadmap", in VERMESAN O., FRIESS P. (eds), *Internet of Things – Global Technological and Societal Trends*, River Publishers, 2011.

[WEI 91] WEISER M., "The computer for the XXIe century", *Scientific American*, vol. 265, no. 3, pp. 3–11, 1991.

[WEI 93] WEISER M., "Hot topics: ubiquitous computing", *IEEE Computer*, October 1993.

[WOO 11] WOOD L., "Today, the Internet, tomorrow – the Internet of Things", *Computer World*, available at: http://www.computerworld.com/s/article/ 9221614/Today_the_Internet_tomorrow_the_Internet_of   Things, November 2011.

2

Deep Learning Approach
of Raw Human Activity Data

This chapter proposes to study the recognition of certain daily physical activities by using a network of smart objects. The approach consists of the classification of certain human activities: walking, standing, sitting and lying down. The study exploits a network of common connected objects: a smartwatch, connected remote control and a smartphone, worn by participants during an uncontrolled experiment. The sensor data of the three devices were classified by a deep neural network (DNN) algorithm without prior data preprocessing. We show that DNN provides better results than decision tree (DT) and support vector machine (SVM) algorithms. The results also show that some participants' activities were classified with an accuracy of more than 98%, on average.

2.1. Introduction

Nowadays, connected objects have become indispensable devices in daily life. The areas of application are broad as they cover the domain of security, home automation and health.

With the development of the Internet of Things (IoT) in daily life, new uses have emerged, paving the way to many perspectives in the field of human activity recognition in terms of use and application.

Chapter written by Hamdi Amroun, M'Hamed (Hamy) Temkit and Mehdi Ammi.

Many studies have been carried out on the recognition of human activity using standard and portable connected objects [MIL 06]. These methods provide easy-to-use, flexible, and above all lightweight devices and platforms for effective human activity control on a daily basis, and include many sensors (inertial unit, pressure sensor, oxygen measurement, etc.) [LES 06, GER 04].

Ongoing research does not exploit these technologies and platforms in a sufficiently comprehensive and mature way. In fact, the majority of research on activity recognition is done in controlled environments where the participants are asked to perform specific daily tasks (e.g. preparing to eat, standing still, walking up the stairs) [ZHU 09], or to annotate their activities or give the location of a device at the beginning of the experiment (e.g. putting the smartphone in the pants pocket or in the bag) [BAO 04, BRU 10].

Generally, human activity recognition is subject to a preliminary preprocessing of training data before an algorithm (SVM, Random Forest, HMM) is applied [ZHU 09, GHO 14, RAH 15]. This preprocessing generally takes only relevant information with respect to classification, without bothering about other types of data that can sometimes cause performance issues. However, all this previous research was mainly done in controlled environments. It is not very robust and has low recognition rates, which are sometimes very demanding in terms of computing time and memory space [WEI 12, KWA 11, GHO 14, RAH 15, NGI 11, MUR 14, LIU 11, HIN 06, SAL 09, RAV 05, VAN 08, HAN 10, HUE 03, EIS 07, ANG 12, ANG 13a, AHM 16, MAG 12, SAZ 11, AMR 16, ZHU 09, GHO 14, GAO 12, SIM 09, LIA 10, LIA 09, IGU 15, AGU 16, WEB 16, MUR 12, FRE 07, SEO 16, BAY 14, BIT 06, BRO 14, HOE 15, MIR 15, DAU 15, SEI 11, BAT 95, BRY 81, HAT 80, TAY 07, TOD 04, MOM 07, WAN 16, GAL, MCC 15, SHE 13, KAR 12, KOZ 91].

Deep neural networks (DNN) are a promising alternative. In fact, they were successfully introduced and applied to various issues such as handwriting classification and gesture recognition [OUC 13], where DNNs were applied directly to data flow without data preprocessing or feature selection. The results show a very good recognition rate [OUC 13, WEI 12, KWA 11, GHO 14, RAH 15, NGI 11, MUR 14, LIU 11, HIN 06, SAL 09,

RAV 05, VAN 08, HAN 10, HUE 03, EIS 07, ANG 12, ANG 13a, AHM 16, MAG 12, SAZ 11, AMR 16, ZHU 09, GHO 14, GAO 12, SIM 09, LIA 10, LIA 09, IGU 15, AGU 16, WEB 16, MUR 12, FRE 07, SEO 16, BAY 14, BIT 06, BRO 14, HOE 15, MIR 15, DAU 15, SEI 11, BAT 95, BRY 81, HAT 80, TAY 07, TOD 04, MOM 07, WAN 16, GAL, MCC 15, SHE 13, KAR 12, KOZ 91, BAY 11, PAT 14, KWA 11, SAP 08, KHA 10, DO 11].

In this chapter, we aim to study human activity recognition, in an uncontrolled environment, using an iPhone, an Apple Watch and an Apple TV remote. The iPhone and the Apple Watch contain an accelerometer, a gyroscope and a microphone. The Apple TV remote contains an accelerometer and a gyroscope.

After extracting sensor data from these three devices, they are then given as input to a DNN without prior and specific preprocessing of these data, that is, by taking raw data alone. The iPhone is then put in the pants pocket of participants, while the Apple TV remote is held in the hand.

The remainder of this chapter is structured as follows: a brief state of the art is presented in section 2.2 and a description of the experiment is presented in section 2.3. In section 2.4, we will detail the process of activity recognition using DNN with raw data input. Section 2.5 will present the findings obtained, while section 2.6 will discuss these findings and compare them with existing research. We will end with the conclusion.

2.2. State of the art

Extensive research has addressed the problem of physical activity recognition. In [ANG 13b], Anguita *et al.* proposed one of the multi-class support vector machine (SVM) classification methods for physical activity recognition with smartphones. Detected activities were as follows: standing still, sitting, lying down, walking, walking up the stairs and walking down the stairs. Today, preserving the phone's battery is essential for an application. Hence, this research put special emphasis on smartphone battery drain. Their results show that it is possible to use their method to an unmodified SVM type multi-class classification method as reduce smartphone energy consumption.

In addition, San-Segundo *et al.*, [SAN 16a] proposed a new approach using a statistical model called the hidden Markov model. In the article [SAN 16b], they expose their methodology to extract relevant descriptors used in their statistical model. The descriptors are statistical frequency and time values taken in 2.56s windows on the raw data of a smartphone's accelerometer and gyroscope (x, y, z). They sought to detect the following activities: walking, walking up the stairs, walking down the stairs, sitting, standing still and lying down. Their approach achieves 95% success in detecting activities using public datasets[1].

Weiss *et al.* successively detailed two approaches to activity detection: one using a smartphone [WEI 16a], and the other using a connected watch [WEI 16b]. The study on smartphones bears similarities with our project though it is in the area of health. An application was designed as part of this study and is available on the Google Play Store[2]. It was not only designed for a scientific purpose, but was also intended to provide users with real utility, with activity detection, like other fitness applications and pedometers, that can give an estimate of burned calories in real time. Two models were tested: a generic model and a customized model. Each model was tested with machine learning and random forest algorithms. They were able to show that the generic model is not very effective, while the customized model achieves 95% success in activity detection (walking, running, standing still, sitting/lying down, walking up/down stairs). Thanks to the large sample of collected data, they had considerable feedback from users of the application. A problem emerged: the application requires the smartphone to be constantly in the pocket for it to have good prediction, which is very restrictive, especially for women who almost never have their smartphones in their pants pockets (due to lack of space).

---

1 Human Activity Recognition Using Smartphones Data Set – UCI Machine Learning Repository.
2 https://play.google.com/store/apps/details?id=edu.fordham.cis.wisdm.actitracker.client&hl=fr.

Figure 2.1. *Actitracker logo*

With this in mind, they studied physical activity recognition with a connected watch. While only data from the accelerometer was used in the study on smartphones, this time, gyroscope data from the connected watch (in addition to data from the accelerometer) was used for the classification of activities. They were able to show that the connected watch was able (unlike the smartphone) to detect manual activities, such as drinking. With this ability, connected watches could be used to characterize the nutritional habits of the user. More generally, the connected watch was more effective in detecting physical activities identified in the previous study.

Deep neural networks are widely used prediction tools, having achieved success in real applications thanks to their predictive power [MUR 14]. They were used to carry out predictive models relating to several domains including plagiarism and spam detection, activity recognition and perception (reading, vision, etc.).

In addition, real intelligent systems require other skills that go beyond perception, such as reasoning, inference and the expression of uncertainty. These are not ensured by neural networks that are black boxes which give results without interpretation (no explanation for the network structure (number of hidden nodes, hidden layers, weight) nor for the results found) [AHM 16, MAG 12, SAZ 11, AMR 16, ZHU 09, GHO 14, GAO 12, SIM 09, LIA 10, LIA 09, IGU 15, AGU 16, WEB 16, MUR 12, FRE 07, SEO 16, BAY 14, BIT 06, BRO 14, HOE 15, MIR 15, DAU 15, SEI 11, BAT 95, BRY 81, HAT 80, TAY 07, TOD 04, MOM 07, WAN 16, GAL, MCC 15, SHE 13, KAR 12, KOZ 91, BAY 11, PAT 14, KWA 11, SAP 08, KHA 10, DO 11, AMR 18, SAL 15, HOU 08, MON 09, BOU 16, ZHU 09, GHO 14,

LI 11, ZAD 84, BEY 00, YAG 87, SEN 02, CHE 05, VOO 91, SEL 98, OLI 02, ZHA 11, KOS 12, XIA 13, FIG 10, EYB 10, DUR 88, DAV 96, HAM 16].

Other research studies have proposed Bayesian networks, which are probabilistic tools that show how the occurrence of certain events influences the probability of other events. They produce the probabilistic model for a problem where the explanatory variables are the "features" and the variables to be explained represent the events to be predicted. This represents an interpretable structure that applies Bayesian inferences to infer results or to refer to queries [SAZ 11].

Other uses have emerged recently that are based on physical activity recognition as in the field of health. In 1993, Ainsworth *et al.* published a compendium (body of knowledge) of physical activities and their associated metabolic equivalents [AIN 93]. The metabolic equivalent (MET) of a physical activity is defined as the intensity of its demand on the basic metabolism (sitting at rest, for example). 1 MET equals 3.5 ml of exhaled oxygen during activity per kilogram and per minute. The compendium takes the form of an equivalence table between physical activities and MET. This compendium has been expanded over the years, especially in 2006 and 2011. The idea behind this compendium is to compile a good number of research studies on energy consumption so as to facilitate comparisons between research studies and allow the association of a broad list of physical activities as well as understanding the functioning of the human body especially in the case of metabolism.

Based on this compendium, Wagner [WAG 12] published a study which aimed to classify physical activities in order to model the energy consumption of the person. In order to do this, they used an accelerometer positioned at the waist (linear relationship between energy consumption and movement of the measured body near the center of mass) and a heart monitor. By exploiting the linear relationship between heart rate and oxygen consumption, and by using classification algorithms (decision trees, artificial neural networks, support vector machine, etc.), they managed to get back to the energy consumption measured according to the MET at 92% success. There are also other areas where the knowledge of physical activity can be used to diagnose certain diseases [GAL, MCC 15, SHE 13, KAR 12,

KOZ 91, BAY 11, PAT 14, KWA 11, SAP 08, KHA 10, DO 11, AMR 18, SAL 15, HOU 08, MON 09, BOU 16, ZHU 09, GHO 14, LI 11, ZAD 84].

All these studies did not take into account the audio factor on the process of physical activity recognition and how the sensor data can be more useful and enriched. In addition, the use of deep learning algorithms has not been applied in this specific context. This is what we propose to study later in this chapter.

Section 2.3 describes the experimental environment and the process of data collection from the network of connected objects.

2.3. Experimental configuration

The experiment took place in a house for a period of 1 week. Seven participants, aged between 25 and 48 (four men and three women), participated in the experiment for 1 week each. Three IP cameras were mounted at different places in the room to record the activity of participants. Videos were saved on a local server. Participants were asked to wear an iPhone, an Apple Watch and an Apple TV remote during the experiment. The iPhone and Apple Watch contain three sensors each: an accelerometer, a gyroscope and a microphone. The Apple TV remote is embedded with an accelerometer and a gyroscope. The sampling frequency of iPhone, Apple Watch and Apple TV sensors were fitted at 120 Hz, 128 Hz and 132 Hz respectively and at an 8 KHz sampling frequency for the microphone. The recording time was 3 hours: 50 minutes twice a day for a week. We developed an iOS, Apple Watch and Apple TV application to access, save and send sensor data via WiFi to a local server, which was stored in a SQL SERVER database.

A data warehouse was created to integrate data automatically from the database at the end of each recording. The video recordings and sensors have been synchronized to start simultaneously. Video recordings and sensor signals were tagged with the ELAN Software. The iPhone was put in the pants pocket, the Apple TV remote was placed in the hand, while the Apple Watch was placed at arm level.

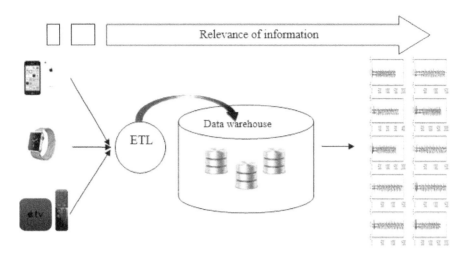

Figure 2.2. *Data collection. For a color version of this figure, see www.iste.co.uk/saleh/challenges.zip*

2.4. Analysis of the activity

In this section, we will detail the activity recognition model we used. Before that, we will discuss the different architectures that can be used.

2.4.1. *Neural network architecture*

Neural network architecture is the link between the different layers and neurons of a network. In the literature, several architectures can be found, with the most used being the following.

MLP (multilayer perceptron)

MLP is a nonlinear transformation sequence that maps input data onto output data. Each neuron in a layer is connected to all the neurons in the next layer in a strongly connected fashion (each node is connected to all the nodes of the next layer if it exists). MLP is a model for supervised learning techniques. There are several techniques to train the MLP-type neural network (the gradient descendant, PSO, etc.) [HOE 15, MIR 15, DAU 15, SEI 11, BAT 95, BRY 81, HAT 80, TAY 07, TOD 04, MOM 07, WAN 16, GAL, MCC 15, SHE 13, KAR 12, KOZ 91, BAY 11, PAT 14, KWA 11,

SAP 08, KHA 10, DO 11, AMR 18, SAL 15, HOU 08, MON 09, BOU 16, ZHU 09, GHO 14, LI 11, ZAD 84].

CNN (convolutional neural network)

CNN is a network of acyclic neurons, in which the connection pattern between layers is based on the visual cortex. It is used in image and video recognition, and natural language processing. It inputs a matrix and outputs a label (the class of input matrix) [VAN 08, HAN 10, HUE 03, EIS 07, ANG 12, ANG 13a, AHM 16, MAG 12, SAZ 11, AMR 16, ZHU 09, GHO 14, GAO 12, SIM 09, LIA 10, LIA 09, IGU 15, AGU 16, WEB 16].

A CNN consists of:

– the convolutional layer: processes input data;

– the pooling layer: allows the compression of an intermediate image resulting from the convolutional layer;

– the correction layer (ReLU): performs linear corrections on the image;

– the "fully connected" (FC) layer: an ordinary layer of neurons;

– the loss layer (LOSS).

BNW (belief neural network)

BNW is a type of multi-layer neural network with connections between the layers. It can be considered as a set of unsupervised networks as well as a layer-by-layer procedure for unsupervised learning. In a BNN, there are recurrent connections between layers, which are also trained in an unsupervised way [EIS 07, ANG 12, ANG 13a, AHM 16, MAG 12, SAZ 11, AMR 16, ZHU 09, GHO 14, GAO 12, SIM 09, LIA 10, LIA 09, IGU 15, AGU 16, WEB 16, MUR 12, FRE 07, SEO 16, BAY 14, BIT 06, BRO 14, HOE 15, MIR 15, DAU 15, SEI 11, BAT 95, BRY 81, HAT 80, TAY 07, TOD 04, MOM 07, WAN 16, GAL, MCC 15, SHE 13, KAR 12, KOZ 91, BAY 11, PAT 14, KWA 11, SAP 08, KHA 10, DO 11, AMR 18, SAL 15, HOU 08, MON 09].

RNN (recurrent neural network)

RNNs are neural networks with at least one recurrent connection, the result of which allows activations to pass between different layers.

This allows networks to carry out temporal and learning processing [BIT 06, BRO 14, HOE 15, MIR 15, DAU 15, SEI 11].

Deep Bayesian network

Bayesian neural networks are deep "multi-layered" probabilistic models, wherein the weights of a typical neural network follow a Gaussian distribution.

– Let X be the set of input data with $X = \{x^i | i = 0 \dots N\}$ and Y the set of outputs: $Y = \{y^i | i = 0 \dots N\}$.

– Let W be the set of weights of the model, wherein each w_i follows the distribution in principle $p(w_i)$.

– Let the likelihood be $p(Y|w_i, X)$, which represents the probability of having an output knowing the input and the model.

– Let the *a posteriori* probability be $p(w_i|Y, X)$, which represents the probability of having a model knowing the input data and the output data. The posteriori probability is given with Bayes' theorem:

$$p(wi|Y, X) = \frac{p(Y|w_i, X)\, p(wi)}{p(Y|X)}$$

– The distribution of the prediction is given by:

$$p(Y^*|X^*, X, Y) = \int p(Y^*|w, X^*) p(w|X, Y) dw$$

This is what is difficult to evaluate. It is for this reason that we use approximate methods like MCMC [RAV 05].

In this research, the deep learning algorithm (DNN) was used as a classifier to recognize physical activities, which can extract features by itself without any specific knowledge of the data (accelerometer, gyroscope and microphone).

By overlooking the extraction procedure of features, the model could become more responsive.

The DNN learning process is subdivided into two stages: pre-training and tuning. Pre-training is an unsupervised step where an initial network is created using a learning algorithm. Fine-tuning is supervised and the parameters of all the layers will be updated using the gradient back-propagation algorithm. The following notations are used to designate network parameters:

– $I = h_0$: the network input;

– h_i (i=1, 2, ..., τ-1): i^{th} hidden layer;

– $O = h_\tau$: the network output;

– w_i (i=1, ..., τ): the connection weight matrix between h_i and h_{i+1};

– ρ_i (i=1, ..., τ): the bias for neurons in the layer h_i when they are activated by the layer h_{i+1};

– ς_i (i=1, ..., τ): biases of the neurons from the layer h_i when they are activated by the layer h_{i-1};

– Θ: all of the network settings;

– Ŧ: the learning set;

– $[f_{\theta(x)}]_i$: the score associated with the ith label by the network parameter.

According to [LIU 11], there are two adjacent layers: h_{i-1} and h_i. The activation function is defined by

$$p\,(h_{i-1,s} = 1|h_i\,) = \Gamma(\rho_{i,s} + \textstyle\sum_j w_{i,j}, h_{i,j}) \qquad [2.1]$$

$$p\,(h_{i,t} = 1|h_{i-1}\,) = \Gamma(\varsigma_{i,t} + \textstyle\sum_j w_{i,j} h_{i,j}) \qquad [2.2]$$

$$\Gamma(x) = \frac{1}{(1+e^{-x})} \qquad [2.3]$$

as $\Gamma\,(.)$ is the logistic function.

Pre-training

The objective of pre-training is to maximize the probability of generating learning data. The probability of each learning datum assigned by the network was calculated using the energy function [2.4]:

$$P(I) = \textstyle\sum_{h\in H} p(v,h) = \frac{\sum_h exp(-E(I,h))}{\sum_{u,g} exp(-E(u,g))} \qquad [2.4]$$

Hinton [HIN 06] proposed a method based on a pre-training layer. This method is used to obtain an appropriate neural network by placing the lower layer as visible v, and the upper layer as hidden layer h. Each pair of adjacent layers can be considered as a restricted Boltzmann machine (RBM). The entire network is built by forming an RBM which has the following energy function:

$$E (v, h) = -\sum_{s,t} v_s \, w_{st} h_t - \sum_s b_s \, b_v - \sum_t c_i \, h_i \qquad [2.5]$$

Fine-tuning

The model was trained by using the maximum likelihood of a decent stochastic gradient. We have maximized the log-likelihood:

$$\Theta \to \sum_{(x,y) \in \uparrow} \log(y|x, \Theta) \qquad [2.6]$$

such that x is the input data and corresponds to the labels. Let x be a given example, the probability p is then calculated from the outputs of a neural network by means of a softmax function:

$$P(i|x,\theta) = e^{[f_{\theta}(x)]_i} \qquad [2.7]$$

This makes it easy to express the log-likelihood:

$$\text{Log p} (y|x, \theta) = [f_{\theta}(x)]_y - \log(\sum_j e^{[f_{\theta}(x)]_j}) \qquad [2.8]$$

The maximization of the log-likelihood using a stochastic gradient is performed by randomly selecting a learning example (x, y) and carrying out a gradient descent:

$$\Theta \to \Theta + \varphi \frac{\delta \log py|x,\Theta)}{\delta \Theta} \qquad [2.9]$$

where φ is the learning rate. All of the proposed architecture is carried out using the Theano library. The effectiveness of the proposed method was evaluated on the basis of data from sensors used and tested by cross-validation (10-fold cross-validation).

The number of hidden layers of our model is set at five and the number of neurons in the hidden layers is set at 850-340-430-920-870. Other network parameters are set at the default setting for Hinton's DBN [HIN 06]

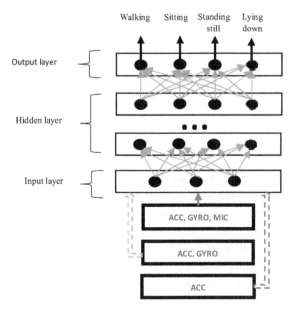

Figure 2.3. *Architecture of the model used. For a color version of this figure, see www.iste.co.uk/saleh/challenges.zip*

Presence recognition

Deep neural networks have proven their effectiveness in several perception problems especially with image recognition and audio classification.

CNNs are neural networks designed to recognize and classify images. The particularity of these networks is that they allow the exploration of features: they take as input an image in the form of a 32 × 32 × 3 table (32 × 32 represents the image resolution and 3 represents the RGB representation) and they provide as output, a label which represents the class of the image.

CNN can also be used for sound recognition and classification. In fact, several research works have used CNNs to classify audio data as in [SAZ 11], who used a CNN to classify urban sounds, and [AMR 16] who used one for goal recognition (football context). A CNN was also used in [ZHU 09] to detect the language of an audio excerpt. Since CNNs are designed to learn the features of images, it is necessary to carry out some processing to adapt sound data to the structure of the deep neural network.

In what follows, we shall present the procedure used to convert sound data to the format compatible with the CNN structure, and then we shall present the CNN architecture used and the steps taken to improve the prediction accuracy.

Data processing

In order to recognize whether a person is in a group or alone, we have recorded several conversations as well as recorded people who were alone in several environments. This was done by using a mobile application designed to collect different context data connected with our research. The figure below shows the difference between two waves, where the first (a) represents the recording of a single person and the second (b) represents the recording of a person in a group.

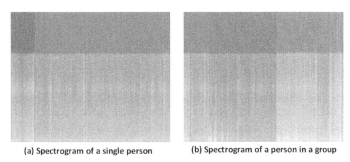

(a) Spectrogram of a single person   (b) Spectrogram of a person in a group

Figure 2.4. *Audio-recording spectrogram of two people (alone (a); in a group (b)). For a color version of this figure, see www.iste.co.uk/saleh/challenges.zip*

In order to obtain the spectrogram of the recording, it is first necessary to convert the recording to the WAV format by using the Pydub library.

Our final dataset contains the following columns: identifier of the recording, the path toward the spectrogram of the recording, and the label (alone or in a group). These data represent CNN input whose architecture is presented in the following section.

Architecture of convolutional neural network (CNN):

In order to build our physical activity recognition system (whether the person is alone or in a group), we used an AlexNet designed to do complex image recognition. It contains only eight layers: the first five are convolutional layers followed by three fully connected layers. Its architecture is described in Table 2.1.

Layer	1	2	3	4	5	6	7	8
Type	Conv + max + norm	Conv + max + norm	Conv	Conv	Conv + max	Full	Full	Full
Channels	96	256	384	384	256	4,096	4,096	1,000
Filter Size	11*11	5*5	3*3	3*3	3*3	–	–	–
Convolution Stride	4*4	1*1	1*1	1*1	1*1	–	–	–
Pooling Size	3*3	3*3	–	–	3*3	–	–	–
Pooling Stride	2*2	2*2	–	–	2*2	–	–	–
Padding Size	2*2							

Table 2.1. *AlexNet architecture*

2.5. Results

Figure 2.5 shows the four activities studied.

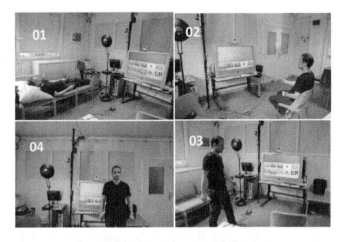

Figure 2.5. *The four activities studied*

Data flow from acceleration signals, gyroscopes and recorded audio sensors have all been reframed, so that they have the same size with an overlap between the samples of the 256-point signals. The length of the window of the acceleration signal, the gyroscope and the audio data is about 4.16 seconds per sensor. Data signals were concatenated and then used as input for the classifier (Figure 2.1).

The recordings were triggered automatically via an application whenever participants returned home. Table 2.2 presents classification results for the four activities by the DNN algorithm.

Activity	iPhone	iPhone, watch	iPhone, watch, TV
Standing still	95.26%	96.08%	98.44%
Seated	94.84%	95.99%	97.89%
Lying down	95.88%	96.47%	99.26%
Walking	98.01%	98.66%	98.98%

Table 2.2. *Classification accuracy (iPhone in pants pocket, Apple TV remote control in hand)*

It should be noted that all activities were recognized with good classification accuracy. The concatenation of these signals significantly improves the recognition accuracy.

2.6. Discussion

The recognition of physical activity was carried out using a classic iPhone, Apple Watch and Apple TV remote, as defined on the official Apple website. Different devices have been used with some configurations.

The iPhone remained in the participants' pants pocket, while the Apple TV remote remained in the hands of participants.

The classification accuracy using the DNN algorithm gives an average accuracy of 95.32% for the iPhone; this accuracy improves significantly and amounts to 96.18% by concatenating data for the two devices (iPhone and Apple Watch) and then reaches almost 98.53% using the Apple TV remote as well. This confirms the contribution of the concatenation of different data sources to the improvement of the recognition accuracy.

To prove the relevance of our results, we compared our recognition results by applying two different algorithms: SVM and DT. The results are summarized in Table 2.3.

For these two algorithms to be applied and compared with the DNN, we selected descriptors, as in [GAO 12], and applied a principle component analysis (PCA) to reduce the dimensionality of the learning data.

	SVM	DT	DNN
Standing	91.66%	92.66%	98.44%
Seated	91.84%	93.49%	97.89%
Lying down	92.89%	94.05%	99.26%
Walking	91.01%	93.66%	98.98%

Table 2.3. *Comparison of classification accuracies of DNN, SVM and DT*

We noted that the classification accuracy of the three algorithms was relatively good. In fact, the SVM had an average classification accuracy of 92.13%, while the average accuracy was 93.4%. The DT algorithm was better than the SVM algorithm because it did not allow over-learning issues, as opposed to the application of the SVM algorithm which required us to manually select descriptors.

The selection of characteristics plays an important role in the reduction of data and information relevant to the recognition of human activity. However, the act of reducing dimensionality penalizes the classification accuracy to an extent. Unlike the DNN model that extracts these descriptors automatically, the risk of losing information relevant to the classification is therefore not expected.

The proposed approach gives better results than similar research studies for the classification of the activities studied. For example, Kazuya Murao and Tsutomu Terada [MUR 14] obtained a precision of 70% for walking and 91.7% for the "sitting" activity when holding a phone in a controlled environment.

2.7. Conclusion

In this chapter, we have shown that we can recognize human activities (standing still, sitting, lying and walking) with very good classification accuracy by using a network of intelligent objects and applying a DNN algorithm without the preprocessing of input signals. The DNN can extract functions by itself without any specific preprocessing for acceleration, gyroscope and audio sensor data. Therefore, the use of a DNN has saved the computation of descriptors and therefore the loss of information by reducing the size of data, as is the case for the SVM algorithm [RAV 05, VAN 08, HAN 10]. In the future, we will focus on calculating the best descriptors for this research.

2.8. References

[AGU 16] AGUILAR M., FERNÁNDEZ S., CASSANY D., "Analysis of user behavior with a multicamera HbbTV app in a live sports event", *Proceedings of the ACM International Conference on Interactive Experiences for TV and Online Video*, pp. 43–48, 2016.

[AHM 16] AHMAD J., MUHAMMAD K., KWON S. *et al.*, "Dempster-Shafer Fusion based gender recognition for speech analysis applications", *International Conference on Platform Technology and Service (PlatCon)*, pp. 1–4, 2016.

[AIN 93] AINSWORTH B.E., HASKELL W.L., LEON A.S. *et al.*, "Compendium of physical activities: classification of energy costs of human physical activities", *Medicine and Science in Sports and Exercise*, vol. 25, no. 1, pp. 71–80, 1993.

[AMR 16] AMROUN H., OUARTI N., AMMI M., "Recognition of human activity using internet of things in a non-controlled environment", *14th International Conference on Control, Automation, Robotics and Vision (ICARCV)*, pp. 1–6, 2016.

[AMR 18] AMROUN H., AMMI M., "Who used my smart object? A flexible approach for the recognition of users", *IEEE Access*, vol. 6, pp. 7112–7122, 2018.

[ANG 12] ANGUITA D., GHIO A., ONETO L. *et al.*, "Human activity recognition on smartphones using a multiclass hardware-friendly support vector machine", *International Workshop on Ambient Assisted Living*, pp. 216–223, 2012.

[ANG 13a] ANGUITA D., GHIO A., ONETO L. *et al.*, "A public domain dataset for human activity recognition using smartphones", *European Symposium on Artificial Neural Networks*, 2013.

[ANG 13b] ANGUITA D., GHIO A., ONETO L. *et al.*, "Energy efficient smartphone-based activity recognition using fixed-point arithmetic", *Journal of Universal Computer Science*, vol. 19, no. 9, pp. 1295–1314, 2013.

[ATA 11] ATALLAH L., LO B., KING R., YANG G.-Z., "Sensor positioning for activity recognition using wearable accelerometers", *IEEE Transactions on Biomedical Circuits and Systems*, vol. 5, no 4, pp. 320–329, 2011.

[BAO 04] BAO, L., INTILLE S.S., "Activity recognition from user-annotated acceleration data", in FERSCHA A., MATTERN F. (eds), *Pervasive Computing*, Springer, Berlin-Heidelberg, pp. 1–17, 2004.

[BAT 95] BATEL P., PESSIONE F., Maitre C. *et al.*, "Relationship between alcohol and tobacco dependencies among alcoholics who smoke", *Addiction*, vol. 90, pp. 977–980, 1995.

[BAY 14] BAYAT A., POMPLUN M., TRAN D.A., "A study on human activity recognition using accelerometer data from smartphones", *Procedia Computer Science*, vol. 34, pp. 450–457, 2014.

[BEY 00] BEYNONM M., CURRY B., MORGAN P., "The Dempster–Shafer theory of evidence: an alternative approach to multicriteria decision modelling", *Omega*, vol. 28, no. 1, pp. 37–50, 2000.

[BIT 06] BITTOUN R., "A combination nicotine replacement therapy (NRT) algorithm for hard-to-treat smokers", *Journal of Smoking Cessation*, vol. 1, 3 pp., 2006.

[BOU 16] BOUKARY N.A., A comparison of time series forecasting learning algorithms on the task of predicting event timing, PhD thesis, Royal Military College of Canada, 2016.

[BRO 14] BROWN J., BEARD E., KOTZ D. *et al.*, "Real-world effectiveness of e-cigarettes when used to aid smoking cessation: a cross-sectional population study", *Addiction*, vol. 109, pp. 1531–1540, 2014.

[BRU 10] BRUSH A.J., KARLSON A.K., SCOTT J., *et al.*, "User experiences with activity-based navigation on mobile devices", *Proceedings of the 12th International Conference on Human Computer Interaction with Mobile Devices and Services*, pp. 73–82, 2010.

[BRY 81] BRYSON R., BINER P.M., MCNAIR E. *et al.*, "Effects of nicotine on two types of motor activity in rats", *Psychopharmacology*, vol. 73, pp. 168–170, 1981.

[CHE 05] CHEN T.M., Venkataramanan V., "Dempster-Shafer theory for intrusion detection in ad hoc networks", *IEEE Internet Computing*, vol. 9, no. 6, pp. 35–41, 2005.

[DAU 15] DAUTZENBERG B., BRICARD D., "Real-time characterization of e-cigarettes use: the 1 million puffs study", *Journal of Addiction Research and Therapy*, vol. 6, 2015.

[DAV 96] DAVIS J.W., Appearance-based Motion Recognition of Human Actions, Master's thesis, Massachusetts Institute of Technology, 1996.

[DO 11] DO T.M.T., GATICA-PEREZ D., "Groupus: smartphone proximity data and human interaction type mining", *15th Annual International Symposium on Wearable Computers (ISWC)*, pp. 21–28, 2011.

[DUR 88] DURRANT-WHYTE H.F., "Sensor models and multisensor integration", *The International Journal of Robotics Research*, vol. 7, no. 6, pp. 97–113, 1988.

[EIS 07] EISEND M., MÖLLER J., "The influence of TV viewing on consumers' body images and related consumption behavior", *Marketing Letters*, vol. 18, nos 1–2, pp. 101–116, 2007.

[EYB 10] EYBEN F., WÖLLMER M., SCHULLER B., "Opensmile: the Munich versatile and fast open-source audio feature extractor", *Proceedings of the 18th ACM International Conference on Multimedia*, pp. 1459–1462, 2010.

[FIG 10] FIGO D., DINIZ P.C., FERREIRA D.R. *et al.*, "Preprocessing techniques for context recognition from accelerometer data", *Personal and Ubiquitous Computing*, vol. 14, no. 7, pp. 645–662, 2010.

[FRE 07] FREY B.S., BENESCH C., STUTZER A., "Does watching TV make us happy?", *Journal of Economic Psychology*, vol. 28, no. 3, pp. 283–313, 2007.

[GAL 15] GAL Y., Modern Deep Learning through Bayesian Eyes, Lecture notes, University of Cambridge, 2015.

[GAO 12] GAO L., BOURKE A.K., NELSON J., "A comparison of classifiers for activity recognition using multiple accelerometer-based sensors", *IEEE 11th International Conference on Cybernetic Intelligent Systems (CIS)*, pp. 149–153, 2012.

[GER 04] GEROCH M.S., "Motion capture for the rest of us", *Journal of Computing Sciences in Colleges*, vol. 19, no. 3, pp. 157–164, 2004.

[GHO 14] GHOSH A., RICCARDI G., "Recognizing human activities from smartphone sensor signals", *Proceedings of the 22nd ACM International Conference on Multimedia*, pp. 865–868, 2014.

[HAM 16] HAMMERLA N.Y., HALLORAN S., PLOETZ T., "Deep, convolutional, and recurrent models for human activity recognition using wearables", arXiv preprint arXiv:1604.08880, 2016.

[HAN 10] HAN C.W., KANG S.J., KIM N.S., "Implementation of home-based human activity recognition using single triaxial accelerometer", *Communications and Computer Sciences*, vol. 93, no. 7, pp. 1379–1383, 2010.

[HAT 80] HATCHELL P.C., COLLINS A.C., "The influence of genotype and sex on behavioral sensitivity to nicotine in mice", *Psychopharmacology*, vol. 71, pp. 45–49, 1980.

[HIN 06] HINTON G.E., SALAKHUTDINOV R.R., "Reducing the dimensionality of data with neural networks", *Science*, vol. 313, no. 5786, pp. 504–507, 2006.

[HOE 15] HOEPPNER B.B., HOEPPNER S.S., SEABOYER L. *et al.*, "How smart are smartphone apps for smoking cessation: A content analysis", *Nicotine & Tobacco Research*, vol. 18, no. 5, pp. 1025–1031, 2015.

[HOU 08] HOUGH P., "'Make goals not war': the contribution of international football to world peace", *The International Journal of the History of Sport*, vol. 25, pp. 1287–1305, 2008.

[HUE 03] HUESMANN L.R., MOISE-TITUS J., PODOLSKI C.L. *et al.*, "Longitudinal relations between children's exposure to TV violence and their aggressive and violent behavior in young adulthood: 1977–1992", *Developmental Psychology*, vol. 39, no. 2, 201 pp., 2003.

[IGU 15] IGUCHI K., HIJIKATA Y., NISHIDA S., "Individualizing user profile from viewing logs of several people for TV program recommendation", *Proceedings of the 9th International Conference on Ubiquitous Information Management and Communication*, Article no. 61, 2015.

[KAR 12] KARSOLIYA S., "Approximating number of hidden layer neurons in multiple hidden layer BPNN architecture", *International Journal of Engineering Trends and Technology*, vol. 3, pp. 714–717, 2012.

[KHA 10] KHAN A.M., LEE Y.-K., LEE S. *et al.*, "Human activity recognition via an accelerometer-enabled-smartphone using kernel discriminant analysis," *5th International Conference on Future Information Technology (FutureTech)*, pp. 1–6, 2010.

[KOS 12] KOSE M., INCEL O.D., ERSOY C., "Online human activity recognition on smart phones", *Workshop on Mobile Sensing: From Smartphones and Wearables to Big Data*, vol. 16, pp. 11–15, 2012.

[KOZ 91] KOZA J.R., RICE J.P., "Genetic generation of both the weights and architecture for a neural network," *IJCNN-91 Seattle International Joint Conference on Neural Networks*, pp. 397–404, 1991.

[KWA 11] KWAPISZ J.R., WEISS G.M., MOORE S.A., "Activity recognition using cell phone accelerometers", *ACM SigKDD Explorations Newsletter*, vol. 12, pp. 74–82, 2011.

[LES 06] LESTER J., CHOUDHURY T., BORRIELLO G., "A practical approach to recognizing physical activities", in FISHKIN K.P., SCHIELE B., NIXON P. *et al.* (eds), *Pervasive Computing*, Springer, Berlin-Heidelberg, 2006.

[LI 11] LI N., HOU Y., HUANG Z., "A real-time algorithm based on triaxial accelerometer for the detection of human activity state", *Proceedings of the 6th International Conference on Body Area Networks*, pp. 103–106, 2011.

[LIA 09] LIAO J., BI Y., NUGENT C., "Evidence fusion for activity recognition using the Dempster-Shafer theory of evidence", *9th International Conference on Information Technology and Applications in Biomedicine (ITAB)*, pp. 1–4, 2009.

[LIA 10] LIAO J., BI Y., NUGENT C., "Activity recognition for smart homes using Dempster-Shafer theory of evidence based on a revised lattice structure", *Sixth International Conference on Intelligent Environments (IE)*, pp. 46–51, 2010.

[LIU 11] LIU T., LI M., ZHOU S. *et al.*, "Sentiment classification via l2-norm deep belief network", *Proceedings of the 20th ACM International Conference on Information and Knowledge Management*, pp. 2489–2492, 2011.

[MAG 12] MAGUIRE B., DESAI S., "Dempster-Shafer fusion for personnel detection: application of Dempster-Shafer theory with ultrasonic micro-Doppler and PIR sensors", *15th International Conference on Information Fusion (FUSION)*, pp. 2209–2214, 2012.

[MCC 15] MCCAFFREY J.D., "Particle swarm optimization using Python", available at: https://jamesmccaffrey.wordpress.com/2015/06/09/particle-swarm-optimization-using-python/, 2015.

[MIL 06] MILENKOVIĆ A., OTTO C., JOVANOV E., "Wireless sensor networks for personal health monitoring: issues and an implementation", *Computer Communications*, vol. 29, no. 13, pp. 2521–2533, 2006.

[MIR 15] MIRONIDOU-TZOUVELEKI M., TZITZI E., TZITZIS P., "Electronic cigarette (E-Cig) as a way of smoking cessation: benefits and potential harms", *Journal of Drug Addiction, Education, and Eradication*, vol. 11, pp. 235, 2015.

[MOM 07] MOMPEROUSSE D., DELNEVO C., LEWIS M., "Exploring the seasonality of cigarette-smoking behaviour", *Tobacco Control*, vol. 16, pp. 69–70, 2007.

[MON 09] MONTAVON G., "Deep learning for spoken language identification", *NIPS Workshop on Deep Learning for Speech Recognition and Related Applications*, pp. 1–4, 2009.

[MUR 12] MURRAY J., GOLDENBERG S., AGARWAL K. *et al.*, "Story-map: iPad companion for long form TV narratives", *Proceedings of the 10th European Conference on Interactive TV and Video*, pp. 223–226, 2012.

[MUR 14] MURAO K., TERADA T., "A recognition method for combined activities with accelerometers", *Proceedings of the 2014 ACM International Joint Conference on Pervasive and Ubiquitous Computing: Adjunct Publication*, pp. 787–796, 2014.

[NGI 11] NGIAM J., KHOSLA A., KIM M. *et al.*, "Multimodal deep learning", *Proceedings of the 28th International Conference on Machine Learning (ICML-11)*, pp. 689–696, 2011.

[OLI 02] OLIVER N., HORVITZ E., GARG A., "Layered representations for human activity recognition", *Proceedings of the 4th IEEE International Conference on Multimodal Interfaces*, 2002.

[OUC 13] OUCHI K., DOI M., "Smartphone-based monitoring system for activities of daily living for elderly people and their relatives etc.", *Proceedings of the 2013 ACM Conference on Pervasive and Ubiquitous Computing Adjunct Publication*, pp. 103–106, 2013.

[PAT 14] PATEL K., VALA J., PANDYA J., "Comparison of various classification algorithms on iris datasets using WEKA", *International Journal of Advanced Engineering Research and Technology*, vol. 1, 2014.

[RAH 15] RAHMAN S.A., MERCK C., HUANG Y. *et al.*, "Unintrusive eating recognition using Google Glass", *Proceedings of the 9th International Conference on Pervasive Computing Technologies for Healthcare*, pp. 108–111, 2015.

[RAV 05] RAVI N., DANDEKAR N., MYSORE P. *et al.*, "Activity recognition from accelerometer data", *AAAI*, vol. 5, pp. 1541–1546, 2005.

[RUS 11] RUSSELL S., Bayesian networks: Inference and learning, Fall 2011 Lecture notes, University of California, Berkeley, 2011.

[SAL 09] SALAKHUTDINOV R., HINTON G.E., "Deep Boltzmann machines", *International Conference on Artificial Intelligence and Statistics*, pp. 448–455, 2009.

[SAL 15] SALAMON J., BELLO J.P., "Unsupervised feature learning for urban sound classification", *IEEE International Conference on Acoustics, Speech and Signal Processing (ICASSP)*, pp. 171–175, 2015.

[SAN 16a] SAN-SEGUNDO R., ECHEVERRY-CORREA J., SALAMEA C., "Humanscale activity monitoring based on hidden Markov models using a smartphone", *IEEE Instrumentation & Measurement Magazine*, vol. 19, no. 6, 2016.

[SAN 16b] SAN-SEGUNDO R., MONTERO J., BARRA-CHICOTE R. *et al*, "Feature extraction from smartphone inertial signals for human activity segmentation", *Signal Processing*, vol. 120, pp. 359–372, 2016.

[SAP 08] SAPONAS T., LESTER J., FROEHLICH J., *et al.*, "iLearn on the iphone: real-time human activity classification on commodity mobile phones," University of Washington CSE Tech Report UW-CSE-08-04-02, vol. 2008, 2008.

[SAZ 11] SAZONOV E.S., FULK G., HILL J. *et al.*, "Monitoring of posture allocations and activities by a shoe-based wearable sensor", *IEEE Transactions on Biomedical Engineering*, vol. 58, no. 4, pp. 983–990, 2011.

[SEI 11] SEIGEL M., *et al.*, "Electronic cigarettes as a smoking cessation tool", *American Journal of Preventive Medicine*, vol. 40, 2011.

[SEL 98] SELESNICK I.W., BURRUS C.S., "Generalized digital Butterworth filter design", *IEEE Transactions on Signal Processing*, vol. 46, no. 6, pp. 1688–1694, 1998.

[SEN 02] SENTZ K., FERSON S., "Combination of evidence in Dempster-Shafer theory". *Sandia National Laboratories Albuquerque*, vol. 4015, 2002.

[SEO 16] SEO J., LIM J.H., OH C. *et al.* "A system designed to collect users' TV-watching data using a smart TV, smartphones, and smart watches", *Proceedings of the ACM International Conference on Interactive Experiences for TV and Online Video*, pp. 147–153, 2016.

[SHE 13] SHEELA K.G., DEEPA S.N., "Review on methods to fix number of hidden neurons in neural networks", *Mathematical Problems in Engineering*, vol. 2013, 2013.

[SIM 09] SIMON C., WEBER P., "Evidential networks for reliability analysis and performance evaluation of systems with imprecise knowledge", *IEEE Transactions on Reliability*, vol. 58, no. 1, pp. 69–87, 2009.

[TAY 07] TAYLOR A.H., USSHER M.H., FAULKNER G., "The acute effects of exercise on cigarette cravings, withdrawal symptoms, affect and smoking behaviour: a systematic review", *Addiction*, vol. 102, pp. 534–543, 2007.

[TOD 04] TODD M., "Daily processes in stress and smoking: effects of negative events, nicotine dependence, and gender", *Psychology of Addictive Behaviors*, vol. 18, pp. 31, 2004.

[VAN 08] VAN KASTEREN T., NOULAS A., ENGLEBIENNE G. *et al.*, "Accurate activity recognition in a home setting", *Proceedings of the 10th International Conference on Ubiquitous Computing*, pp. 1–9, 2008.

[VOO 91] VOORBRAAK F., "On the justification of Dempster's rule of combination", *Artificial Intelligence*, vol. 48, no. 2, pp. 171–197, 1991.

[WAG 12] WAGNER A., DALLONGEVILLE J., HAAS B., *et al.*, "Sedentary behaviour, physical activity and dietary patterns are independently associated with the metabolic syndrome", *Diabetes & Metabolism*, vol. 38, no 5, pp. 428–435, 2012.

[WAN 16] WANG H., YEUNG, D-Y., *Towards Bayesian Deep Learning: A Survey*, arXiv preprint, arXiv:1604.01662, 2016.

[WEB 16] WEBER D., MAYER S., VOIT A. *et al.* "Design guidelines for notifications on smart TVs", *Proceedings of the ACM International Conference on Interactive Experiences for TV and Online Video*, pp. 13–24, 2016.

[WEI 12] WEISS G.M., LOCKHART J.W., "The impact of personalization on smartphone-based activity recognition", *AAAI Workshop on Activity Context Representation: Techniques and Languages*, pp. 98–104, 2012.

[WEI 16a] WEISS G.M., LOCKHART J., PULCKAL T. *et al.*, "Actitracker: a smartphone-based activity recognition system for improving health and well-being", *IEEE International Conference on Data Science and Advanced Analysis (DSAA)*, 2016.

[WEI 16b] WEISS G.M., TIMKO J.L., GALLAGHER C.M. *et al.*, "Smartwatch-based activity recognition: A machine learning approach", *2016 IEEE-EMBS International Conference on Biomedical and Health Informatics (BHI)*, pp. 426–429, 2016.

[XIA 13] XIA L., AGGARWAL J.K., "Spatio-temporal depth cuboid similarity feature for activity recognition using depth camera", *Proceedings of the IEEE Conference on Computer Vision and Pattern Recognition*, pp. 2834–2841, 2013.

[YAG 87] YAGER R.R., "On the Dempster-Shafer framework and new combination rules", *Information Sciences*, vol. 41, no. 2, pp. 93–137, 1987.

[ZAD 84] ZADEH L.A., "Review of a mathematical theory of evidence", *AI Magazine*, vol. 5, no. 3, 81 pp., 1984.

[ZHA 11] ZHANG H., PARKER L.E., "4-dimensional local spatio-temporal features for human activity recognition", *IEEE/RSJ International Conference on Intelligent Robots and Systems (IROS)*, pp. 2044–2049, 2011.

[ZHU 09] ZHU C., SHENG W., "Multi-sensor fusion for human daily activity recognition in robot-assisted living", *Proceedings of the 4th ACM/IEEE International Conference on Human Robot Interaction*, pp. 303–304, 2009.

Study and Development of a Smart Cup for Monitoring Post-stroke Patients' Activities at Home

3.1. Introduction

A total of 15 million people worldwide are affected by strokes each year and experience various cognitive and motor deficits [KIM 92]. Of them, 5 million people die and 5 million remain disabled. Post-stroke disabilities are diverse and vary depending on the area of the brain affected. Motor deficits such as spasmodic paralysis or muscle weakness and ocular disorders are often experienced [KIM 92, DET 93]. Post-stroke rehabilitation is expensive in terms of infrastructure and medical staff. Yet, follow-ups at home can be valuable to evaluate the evolution of patients' health status. In general, progress is assessed by a therapist before each rehabilitation session by empirical measurements based on visual estimations [PAN 14].

Several research groups have proposed new technological approaches, such as serious games, to provide new tools for stroke rehabilitation [FRI 15, VOG 14]. These tools provide playful environments that include a series of suitable tasks and specific exercises for rehabilitation. However, these applications are expensive in terms of equipment and rather constraining. Indeed, they require being in front of screens, which limits the frequency and duration of physical exercise.

Chapter written by Mehdi AMMI, Mehdi BOUKALLEL, Margarita ANASTASSOVA, Hamdi AMROUN and Maxence BOBIN.

To overcome the limitations of existing platforms and post-stroke follow-up approaches for rehabilitation, we imagined an ecosystem of smart objects interacting with each other, which will be able to monitor the activities of patients at home in a transparent way (eating, walking, cleaning etc.). In order to perform monitoring at home without disturbing the daily activities of patients, we decided to develop an ecosystem of objects used during the activities of daily living (ADLs). As a first step, we offer the first object of the ecosystem, called SyMPATHy (see Figure 3.1), a smart cup that integrates a sensor network to monitor the activities of post-stroke patients at home. The cup is a common object that patients use regularly (for drinking water, coffee, etc.). During handling of the cup, information can be recovered on the way the patient fills, grasps, holds and manipulates the cup, which reflects his/her arm and hand motor activity. SyMPATHy also embeds visual displays for filling and manipulation. These displays provide a relevant feedback strategy that enables the patient to adjust his/her movements when he/she presents visual or cognitive disabilities limiting his/her perception of the environment. Second, the cup detects the apparition and the evolution of tremors which leads to the detection of neurological or motor disorders [MUR 11]. Finally, the cup monitors four everyday life activities (sitting, standing, walking and drinking), allowing the therapist to assess the overall body activity of the patient and detect sedentariness or dependence for some daily basic tasks. All this information (arm and hand motor activity, body activity and tremor assessment) is crucial to evaluate the patient's independence and recovery. Post-stroke patients are often dependent to perform basic tasks and require the help of someone, which is a responsibility of either the patient's family or society (as a nursing auxiliary needs to take care of the patient). Furthermore, modification of the rehabilitation program at the hospital or even a reinstatement can be proposed to the patient if his/her physical state evolves.

In this chapter, we present a review of the state of the art, including existing platforms for stroke monitoring and an activity recognition algorithm. Then, the design concept, including monitored data and sensory feedback of the cup, is introduced. Third, the implementation of the prototype is detailed. Afterward, data processing and analysis is detailed for orientation calculation, tremor detection and characterization as well as the activity analysis method. Furthermore, planned studies are presented. Finally, a conclusion and future prospects for the SyMPATHy platform are detailed.

Figure 3.1. *SyMPATHy during (a) filling, (b) grasping,*
(c) manipulation and (d) positioning. For a color version of
this figure, see www.iste.co.uk/saleh/challenges.zip

3.2. Related work

In this section, we present the state of the art for motor assessment of the upper limbs, activity analysis and post-stroke rehabilitation.

3.2.1. *Upper limbs motor assessment tools*

There are different methods to evaluate the recovery of a patient, but they remain empirical and are based on visual estimations. S. Brunnstrom defined the motor recovery stage (BRS) [SAW 92] after many longitudinal observations. The BRS test is divided into two parts: BRS-A for the arm and BRS-H for the hand. The former includes seven stages evaluating basic and complex arm controls such as bending, extension or moving forward without moving the trunk, while the latter includes six stages that evaluate grasping, lateral prehension or palmar prehension. BSR is mostly used as a clinical method to evaluate the level of post-stroke motor recovery. The higher the stage, the better the recovery. On the basis of BSR, Fugle and Meyer created the Fugle–Meyer assessment (FMA) [FUG 75]. The FMA is the first stroke-specific assessment tool that follows the natural progression of a post-stroke hemiparetic patient [DIP 07], where five domains are assessed, including motor function, sensory function, balance, joint range of motion and joint pain. Finally, the action research arm test (ARAT) is divided into four categories: grasp, grip, pinch and gross movements [VAN 01]. However, ARAT grip and gross movements are used more than grasp and pinch [KWA 07]. All these estimation methods evaluate arm and hand function via different tasks and scales. The most common tasks are hand grasp and elbow flexion. However, these empirical methods are time-consuming and require a therapist.

3.2.2. *New platforms for stroke assessment*

New information and communications technologies (NICTs) have been used in the field of health and, in particular, to provide new approaches for rehabilitation. Serious games were widely studied to enable patients to practice rehabilitation exercises (motor and cognitive) in a playful way at home. Vogiatzaki *et al.* proposed virtual, augmented and immersive environments for training and rehabilitation of post-stroke patients [VOG 14]. These environments provide 3D physical and visual feedback through mixed-reality interactions. Although the patient can perform rehabilitation exercises at home, wearing sensors and using specific devices is required.

Some researchers showed that self-monitoring for rehabilitation is effective for improving physical function and quality of life particularly in early post-stroke patients [KWO 15]. For example, MagicMirror is a self-monitoring platform that uses motion tracking with a Kinect [BAG 10]. Rehabilitation exercises are performed following a "reference" exercise recorded at the hospital by the patient with the help of a therapist. However, these exercises are stroke-specific and monopolize the therapist during the session at the hospital. Another study focused on the process of cooking in terms of cognitive functions [MIY 12]. Cameras are used to monitor the patient during his/her rehabilitation exercise, and speakers are used to allow the therapist to provide advice and encouragements. However, this system is intrusive and requires different pieces of equipment.

3.2.3. *Activity analysis and monitoring*

Many approaches allow us to perform activity recognition. First, different vision systems are used to track human activity. These systems can be fixed or mobile (smartphones, smartwatches, etc.) [SOU 14]. However, these devices are inadequate for monitoring post-stroke patients at home and present several constraints due to the hardware and software complexity of platforms (expansive calculation, robustness of tracking, covering large spaces, etc.).

Moreover, many studies have investigated the recognition of human activity using standard smart objects [GER 04, FON 14, ISO 15, ISH 14]. In fact, this approach provides cheap and lightweight platforms for transparent monitoring of activities with different types of embedded sensors (e.g. inertial measurement units, proximity sensors, force sensors, temperature sensors and health rate sensors). Several other studies have also used these objects to recognize physical activities in specific configurations: by asking participants to perform specific tasks (e.g. standing, sitting or walking upstairs) [ZHU 09] or to details the placement of the device at the beginning of the activity (e.g. in pocket, purse or hand) [GHO 14]. The aforementioned activity recognition approaches present several constraints such as performing specific tasks or placing the sensors in a specific place. However, the tasks and rehabilitation exercises are diverse.

3.2.4. *Tasks and rehabilitation exercises for strokes*

Many patients encounter motor impairments such as hemiparesis and spasticity after a stroke [OLE 14]. They also encounter visual impairments such as vision loss or vision perception problems (double vision, depth and distance perception or color detection problems) [ROW 08]. These motor, sensory and cognitive disabilities have a direct impact on their daily activities. Previous studies [MUR 11, APR 14, VAN 12] have shown that stroke patients face problems in manipulating everyday objects (cup, fork, pen, etc.). They tend to use compensatory strategies (moving the chest forward instead of extending the arm) to reach and move the cup to their mouth. Moreover, performances of ADLs are considered as a good outcome predictor for strokes [GIA 13]. In fact, they reflect the real motor activity and highlight the motor, sensory and cognitive weaknesses of the patients. Finally, [DET 93, KIM 92, SIN 12] showed that tremors can appear after a stroke in addition to fatigue, hemiparesis, spasticity or vision problems.

The state of the art showed that stroke evaluation methods are empirical and based on visual estimations carried out by the therapist during rehabilitation sessions. Other solutions also emerged for home monitoring and rehabilitation, such as serious games and self-monitoring platforms, but they present certain constraints (expansive, specific exercises, short-term monitoring, etc.). Moreover, data processing and activity analysis methods using the Internet of Things (IoT) have only been used in specific configurations. The evaluation of ADLs is an interesting alternative to provide relevant information to therapists on the patients' daily activities. The manipulation of a cup (filling, drinking, etc.) seems to be a relevant task to provide consistent information on arm and hand motor activity, which plays an important role in stroke assessment. Moreover, the data collected with the cup can be used to analyze the patients' daily activities and provide information on their habits and lifestyle.

3.3. Design concept

We developed a smart cup, called SyMPATHy, designed to monitor the motor activities of post-stroke patients. A common ADL is monitored to provide information on patients' activities at different times of the day (e.g. drinking coffee in the morning, drinking water during lunch, walking through the house). In addition, SyMPATHy embeds real-time sensory feedback in order to correct patients' movements. SyMPATHy also provides relevant data to the therapist that allows him/her to adapt the rehabilitation program according to the patient's progress.

The design process of SyMPATHy includes three main steps and is based on the following methodology:

– identification:

  - task to perform,

  - information to monitor,

  - sensory feedback for the patient;

– implementation of the prototype;

– data processing:

  - tremor detection,

  - activity recognition.

3.3.1. *Task identification*

Interviewing two qualified health professionals working in a stroke rehabilitation center helped us to better understand the importance of ADLs, which would allow for an easier acceptance of monitoring systems. Then, Timmermans *et al.* showed that positioning and manipulating are the most suitable exercises for stroke patients [TIM 09], which require good coordination of upper limbs' movements as well as the use of several sensory channels (vision, tactility, proprioception, audio, etc.). A daily activity involving positioning and manipulating tasks is drinking. Indeed, the patient has to grasp the bottle and the cup, raise the bottle above the cup and control the amount of liquid poured into the cup. These activities involve motor actions of different parts of the upper limbs (hand, arm, etc.). Moreover, they simultaneously involve vision, tactility, proprioception and audio sensory feedback.

Several studies in the medical field investigated such tasks (manipulation of a cup, drinking from a cup) in order to assess the performance of stroke patients [MUR 11, APR 14, VAN 12] and showed that kinematic measurements can be used as an objective assessment of upper-extremity motor performance.

On the basis of the results of previous research and interviews, this work focuses on the task of reaching, filling and transporting a cup by stroke patients. This task includes different motor sub-tasks (arm movement, hand grasping, etc.) with the upper limb, which is involved in other common ADLs (cleaning, taking a shower, etc.).

3.3.2. *Monitored information*

The interviews highlighted six main relevant pieces of information to assess patients' recovery progress with the drinking task, which can be divided into two categories: (1) arm and hand motor activity and (2) overall body activity.

– Arm and hand motor activity:

- grasping force applied on the cup;

- liquid level during cup filling;

- orientation of the cup during manipulation;

- cup position relative to a reference position;

- the apparition and evolution of tremors.

– Overall body activity (activity analysis).

3.3.2.1. *Arm and hand motor activity*

Five types of data allow the therapist to assess the arm and hand motor activity of the patient. First, we monitor the pressure exerted by the patient on the cup, which is a good indicator of the recovery state of the hand function [SUN 89].

Second, we monitor the liquid level to evaluate the accuracy and coordination of movements during filling as pouring water into a cup is a challenge for motor-deficient stroke patients.

Third, we monitor the orientation of the cup during manipulation, which allows the therapist to understand the way the patient holds the cup (vertically or not) and to potentially detect motor disorders. Indeed, incorrect posture is generally spotted when the patient presents motor, sensory or cognitive disabilities.

Then, we monitor the movements of the cup in the 3D space in order to evaluate the overall coordination of the upper limbs and particularly whether the patient places the cup on a reference target, for example, a drink coaster placed on the table.

Finally, SyMPATHy also detects the tremors of the patient's hand, which are involuntary muscle contractions and relaxations involving oscillations or twitching movements of one or more body parts with low amplitudes. A previous study highlighted that post-stroke tremors have a frequency below 5 Hz and are perpendicular to the direction of movement [SMA 03]. Moreover, several studies showed that the evolution of the frequency of tremors along with their power allows the therapist to detect the evolution of neurological or motor disorders [MUR 11].

3.3.2.2. *Overall body activity*

The data collected by the sensors are used to analyze the overall body activity of the patient. With activity recognition, the therapist can obtain the sequence of activities carried out by the patient as well as the distribution of the patient's activities over the day. He/she can also assess the patient's progress, the evolution of the patient's dependence and sedentariness. As a reminder, this is the first development of the ecosystem and activity recognition is intended to be performed through all the objects of the ecosystem.

3.3.3. *Sensory feedback*

Providing alert and guidance information during the filling and drinking steps enhances not only the performances of patients (motor control, accuracy of movement), but also their motivations [STA 15]. SyMPATHy focuses on providing information on (1) liquid level, (2) cup orientation and (3) position of the cup relative to a specified target on the table. We decided not to add feedback for tremors and grasping force in order to avoid sensory overload. Only the therapist can access these parameters for the diagnosis. We selected feedback on the advice of an informal study.

The feedback for cup orientation is a visual one. We added a circle of LEDs around the top of the cup to highlight the tilt angle. Indeed, audio feedback cannot provide angle information easily. Distinguishable colors (green: 0–20°; yellow: 20–35°; orange: 35–50° and red: >50°) have been selected to display the cup's orientation in accordance with the European culture. Using distinguishable colors contributes to avoiding the ambiguity of perception for the patient. An in-depth study is required to configure these angles according to therapists' recommendations and patients' behaviors.

The feedback of liquid level also uses the visual channel by displaying colors vertically along the cup (red to green). These colors simplify the information display by providing a discrete representation of the liquid level. The color choice is also based on European culture.

For positioning, binary audio feedback is used to indicate to the patient that the target is reached. We wanted to unload the visual channel by using a speaker integrated in the cup. It plays a tone when the patient brings the cup to the correct position.

3.4. Implementation of the prototype

The SyMPATHy prototype collects data via sensors embedded into the cup. The data are stored in a remote computer via wireless communication.

3.4.1. *Grasping force detection*

In order to encourage the patient to grasp the cup correctly, we designed SyMPATHy with a handprint. Five pressure sensors corresponding to the five fingers were placed on the handprint (see Figure 3.2). We used "force sensing resistors" (FSR) 402, which provides the mean applied force (pressure) on the surface of the sensor. The resistance of the sensor decreases almost linearly with the increase of force applied from 11 to 10,000 g.

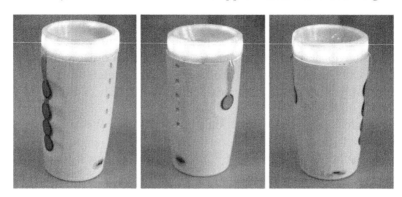

Figure 3.2. *Placement of the FSR around the cup*

The adopted sensors and spatial configurations aim to provide initial measures on the way patients grasp the cup (force ranges, mean force, etc.). Further studies are planned to find the most suitable positions and metrological features for the sensors.

3.4.2. *Liquid level detection*

Because of the constraints of industrial liquid level sensors (low reactivity, size, etc.), we created our own custom sensor based on the measurement of liquid conductivity. Five conductive electrodes were placed vertically inside the cup at a distance of 1 cm from each other corresponding to a volume of 100 ml (see Figure 3.3). Electrodes act as switches, and liquid allows the circuit to be closed. When the liquid is poured into the cup, one or several tension divider bridges are activated, which modify the measured resistance.

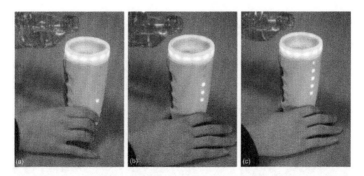

Figure 3.3. *Liquid level feedback using custom sensor: (a) first level filled, (b) third level filled and (c) fifth level filled. For a color version of this figure, see www.iste.co.uk/saleh/challenges.zip*

3.4.3. *Orientation detection*

SyMPATHy embeds an inertial measurement unit (IMU) that retrieves raw movement data (Invensense MPU-9150) via an accelerometer, a gyroscope and a magnetometer. This presents a good compromise between performance, energy efficiency, size and cost. Moreover, data are sampled at 30 Hz in order to light LEDs smoothly (see Figure 3.4).

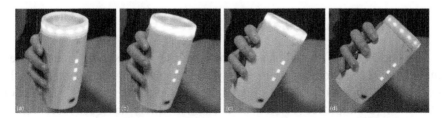

Figure 3.4. *LEDs lighting according to the tilt angle: (a) 0–20°, (b) 20–35°, (c) 35–50° and (d) > 50°. For a color version of this figure, see www.iste.co.uk/saleh/challenges.zip*

3.4.4. *Relative position detection*

We detect whether the patient correctly reaches the target placed on the table using a near-field communication (NFC) reader and an NFC tag as a target (see Figure 3.5). The NFC reader detects the NFC tag, which is a sticker with a microchip, at very short range. The minimum vertical detection distance is approximately 5 mm due to the bottom of the cup. One or several NFC tags can be placed on the table to define different targets to reach.

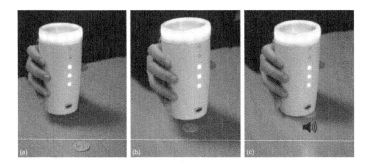

Figure 3.5. *(a) Patient moves the cup toward the target, (b) puts the cup on the target and (c) a tone is played to alert the patient*

3.5. Data processing

In this section, we present the data processing for: (1) orientation detection, (2) tremor detection and characterization and (3) activity recognition.

3.5.1. *Orientation calculation*

On the basis of the values returned by the IMU sensor (nine values, including acceleration, angular velocity and magnetic field), we calculate the position of the sensor (3D orientation of the cup). The RTQF fusion algorithm (a simplified version of a Kalman filter) has been used for an effective fusion of data. RTQF calculates the following two quaternions at every step: (1) a predicted quaternion from the gyroscope for measurement and (2) a ground frame-referenced measured quaternion from the accelerometer and magnetometer. Then, the SLERP (spherical linear interpolation) technique is used to find an intermediate quaternion (3D orientation of the cup) between the two calculated quaternions. On the basis of this quaternion, we computed the tilt angle by calculating the ϕ angle expressed in the spherical coordinate frame. Then, the LED colors (green, yellow, orange and red) are generated to provide the right visual sensory feedback to patients.

3.5.2. *Tremor detection*

3.5.2.1. *Tremor characterization*

Tremor detection is performed with the three axes of the gyroscope. The data collected by the IMU sensor are also used to analyze and classify the activities of the patient. Data processing is performed offline on a computer. Indeed, as the activity recognition visualization is realized on a remote computer, this design choice seemed the best solution in terms of power consumption, power computation and rollout.

Tremor detection uses a spectral analysis tool provided by the MATLAB® software: fast Fourier transform (FFT). FFT highlights the frequency components of a noisy time domain signal. We applied FFT on the measures of each axis of the gyroscope. Then, we computed the power spectral density (PSD) for each axis, which is a measure of energy at various frequencies. This describes how the power of the signal is distributed over frequency. The maximum value of the PSD corresponds to the fundamental frequency of the signal. Figure 3.6 shows the PSD on the vertical axis and the frequency on the horizontal one. A marker is placed on the maximum PSD peak as well as the corresponding PSD and frequency values (see Figure 3.6).

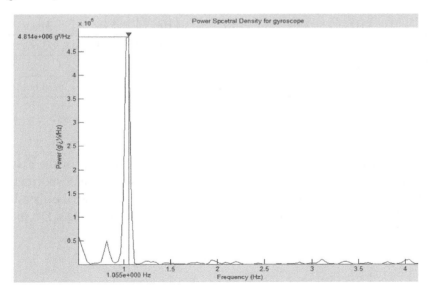

Figure 3.6. *Example of tremor detection on the z axis of the gyroscope. For a color version of this figure, see www.iste.co.uk/saleh/challenges.zip*

3.5.2.2. *Tremor reliability study*

This technical study focuses on assessing the reliability and accuracy of tremor detection. This information is very important for therapists to monitor the progress of patients and to detect health problems.

3.5.2.2.1. Protocol

To generate controlled gyroscopic tremors, a stepper motor was used. A potentiometer was added to the motor to calibrate the frequency of the tremor and to generate a precise frequency. When the potentiometer detects a minimum (or maximum) value, the rotation is reversed. The time between two minimums (or maximums) is used to calculate the frequency of the motor: $1,000 = \Delta t$ (Δt expressed in ms). We performed 30 measurements on each axis for five different tremor frequencies (1, 2, 3, 4 and 5 Hz) according to the specifications demonstrated by Smaga *et al.* [SMA 03].

3.5.2.2.2. Results

We calculated the means of each sample (1–5 Hz on X, Y and Z) as well as the error percentage. Then, we calculated the percentage of general error for each axis to compare it with the percentage of error in the documentation.

	1 Hz	2 Hz	3 Hz	4 Hz	5 Hz	Mean
X	3.12	4.00	3.55	3.96	3.71	3.66
Y	3.32	4.00	3.55	3.86	3.69	3.68
Z	2.93	4.00	3.61	3.80	3.77	3.66

Table 3.1. *Percentage error measured for a specification of ±3%*

Table 3.1 shows that the error percentage is independent of the axis of rotation. In addition, the IMU conforms to the datasheet which specifies an error range of 3%. The difference between our results and the datasheet could be reduced by increasing the sampling frequency or using a DC motor to avoid parasitic vibrations.

3.5.3. *Activity recognition*

In this section, we present the methodology followed to recognize user activities. This preliminary study is conducted on healthy subjects in order to demonstrate the feasibility of activity recognition with the IMU data collected during cup usage.

3.5.3.1. *Protocol*

A total of 15 participants were selected for this experiment. The data were recorded at a sampling frequency of 30 Hz via WiFi under controlled conditions in a laboratory corridor.

In order to simulate more realistic everyday tasks, the participants were asked to perform the following tasks (see Figure 3.7) for 10 min continuously: (1) sitting, (2) standing, (3) walking and (4) drinking. This behavior is similar to the activities of post-stroke patients at home during the day and is easily controllable.

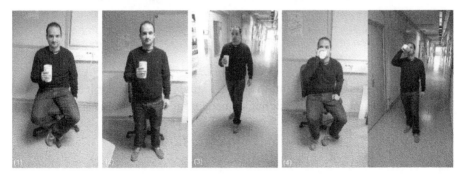

Figure 3.7. *The five tasks performed by a participant*

The activity analysis method includes the following steps:

– extraction of a useful signal;

– calculation of the signal's representative key points;

– classification performances;

– creation of database for future learning.

3.5.3.2. *Extraction of useful signal*

Figure 3.8 shows an illustration of the accelerometer signals recorded during the walking task. The abscissa axis represents time (in s), and the ordinate axis represents acceleration (in multiples of g, the gravity).

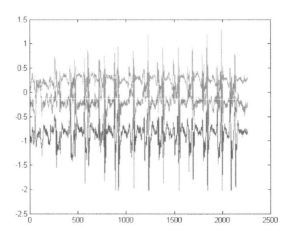

Figure 3.8. *Representation of signals of the "walking" activity. For a color version of this figure, see www.iste.co.uk/saleh/challenges.zip*

We performed a segmentation of the signals to allow stable, similar and therefore non-noisy periodic signal sequences, as shown in Figure 3.9.

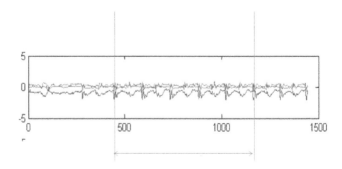

Figure 3.9. *Segmentation, cleaning and extraction of a useful signal. For a color version of this figure, see www.iste.co.uk/saleh/challenges.zip*

3.5.3.3. *Calculation of the signal's representative key points*

Before using any learning algorithm, we compressed the data; that is, we found representative key points of a signal (called descriptors) that characterize the signal. We decided to use the discrete cosine transform DCT-II as a descriptor \cite{de2008face} because the DCT is a good signal decorrelator, and it also has the peculiarity of regrouping the energy in the low-frequency coefficients thanks to its approximation of the Karhunen–Loeve transform of main component analysis.

The DCT of a sample $X_n, n \in [0, 1, .., N-,]$ is given by:

$$X_0 = \frac{1}{\sqrt{N}} \sum_{n=0}^{N-1} x(n) \tag{3.1}$$

$$X_c(k) = \sqrt{\frac{2}{N}} \sum_{n=0}^{N-1} x(n) \cos \frac{(2n+1)\pi k}{2N}, k \in [1..N-.] \tag{3.2}$$

As $X_c(k)$ is the kth DCT coefficient, we calculated all the N coefficients of the DCT using a fast 2N points Fourier transform. It is shown that when the sampling frequency is normalized to 1, $X_c(k)$ is a bandpass filter having center frequency at $\frac{2k+1}{2N}$; therefore, the amplitude of the output of $X_c(k)$ is greater when k is small. In other words, DCT can be concentrated in the low-DCT indices if the remaining coefficients can be zeroed without significant impact on signal energy.

As the IMU signals were not homogeneous, we decided to cut signals in regular portions (see Figure 3.10). Indeed, using the whole signal can cause an overfitting; that is, the learning model will learn the data by heart and the generalization will be inaccurate.

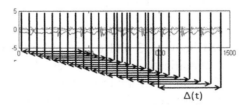

Figure 3.10. *Cutting of the signal. For a color version of this figure, see www.iste.co.uk/saleh/challenges.zip*

3.5.3.3.1. Size of the signal cutting window

All results have been obtained by using support vector machines (SVM), which is a linear classification algorithm.

The aim is to choose the size of the signal cutting window and decide if the overlap can bring more precision to the calculations. Two cutting sizes (Δt) were investigated: the first one has a length of 256 samples (2.13 s) and the second one has 512 samples (4.26 s). We did not use more than 512 points per window because this could compromise the real-time aspect of the response.

We computed the average performance with each sensor of the IMU with different cutting sizes (128, 256 and 512) for each tracked activity. The average performance is 93.37% for the accelerometer signals, 85.49% for the gyroscope and 82.86% for the magnetometer with overlap between the windows and a cutting size of 512.

3.5.3.3.2. Descriptor size

After setting the cutting size, we determined the descriptor size (see Figure 3.11), which results in better performances for classification.

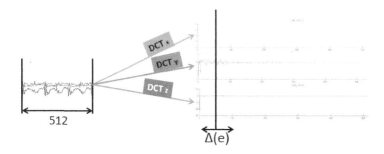

Figure 3.11. *Calculating descriptors for each axis for each sensor. For a color version of this figure, see www.iste.co.uk/saleh/challenges.zip*

The $\Delta(e)$ was tested between 2 and 64, in order to find the best $\Delta(e)$, which gives the best classification performances. A descriptor of size 32 gives better classification performance for the accelerometer and magnetometer. For the gyroscope, the best classification performances are obtained with a descriptor of size 48.

3.5.3.4. *Classification performances*

As each sensor is composed of three axes, it is important to find whether the use of only one axis or the merge axis will allow us to have better precision. The attention was focused on the descriptors constructed not only from the three axes, X, Y and Z, but also from the X axis and from the Y axis. It should be noted that the obtained classification performances use a 512 cutting window with an overlap and a descriptor size of 144 (48 × 3) for the gyroscope and 96 (32 × 3) for the accelerometer and magnetometer.

The concatenation of the three axes of the accelerometer, gyroscope and magnetometer allows us to achieve better performance for classification.

3.5.3.5. *Creation of database for future learning*

The determined DCTs of each axis (X, Y and Z) of each sensor are concatenated to form descriptors, which are stored in a database used for the classification step, in which the data set will be subdivided into a training set and test set. The learning phase is performed by the 10-fold cross-validation method.

The concatenation of the three sensor signals gives the best result with a precision of 94.33% for activity recognition with the SVM classification. The concatenation of the sensor signals for the "drinking" activity gives the best results with a precision of 96.98%.

3.5.3.6. *Results*

After extracting a non-noisy periodic signal by segmentation, we calculated descriptors by using the DCT algorithm that allows us to easily identify a signal. Then, we found that the use of overlapping resulted in much better performance for each sensor (accelerometer, gyroscope and magnetometer). Afterward, three cutting sizes were investigated (128, 256 and 512). The best results are obtained with the 512 cutting size for each sensor. Next, we fixed the descriptor size at 32 for the accelerometer and magnetometer and 48 for the gyroscope. We also demonstrated that the concatenation of the three descriptors (X, Y and Z) for each sensor shows better results for activity recognition. Finally, we performed fusion to enhance the precision of activity recognition. The fusion of the three sensors gives the best results (94.33% on average and 96.98% for the "drinking" activity).

A comparative study will be carried out to compare SVM to a nonlinear classification algorithm, multilayered perceptron (MLP).

3.6. Planned studies

On the basis of this prototype of SyMPATHy, two studies are planned with therapists and patients. The first objective is to collect feedback in order to improve the design and functionalities of the cup. The usability and acceptability of the platform will also be studied. Finally, the impact of SyMPATHy on the health status of patients will be assessed.

3.6.1. *Studies with therapists*

SyMPATHy provides a large amount of relevant data on patient activity (time records, average values, etc.). The data collected must be displayed in order to provide useful information for therapists. A study with therapists working in a rehabilitation center will be carried out in order to create a visualization tool that meets their expectations. This study should highlight the most important information to display and how to display it. More fundamentally, this study will evaluate the usefulness of the data collected by this type of platform to monitor ADLs.

3.6.2. *Studies with patients*

Another study with patients in a rehabilitation center should be conducted. The objective of this study is to assess the acceptability of the cup in the rehabilitation process. First, the cup (features and display) will be presented to the patients. Then, the patients should use the cup without feedback. After that, feedback will be activated. During each step, the acceptability and usability of SyMPATHy will be assessed with patients and therapists. The results of this study should highlight the functionalities to be improved and allow us to identify the weaknesses that could lead to rejection of this technological concept [ANA 07].

3.7. Conclusion and perspectives

In this chapter, we presented the design methodology and the prototype of SyMPATHy, a self-contained smart cup for monitoring post-stroke patients at home. SyMPATHy is the fundamental element of an ecosystem of smart objects for home monitoring. The platform design is based on the activities of daily living, allowing transparent monitoring of the upper limb motor activity of stroke patients and providing feedback to them during their daily activities. Arm and hand motor activity can be assessed by the therapist based on qualitative information (grasping force, liquid level, cup orientation and cup relative position) as well as overall body activity (activity recognition with machine learning). Moreover, the therapist can assess the apparition and evolution of tremors, which is a good indicator of recovery, and modify the rehabilitation program, if necessary. We carried out a preliminary study to assess the precision of the activity recognition with such a device (>92%).

Future works will address several issues. First, based on the SyMPATHy cup, two clinical studies are planned to improve the functionalities of the cup and to create a data visualization tool usable for therapists as well as to evaluate the usability of the cup for patients and therapists. Second, a comparison of the activity recognition algorithm needs to be performed in terms of performances. Furthermore, information retrieval related to movements such as linear acceleration or translation amplitude could provide complementary characteristic information on the patient's movement.

3.8. References

[ANA 07] ANASTASSOVA M., MÉGARD C., BURKHARDT J.M., "Prototype evaluation and user-needs analysis in the early design of emerging technologies", *Human-Computer Interaction. Interaction Design and Usability*, vol. 4550, pp. 383–392, 2007.

[APR 14] APRILE I., RABUFFETTI M., PADUA L. *et al.*, "Kinematic analysis of the upper limb motor strategies in stroke patients as a tool towards advanced neurorehabilitation strategies: a preliminary study", *BioMed Research International*, vol. 2014, Article ID 636123, 2014.

[BAG 10] BAGALKOT N., NAZZI E., SOKOLER T., "Facilitating continuity: exploring the role of digital technology in physical rehabilitation", *Proceedings of the 6th Nordic Conference on Human-Computer Interaction: Extending Boundaries*, ACM, Reykjavik, Iceland, pp. 42–51, 2010.

[DET 93] DETHY S., LUXEN A., BIDAUT L.M. *et al.*, "Hemibody tremor related to stroke", *Stroke*, vol. 24, no. 12, pp. 2094–2096, 1993.

[DIP 07] DIPIETRO L., KREBS H.I., FASOLI S.E. *et al.*, "Changing motor synergies in chronic stroke", *Journal of Neurophysiology*, vol. 98, no. 2, pp. 757–768, 2007.

[FON 14] FONTANA J.M., FAROOQ M., SAZONOV E., "Automatic ingestion monitor: a novel wearable device for monitoring of ingestive behavior", *IEEE Transactions on Biomedical Engineering*, vol. 61, no. 6, pp. 1772–1779, 2014.

[FRI 15] FRIEDRICH R., HIESEL P., PETERS S. *et al.*, "Serious games for home-based stroke rehabilitation", *Studies in Health Technology and Informatics*, vol. 213, pp. 157–160, 2015.

[FUG 75] FUGL-MEYER A.R., JÄÄSKÖ L., LEYMAN I. *et al.*, "The post-stroke hemiplegic patient. 1. A method for evaluation of physical performance", *Scandinavian Journal of Rehabilitation Medicine*, vol. 7, no. 1, pp. 13–31, 1975.

[GER 04] GEROCH M.S., "Motion capture for the rest of us", *Journal of Computing Sciences in Colleges*, vol. 19, no. 3, pp. 157–164, 2004.

[GIA 13] GIALANELLA B., SANTORO R., FERLUCCI C., "Predicting outcome after stroke: the role of basic activities of daily living predicting outcome after stroke", *European Journal of Physical and Rehabilitation Medicine*, vol. 49, no. 5, pp. 629–637, 2013.

[GHO 14] GHOSH A., RICCARDI G., "Recognizing human activities from smartphone sensor signals", *Proceedings of the 22nd ACM International Conference on Multimedia*, ACM, Orlando, FL, pp. 865–868, 2014.

[ISH 14] ISHIMARU S., KUNZE K., KISE K. *et al.*, "In the blink of an eye: combining head motion and eye blink frequency for activity recognition with Google Glass", *Proceedings of the 5th Augmented Human International Conference*, ACM, Kobe, Japan, p. 15, 2014.

[ISO 15] ISODA T., NOHARA Y., INOUE S. *et al.*, "Experiment for nursing activity analysis using mobile sensors and proximity sensors", *Adjunct Proceedings of the 2015 ACM International Joint Conference on Pervasive and Ubiquitous Computing and Proceedings of the 2015 ACM International Symposium on Wearable Computers*, ACM, pp. 153–156, 2015.

[KIM 92] KIM J.S., "Delayed onset hand tremor caused by cerebral infarction", *Stroke*, vol. 23, no. 2, pp. 292–294, 1992.

[KWA 07] KWAKKEL G., KOLLEN B., "Predicting improvement in the upper paretic limb after stroke: a longitudinal prospective study", *Restorative Neurology and Neuroscience*, vol. 25, nos 5–6, pp. 453–460, 2007.

[KWO 15] KWON Y.S., CHOI J.Y., "Effect of self-monitoring rehabilitation program after stroke on physical function, self-efficacy and quality of life", *The Korean Journal of Rehabilitation Nursing*, vol. 18, no. 2, pp. 107–117, 2015.

[MIY 12] MIYAWAKI K., SANO M., YONEMURA S. *et al.*, "Cooking rehabilitation support for self-reliance of cognitive dysfunction patients", *Proceedings of the ACM Multimedia 2012 Workshop on Multimedia for Cooking and Eating Activities*, ACM, Nara, Japan, pp. 19–24, 2012.

[MUR 11] MURPHY M.A., WILLÉN C., SUNNERHAGEN K.S., "Kinematic variables quantifying upper-extremity performance after stroke during reaching and drinking from a glass", *Neurorehabilitation and Neural Repair*, vol. 25, no. 1, pp. 71–80, 2011.

[OLE 14] OLESH E.V., YAKOVENKO S., GRITSENKO V., "Automated assessment of upper extremity movement impairment due to stroke", *PloS One*, vol. 9, no. 8, p. e104487, 2014.

[PAN 14] PANDIAN S., ARYA K.N., "Stroke-related motor outcome measures: do they quantify the neurophysiological aspects of upper extremity recovery?", *Journal of Bodywork and Movement Therapies*, vol. 18, no. 3, pp. 412–423, 2014.

[ROW 08] ROWE F., BRAND D., JACKSON C.A. *et al.*, "Visual impairment following stroke: do stroke patients require vision assessment?", *Age and Ageing*, vol. 38, no. 2, pp. 188–193, 2008.

[SAW 92] SAWNER K.A., LAVIGNE J.M., BRUNNSTROM S., *Brunnstrom's Movement Therapy in Hemiplegia: A Neurophysiological Approach*, Lippincott, Philadelphia, PA, 1992.

[SIN 12] SINISCALCHI A., GALLELLI L., LABATE A. *et al.*, "Post-stroke movement disorders: clinical manifestations and pharmacological management", *Current Neuropharmacology*, vol. 10, no. 3, pp. 254–262, 2012.

[SMA 03] SMAGA S., "Tremor-problem-oriented diagnosis", *American Family Physician*, vol. 68, pp. 1545–1552, 2003.

[SOU 14] SOUCIES N., GIROUARD J., OUARTI N., "Smart moving nightstand, for medical assistance of elderly people: an open project", *Proceedings of the 7th International Conference on Health Informatics: HEALTHINF*, Angers, France, pp. 517–522, 2014.

[STA 15] STANTON R., ADA L., DEAN C.M. *et al.*, "Feedback received while practicing everyday activities during rehabilitation after stroke: an observational study", *Physiotherapy Research International*, vol. 20, no. 3, pp. 166–173, 2015.

[SUN 89] SUNDERLAND A., TINSON D., BRADLEY L. *et al.*, "Arm function after stroke. An evaluation of grip strength as a measure of recovery and a prognostic indicator", *Journal of Neurology, Neurosurgery & Psychiatry*, vol. 52, no. 11, pp. 1267–1272, 1989.

[TIM 09] TIMMERMANS A.A., SEELEN H.A., WILLMANN R.D. *et al.*, "Arm and hand skills: training preferences after stroke", *Disability and Rehabilitation*, vol. 31, no. 16, pp. 1344–1352, 2009.

[VAN 01] VAN DER LEE J.H., BECKERMAN H., LANKHORST G.J. *et al.*, "The responsiveness of the Action Research Arm test and the Fugl-Meyer Assessment scale in chronic stroke patients", *Journal of Rehabilitation Medicine*, vol. 33, pp. 110–113, 2001.

[VAN 12] VAN KORDELAAR J., VAN WEGEN E.E., KWAKKEL G., "Unraveling the interaction between pathological upper limb synergies and compensatory trunk movements during reach-to-grasp after stroke: a cross-sectional study", *Experimental Brain Research*, vol. 221, no. 3, pp. 251–262, 2012.

[VOG 14] VOGIATZAKI E., KRUKOWSKI A., "Serious games for stroke rehabilitation employing immersive user interfaces in 3D virtual environment", *Journal of Health Informatics*, vol. 6, 2014.

[ZHU 09] ZHU C., SHENG W., "Multi-sensor fusion for human daily activity recognition in robot-assisted living", *Proceedings of the 4th ACM/IEEE International Conference on Human Robot Interaction*, ACM, La Jolla, CA, pp. 303–304, 2009.

4

Enabling Fast-prototyping of Connected Things using the WiNo* Family

In order to deploy the various solutions for the Device Layer of the Internet of Things, these proposals must be evaluated in terms of performance, scalability and repeatability. This chapter introduces our test platform that was designed to support these types of tests. We describe the wireless nodes that make up the test platform and present a selection of use cases.

4.1. Introduction

The Internet of Things (*IoT*) is revolutionizing the field of networks and telecommunications. Many experts anticipate an explosion of connected objects for the years to come [SHA 17] in industrialized countries, particularly with applications related to comfort, leisure, quality of life and health. Emerging countries are also likely to benefit from this revolution because of the existence of numerous applications that generate strong needs for smart-metering solutions (sustainable agriculture, renewable energies, etc.). This possibility is strengthened by the simplicity of the deployment of wireless networks in deserts or hostile areas. Among these connected objects are fixed elements monitoring the environment, and mobile elements, worn by a human, attached to cattle or intelligent vehicles. Today, these different classes form separate networks because they use different communication protocols and sometimes non-interoperable technologies. The purpose of IoT is to have them collaborate by giving them all the possibility to communicate via the Internet. This revolution is at several skill levels and opens up great

Chapter written by Adrien VAN DEN BOSSCHE, Réjane DALCÉ and Thierry VAL.

opportunities for contributions. It is associated with the concept of machine-to-machine communications, M2M, where extensive research is in progress [JAE 14]. In this "cloud of objects", studies related to the hardware and lower layers receive renewed attention as these components constitute the (DL-IoT – *Device Layer of the IoT*) collection network, which can be seen as either the first or last link in the global structure of the IoT. The tools and methods for developing networks and protocols must also be adapted to IoT. We are currently witnessing the emergence of numerous research studies [LEE 16] on simulation tools such as NS3 [NS3 17] or Cooja for Contiki, for testing and analyzing the new lower layers of the collection network. Nevertheless, the great evolution of these last few years remains – in parallel with and in addition to these simulators – the strong orientation of the scientific community toward the prototyping and analysis of real performances allowed by hardware test platforms, described as *testbeds*. The low economic cost and the high availability of efficient and fully reprogrammable components foster the development of these techniques. Several new platforms are emerging and they often come from environments that were set up a few years ago for the wireless sensor network (WSN).

Our research takes place within this context and contributes by proposing and providing an open platform for *fast prototyping of nodes* that can be used for connected objects. One of the strategic choices was to position our platform in the open-source ecosystem, from both the hardware and software points of view. Our contributions differ from the competition by the use of components from the Arduino world, the ability to integrate a large number of *transceivers* and, therefore, a very large diversity of existing and future physical layers, as well as ergonomics facilitating the development of protocols and innovative applications.

After this introduction, we will begin this chapter with a presentation of the normative context of the IoT networks and protocols. In section 4.3, we shall present a state of the art of the main existing platforms: this review will take into consideration both the prototyping and performance evaluation aspects of protocols, as well as the ability to test application-level use cases. In section 4.4, we shall detail our architecture model, referred to as "WiNo", as well as the different versions of this model in an evaluation platform, offering a wide variety of physical layers. In section 4.5, we shall illustrate their use on a few typical examples, before concluding and presenting the outlook of our research.

4.2. Context

Since the beginning of the year 2010, the field of personal and local wireless networks (Wireless Personal Area Network, WPAN and Wireless Local Area Network, WLAN) has registered the emergence of numerous disruptive transmission methods. Many physical layer technologies (PHY) and related medium access layers (MAC) – proprietaries or derived from open standards – are now commonly encountered and implemented in devices. This situation reminds us of the fight for supremacy fought among standards in the 1990s: it was expected that this war would lead to a single standard, unifying all short-range wireless communications, WLAN and WPAN. The best illustration of this unified protocol concept is Bluetooth, which, at the dawn of the 21st Century, won the fight for WPAN standards against WiFi and Zigbee. Ten years later, technological and economic circumstances have allowed many innovative transmission protocols to emerge, from innovative transmission methods (using light: LiFi or using ultra-wide band, UWB) to proprietary protocols aiming to establish themselves as standards (Ant+, LoRaWAN). Protocols from the IEEE sphere are also part of this evolution: many extensions of existing protocols are proposed (802.11ac, 802.15.1 BLE, 802.15.4-2011 in CSS and UWB, 802.15.4-2012 for industry) and new standards are introduced (802.15.6). Finally, the very open fields of cognitive or software radio (Software Defined Radio, SDR, Software Defined Network, SDN) completed the kick on the hornet's nest and reshuffled the deck a little more. We are indeed witnessing an explosion in diversity wherein the unique standard once again seems a utopian concept, which is far from the realities of the field.

Nevertheless, what was promising to be a new battle may not be, in reality: on the one hand, the diversity of transmission methods seems to be assumed by both designers and users and, on the other hand, the availability of IPv4 and IPv6, even on very limited hardware targets, ensures convergence over heterogeneous physical layers. Technological and economic advances in terms of electronic integration are such that communicating objects today integrate several low-layer technologies without major difficulty, the latter eventually converging thanks to higher layers. The best example is the tablet or smartphone, which have been integrating a number of different communication technologies for years: 2G/3G/4G, WiFi, Bluetooth, NFC, and soon LTE/5G and NB-IoT (NarrowBand-IoT). Finally, with the software encroaching on the hardware, it sometimes suffices to install an application to make a device compatible with a new transmission method. This last point could well be generalized in the future with the democratization of the SDR. The coming years will tell if the market, as a whole, definitively accepts this diversity.

We decided to rely on the coexistence of different transmission methods rather than on a single radio technology. Therefore, the main objective of our research is to provide a hardware and software architecture that enables the exploitation of these different transmission methods, through various physical layers, while maintaining a coupling between the studied protocols and the communication technologies: our fast prototyping approach aims to produce result sets that are relevant for the deployment use case in a reasonable space of time. This approach makes it easier to integrate new solutions, as well as choose the best physical layer for selected protocol stacks and various applications. In section 4.3, we shall examine existing fast prototyping platforms for IoT and analyze how they address this problem.

4.3. State of the art

The issue of IoT can be approached from the point of view of data as well as infrastructure. In the first case, the problem has to do with the processing and the transformation of a huge mass of data into relevant information (notion of Big Data). Indeed, the nodes of this network capture information on the environment that can range from classic characteristics like temperature and brightness to the traffic at a given location or the intensity of the magnetic field. Grouping sources to correlate information can lead to innovative applications. Similarly, in this context of crowdsourcing, ensuring that the observed data are the most appropriate is another challenge. The development of a middleware becomes the main issue since it makes material differences transparent in relation to the environment. The VITAL IoT platform [VIT 17] is an example of such a study.

More generally, testbeds can be developed for a specific market with the objective of producing data streams that can improve processes. This is, for instance, the case of platforms referenced by the Industrial Internet Consortium (IIC) [IND 17]: the objective of the testbed dedicated to e-health, the Connected Care Testbed, is to propose information from medical devices in order to avoid erroneous diagnostics. In the same way, the FIESTA-IoT platform [FIE 17] aims to federate existing testbeds in order to give access to the data produced by these different facilities. At the time of writing this, a dozen testbeds have joined FIESTA-IoT, among which is SmartSantander [SÁN 13], which we shall present below.

Approaching IoT with an infrastructure-based vision is as much about developing protocols for secure and remote interaction with equipment, as it is about setting up platforms that enable the extensive study of these solutions. Owing to our specialization in wireless networks, we shall focus on communication aspects of issues related to the Internet of Things. The rest of this section shall present an overview of platforms that are currently available, thus enabling us to clearly position our contribution. On the one hand, we shall present some representative testbeds, while focusing on criteria such as the diversity of the supported PHY layers, the network size, mobility support and proposed development tools. We also offer an overview of platforms that may serve as building blocks for a local testbed.

For several years now, a number of development platforms have emerged. Although they have historically been used for real tests and performance evaluation of wireless sensor networks, they are now part of the Internet of Things. The nodes that make up these platforms are often equipped with light and adapted operating systems. TinyOS was one of the first open-source operating systems designed specifically for communicating light-weight embedded systems, and associated with development and simulation tools. Other software and hardware platforms such as RIOT [RIO 17], LiteOS [CAO 08] and Contiki [DUN 04], specifically developed for TI MSP430 and Atmel AVR microcontrollers, exist. TelosB, Tmote or MicaZ Motes are based on this software environment. The testbeds that we will describe later are built mainly above these different nodes.

Closer to us, research projects have made it possible to design complete environments that are accessible to remote users. The term test bench is commonly used to refer to those platforms which host a large number of nodes, which are open and accessible on demand. These platforms make it possible for users to evaluate their protocols, from functional validation to performance analysis, while investigating the scalability of their solution. One of the first public testbeds in France was SensLab, created by INRIA, initially backed by the French National Research Agency (ANR). As marker of the general evolution of wireless sensor networks toward the Internet of Things, SensLab evolved, in 2012, into the FIT/IoTlab platform [FLE 15].

It should also be noted that there are research teams focused entirely on proposing testbed platforms for wireless sensor networks and communicating objects, such as Planet [KER 14], NITOS and Orbit [ORB 17].

The SmartSantander platform for smart cities competes with FIT/IoT-LAB with regard to the scale of the deployment: each of these testbeds gives access to several thousands of nodes. INDRIYA and TWIST each give access to nearly 200 nodes, deployed on several floors. FIT/IoT-LAB nodes communicate via the IEEE 802.15.4-2006 standard, at 860 MHz and 2.4 GHz. In the case of SmartSantander, the heterogeneity of hardware platforms and communication mechanisms is strong because the population of the network includes NFC tags, smartphones, embedded nodes on public transport buses, etc. This diversity is a factor that allows the platform to get closer to the actual situation of the interaction of nodes equipped with heterogeneous technologies. Although we are focusing on diversity at the communication level, we must not neglect the variety of the sensors built into the nodes. Thus, FIT/IoT-LAB nodes comprise accelerometers, magnetometers and gyrometers. As for the INDRIYA platform, it uses only one radio technology but offers light sensors, infrared detectors, magnetometers, accelerometers and acoustic sensors. It also has the particularity of having a cluster of Arduino nodes. SmartSantander and FIT/IoT-LAB both integrate the mobility component. As a matter of fact, the IoT is susceptible to hosting as many fixed nodes as moving nodes, simply because some nodes are attached to a human (their smartphone, for example). SmartSantander implements this mobility by incorporating both smartphones and buses into its network, while the FIT/IoT-LAB platform supports robot-based mobility in indoor environments.

As for software aspects, our studies show that some tools and services have practically become standards, for example, having a web interface for the visualization of results with variable granularities, being able to reprogram nodes remotely, generating traces of execution and also collecting context data such as energy consumption curves during the experiment. This information is usually produced by a parallel network: the communications happen in an out-of-band fashion so as not to affect the results of the current experiment. In the case of FIT/IoT-LAB, data is stored in CSV files, while SmartSantander and INDRIYA store it in a database. Some testbeds offer additional functionalities, for example TWIST makes it possible to test, without the cooperation of the node, the death of a network element by controlling the activation of the USB interface used for the power supply.

Tools recommended to evaluate the code prior to deployment on the embedded operating systems differ from one platform to another. INDRIYA and TWIST use TinyOS, but the first recommends TOSSIM, while the second recommends the use of Cooja, a simulator with a plugin to easily switch from simulation to testbed. In the case of FIT/IoT-LAB, different OS are supported (FreeRTOS, Contiki, RIOT, TinyOS, OpenWSN) and the choice of simulator is left to the user's discretion.

After this overview of existing testbeds for the IoT as well as some comparison criteria, we shall focus on the details of these hardware platforms suitable for implementing a personal testbed. We shall examine them from the point of view of not only the facility of replication but also the explicit support of multiple physical layers. In fact, conducting research using a test platform that can be set up by another team facilitates reproducibility checks.

Taking into account repeatability, the importance of using Arduino-like components as a basic material for these testbeds becomes obvious. On the one hand, the platform tends to integrate the open character of the Arduino ecosystem, from both a hardware and a software perspective. In fact, as the open-source model has shown its effectiveness in the area of software, today, the hardware follows the same guidelines (the design of cards under the BSD, Creative Commons or even GPL license, etc.). The community can then get hold of these systems and efficiently advance innovations in the field of the Internet of Things. On the other hand, beyond protocols and "network" aspects as such, the high accessibility of these platforms, both technically and economically, means that their use is spreading outside of the Telecoms and Networks community: in the Human–Computer Interaction (HCI) community, experiments are conducted on use cases [DUC 15, VEL 13]; in the eHealth community, prototypes [VIG 15, WU 08, SUR 12, ABD 17] are developed with real sensors, etc. This multidisciplinary approach makes it possible for innovative products and services – which go far beyond the field of Telecoms and Networks – to emerge. These devices, designed for fast prototyping, can be used to quickly develop systems with a *Technology Readiness Level* (TRL) high enough (6-7) to convince potential investors, for example, in a crowdfunding approach.

As can be seen from this quick overview, new platforms are emerging in a very diverse way. Performance evaluation solutions are very diverse and tend toward pragmatism, focusing on real performance, as opposed to just simulated performance analysis, and performances as a whole, that is, by including the system, sensors and even usage, rather than sticking to the usual performance criteria (data rate, latency, loss of messages, etc.).

	FIT/IoT-LAB 2,782 nodes on eight websites	SmartSantander 20,000 nodes on four websites
Management tools and interaction	Web client and Python command line tools: control of node status and configuration, resource reservation and control of scenario execution	Web client and shell scripts: resource reservation and experience control
Handling	Multiple tutorials available Possible access to the platform	Tutorial available Online registration on the platform not available
Diversity of radio technologies	IEEE 802.15.4 (2.4GHz) IEEE 802.11a/b/g	GPRS IEEE 802.15.4 (2.4GHz)
Diverse deployment environments	Laboratory-type indoor environment	Laboratory-type indoor, outdoor (parking, gardens, etc.) and mobile (smartphones and vehicles) environments
Physical modularity	N/A	N/A
Deployment control and customization	Limited	Limited

Table 4.1. *Comparison of FIT/IoT-Lab and SmartSantander*

Table 4.1 summarizes the characteristics of two of the largest platforms. They were selected because of their size and longevity. This longevity criterion is linked to the visibility of the platform in terms of evolutions, information provided by the GitHub statistics and websites associated with these testbeds. Despite the promising features listed, it is clear that, in most cases, the platforms under consideration do not provide a mechanism to facilitate the transition from one physical layer to another. While their deployments encompass different sub-networks in terms of communication technologies, evaluating the same solution on both architectures requires the implementation to be developed once again. In addition, it is sometimes necessary to conduct experiments in an environment similar to that envisaged for actual deployment (mines, tunnels, etc.). From this point of view, although the most active platform, FIT/IoT-Lab, allows the selection of subsets of nodes to constitute test topology, the environment remains homogeneous (typically a room in a laboratory). The possibilities of control and customization, as well as the ability to approach the target site, are therefore limited.

Our approach for the cost-effective testbed gets rid of these constraints. In fact, the platform proposed in this chapter respects cost minimization strategies (use of off-the-shelf devices, application of open-source guidelines, etc.), which make it possible to equip locations to be monitored at a reasonable cost. Nevertheless, this desire to keep our solution affordable does not affect the richness of the interaction tools both proposed and under study in the Ophelia project, which aims to provide tools for remote programming, data retrieval and the provision of experimental results.

As far as physical modularity is concerned, the following section will present our solution to this problem by introducing our architecture and instantiating this architecture on different examples.

4.4. Introducing the WiNo* family

As we have seen in previous sections, there is a strong need for an open platform for fast prototyping of network protocols as well as connected devices for wireless sensor networks and the Device Layer of the Internet of Things. Real and pragmatic evaluation is a strong expectation. In this section, we shall present a versatile architectural model that meets these needs.

The proposed architecture is an open node model, "WiNo", a contraction of *Wireless Node*. This architecture is intended to be open and as generic as possible to allow fast prototyping in terms of networks and protocols, as well as the complete prototyping of connected objects that allow pragmatic evaluation through protocol and application use. This architecture was proposed according to the following three principles and objectives:

– rapid integration of new physical layers: one of the difficulties in the context of protocol evaluation is the need to develop new implementations when changing the physical platform;

– form factor adapted to the IoT: from the standpoint of technology transfer from laboratories to the industry, communicating nodes are designed to be integrated as is in most scenarios, without requiring a miniaturization phase;

– ability to support a wide range of sensors for various applications: the platform which we are proposing aims to become a tool for researchers in areas that are different from ours. Applications and interactions with the environment will therefore not be the same.

The architecture includes both hardware and software components. From a hardware point of view, the solution is based on the Arduino ecosystem, well known for its relevance and efficiency in the fast prototyping of small electronic systems. This choice was refined with the selection of a microcontroller module of this ecosystem that is adapted to the identified needs: the selected module, the Teensy 3.x, has more memory and a more powerful processor than most Arduino platforms. The amount of memory is particularly relevant as, during protocol performance evaluation, results are stored in order to not consume CPU time. From a software standpoint, several components have been developed in order to abstract the interface with the transceiver component. Finally, in order to facilitate evaluation through usage (including mobile situations), the model includes a lithium polymer battery (Li-Po). Figure 4.1 shows this WiNo architecture model. It was then declined in four complementary versions, illustrating its good genericity. The features of each of these versions are summarized in Table 4.4 (section 4.4.4); these versions are presented in the following sections. The website [WIN 17] contains all information about the different WiNo nodes.

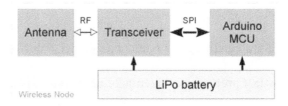

Figure 4.1. *Typical architecture of the WiNo node*

The clear intent of our contribution is to become a reference model. Even if, at first, access to our platform is open to the scientific community, the long-term goal is to inspire the deployment of testbeds that share a set of common features despite being placed under different administrative authorities. In addition to boosting prototype-based research, this strategy will strengthen the guarantee of result repeatability. For the modification of WiNo physical subsystems to be effective, we adopted a modular approach to the software: to avoid a strong coupling between low layers (data link, network) and the physical layer, a library responsible for interaction with the hardware component is developed. This way, a developer can focus on the layer corresponding to the contribution to be analyzed. This strategy enriches the evaluation phase by adding a degree of freedom to experiments, thus choosing the most suitable physical layer for the protocol suite.

The following sections illustrate several instantiations of our model.

4.4.1. WiNoRF22 and TeensyWiNo

WiNoRF22 (Figure 4.2) is the first instantiation of the proposed architecture, while TeensyWiNo, manufactured and distributed by Snootlab.com is an industrialized version of the WiNo architecture, including many additional sensors.

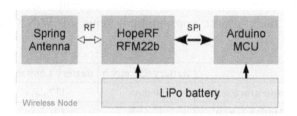

Figure 4.2. WiNoRF22 node architecture

The two nodes (Figure 4.3) share the same features in terms of physical layer. The radio that equips the nodes is a HopeRF RFM22b transceiver; although this "sub-GHz" radio is not compatible with conventional IEEE 802.15.4 transceivers, it shares some features in terms of frame format, while supporting a vast selection of possible configurations on the modulations (OOK, FSK, GFSK), the operating frequency (200–900 MHz), the data rate (1–125 kbps) and the bandwidth (1–125 kHz). This wide panel allows the WiNoRF22 and TeensyWiNo to adapt to many use cases and protocol requirements (low data rate on a star topology, over a range of 300 meters, or higher data rate, to develop mesh protocols with a narrow scope, for example).

Figure 4.3. *WiNo (left) and TeensyWiNo (right)*

IMPORTANT.– In the field of prototypes for sensor networks and connected objects, a very important point concerns the control of energy expenditure related to nodes and communication protocols. In general, if connected objects have lower energy autonomy than their "unconnected" equivalents, their acceptance by users will be difficult. The WiNo design takes this requirement into account and has been evaluated in real-life scenarios. Table 4.2 shows the energy autonomy of a TeensyWiNo measured in real-life scenarios, depending on the capacity of the connected LiPo battery, for two scenarios: temperature sensor (one measurement every ten seconds) or the accelerometer motion sensor (one measurement twice a second). More generally, the main power consumption items of WiNo are shown in Table 4.3.

	Battery 850 mA.h	Battery 1,600 mA.h
Temperature sensor	50 days	117 days
Motion sensor	45 days	101 days

Table 4.2. *Energy autonomy of a TeensyWiNo in a real-life scenarios*

Consumer items	State	Power consumption (Vcc = 3.7 V)
CPU Freescale MK20DX256 VLH7	Active, 96 MHz	129 mW
	Active, 72 MHz	103 mW
	Active, 48 MHz	88.8 mW
	Active, 24 MHz	55.5 mW
	Sleep, wake up by LPTMR	2 mW
	Deepsleep, wake up by LPTMR	650 µW
	Hibernate, wake up by LPTMR	<30 µW

	Transmit (10 dBm)	76 mW
Transceiver HopeRF RFM22b	Receive	57 mW
	Idle	26 mW
	Sleep	<5 μW

Table 4.3. *TeensyWiNo energy consumption*

Compared with WiNoRF22, TeensyWiNo (Figure 4.4) includes many sensors, allowing the prototyping of many communicating objects without additional electronics, as we will see in the next section.

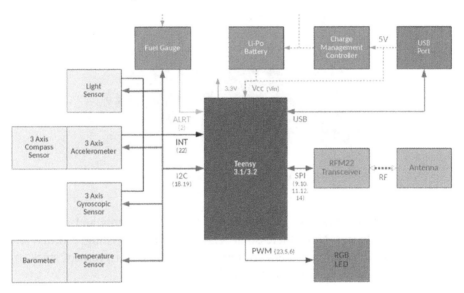

Figure 4.4. *TeensyWiNo node architecture. For a color version of this figure, see www.iste.co.uk/saleh/challenges.zip*

4.4.2. WiNoLoRa

WiNoLoRa is a variation of WiNo that exploits a LoRa (Long-Range) physical layer. LoRa [BOR 16] is a very low-bandwidth transmission method that achieves very high ranges compared with conventional WSN transmission methods; ranges of several hundred meters, or even several kilometers, are attainable with transmission powers of up to tens of milliwatts.

Once more, WiNoLoRa takes the principle of WiNo by replacing the transceiver with a LoRa compatible transceiver: we selected the Hope RFM95, operating in the 868 MHz band. The hardware implementation is shown in Figure 4.6. It is based on the architecture detailed in Figure 4.5.

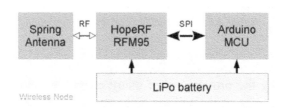

Figure 4.5. *WiNoLoRa node architecture*

Figure 4.6. *WiNoLoRa node prototyping*

WiNoLoRa enables the prototyping of level 2 protocols and more on a LoRa PHY layer. Nevertheless, it can still join existing LoRaWAN networks, depending on the integration of the LoRaWAN protocol stack, of which several open versions are available [IOT 17].

4.4.3. *DecaWiNo*

DecaWiNo is a variation of WiNo that makes the specificities of the UWB physical layer accessible. In addition to the communication function, this PHY allows the implementation of ranging or distance measurement protocols, based on the propagation time of the radio signal. This WiNo variant (Figure 4.7) uses one of the few UWB transceivers available on the market, DecaWave's DW1000. This module has the advantage of complying, to a large extent, with the IEEE 802.15.4-2007 standard describing the operation of a UWB physical layer.

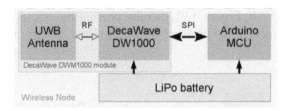

Figure 4.7. *DecaWiNo node architecture*

The control of this transceiver is done through the DecaDuino software library [VAN 16c]. This software library was developed by our team and it provides access to communication functionalities as well as timestamps generated during frame transmission and reception. Our library also provides an estimate of the difference between neighbor nodes' clocks and the possibility of preprogramming the transmission time of a specific bit of the MAC frame, known as RMARKER. This delayed transmission saves messages since the expected transmission time can be carried by the same frame [FOF 16] (Figure 4.8), while the ability to characterize transmission and reception clocks enabled the dynamic correction of propagation time estimates [DAL 15].

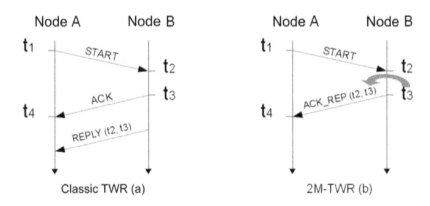

Figure 4.8. *TWR and 2M-TWR protocol sequence diagrams*

DecaDuino provides entry points for the development of new protocols in the form of known protocol implementations such as Two-Way Ranging (TWR) and Symmetric Double-Sided Two-Way Ranging (SDS-TWR). These versions directly access the physical layer through dedicated Service

Access Points (SAP, Figure 4.9), thereby preventing ranging protocols from suffering the effects of the protocol of access to the chosen medium.

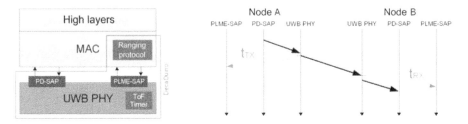

Figure 4.9. *DecaDuino in the protocol stack. For a color*
version of this figure, see www.iste.co.uk/saleh/challenges.zip

4.4.4. Summary of WiNo nodes

The WiNo architecture therefore proposes an open node model and is intended to be as generic as possible to allow fast prototyping in networks and protocols. More generally, it also allows the complete prototyping of connected objects thanks to the simple and fast integration of new physical layers, with a form factor suitable for evaluation through usage as well as the ability to withstand a wide range of sensors for various applications. Table 4.4 summarizes the four variations presented.

	TeensyWiNo	**WiNoRF22**	**WiNoLoRa**	**DecaWiNo**
Use	IoT and RCSF		Long range	Short range, localization
CPU/RAM	PJRC Teensy 3.2, compatible with Arduino (Freescale MK20DX256VLH7) ARM Cortex M4 72MHz, 64kB RAM, 256kB Flash			
Transceiver Modulation	OOK/FSK/GFSK HopeRF RFM22b		LoRa/OOK/FSK/GFSK HopeRF RFM95	UWB DecaWave DW1000
Library	RadioHead			DecaDuino
Sensors	Temp, Lum, Baro, Accelero, Magneto, Gyro		Temperature, brightness	
Others	RGB LED, GPIOs, PWM, ADC/DAC, SPI, I2C, CANbus			
Availability	snootlab.com		DIY	

Table 4.4. *WiNo versions*

Several results and examples of use of the WiNo architecture are detailed in the following section.

4.5. Results and examples of use

Our WiNo platform was used many times for various applications, according to the different WiNo node versions. In this section, we shall present some representative examples of use for the WiNo nodes at 433 MHz (WiNoRF22 and TeensyWiNo), the WiNo equipped with a transceiver to work in LoRa (WiNoLoRa) and the WiNo in UWB version (DecaWiNo), respectively.

4.5.1. *WiNo and TeensyWiNo*

4.5.1.1. *WiNoIR nodes [VAN 16a]*

A classic habitat hosts many devices that are controllable through infrared (IR) remote controls, such as TVs, DVD players, video projectors and home theater systems for the most conventional environments, as well as medical beds, extractor hoods, autonomous robotic vacuum cleaners, Japanese toilets and air conditioning for higher technology habitats. These different devices can form a local IoT through the implementation of gateways between the infrared control system and the local smart habitat network. This IoT can contribute to the resident's comfort as well as serve as a stepping stone toward autonomy for persons with reduced mobility. In this regard, some isolated solutions exist and are often based on the use of the smartphone as a control tool. A first category corresponds to IR-Blasters: in their basic version, they control an IR-emitting diode connected to the audio jack port of the smartphone through a suitable application. Some modern smartphones now integrate this emitting diode.

A second category uses dedicated gateways, such as the Broadlink product [BRO 17]. In this configuration, the smartphone communicates with the gateway and the intelligence of the system, which is usually proprietary, is contained in the gateway. A database of the most conventional IR codes is used and it is often complicated or impossible to control non-traditional or large-scale equipment. The main disadvantage of this class of solutions is the fact that a smartphone is almost indispensable in controlling house equipment.

Other specific solutions exist and are dedicated to disabled people. They are known as telethesis or environmental controls. These systems allow a person with motor disabilities to interact remotely with his environment. The devices are equipped with human–machine interaction techniques adapted to people's situations of disability, whether they are due to deficiencies or to the environment (remote object control), such as the MATT system [VEL 15], the Pictocom system [BOC 16, ACC 17] or the HouseMate Control system [DOM 17], an environmental control via an Android phone or tablet through infrared and radio via D-Box and wireless home automation. Finally, we must not forget the classic and well-known IR remote control systems. Those are mere transponders, usually through a 433 MHz radio layer, which are used to control equipment from a room via the original remote control. The target equipment is located in another room, out of IR range due to distance or obstacles such as walls. The commands are relayed through 433 MHz links. These devices are typically not intended to be interfaced with another network.

The existing body of work shows that, in these situations, it is necessary to propose an open generic remote controller. In order to meet this need, we designed WiNoIR nodes (Figure 4.10), providing IR control of home automation equipment, and connected by a home radio network to other existing equipment and networks. These WiNoIRs are part of an open and scalable equipment control system. This device aims to limit the proliferation of IR remote controls without inhibiting their operation. Control is possible not only from any local source connected to the home network (computer, tablet, smartphone, home automation sensor, control and decision center/unit, etc.), but also from a remote host via the Internet.

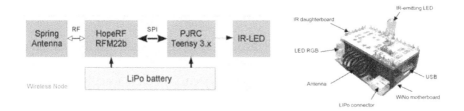

Figure 4.10. *The WiNoIR node*

Since WiNo nodes are based on a Teensy hardware architecture [PJR 17], we naturally turned to the Arduino ecosystem and used the IRremote library initially developed by Ken Shirriff [SHI 17]. This library, developed for Arduino UNO boards, was also adapted to operate on Teensy modules. It offers the possibility to learn codes of existing remote controls (with a specific node equipped with a receptor LED), and replay these codes later. The first step will consist of learning IR codes for a given target. The IRremote library is used to collect IR codes produced by a receiver connected to a Teensy input port. These codes are then processed, recognized and identified among the most common codes (RC5, RC6, Sony, Samsung, etc.) and stored. The next step is to replay these codes via an IR-emitting diode connected to an output port. The IRremote library is generic enough to adapt to the most standard modulations (38 KHz), although it is also possible to modify this parameter. For unrecognized IR codes, it is also possible to work in RAW mode. This mode puts a bigger strain on the memory because it actually encodes each command as a succession of IR pulses of which the duration is stored in milliseconds, as well as the duration between two successive IR flashes. We chose this mode of operation because it works for both known remote controls and those using proprietary IR encoding.

WiNoIR nodes are currently used in the IUT Blagnac smart home [MAI 17], especially during the real testing of the use of the MIB by elderly participants. These tests are part of the SENUM (*Séniors et Numerique*, seniors and digital) research project in partnership with AG2R LA MONDIALE, and are also performed in collaboration with other research programs [BOU 16, VAN 16b]. The WiNoIR nodes allow us to remotely (within the same local network, or potentially from a remote machine connected to the Internet network) control all home equipment, even those for which no IP interface is provided. The methodology used for their design, and especially the learning of IR codes, makes them interoperable with any equipment that has a classic IR remote control.

4.5.1.2. *Example of interaction objects: the cane*

By modifying our WiNo sensors and actuators, we have designed connected objects of interaction: the connected cane and the interaction cube. The general objective is to facilitate communication between the home and the resident, especially in the case of home care for the elderly. In this section, we introduce our connected walking device.

In order to track the elderly, it is common to equip them with medallions or other types of bracelets. These devices can be used to detect falls, as well as measure their activities, movements, etc. Nevertheless, these devices are quite cumbersome as it is common for the elderly to forget to put them back after having dropped them or taken them off before their shower. Taking into consideration the fact that the walking device is equipment commonly used by these people, in 2012 we set up the CANet project, whose objective is to follow the behavior of a person via his/her instrumented walking stick.

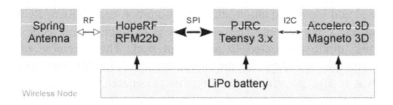

Figure 4.11. *WiNo node architecture specific to the CANet project*

The cane is equipped with a specific WiNo node (Figures 4.11 and 4.12), which is narrow enough to fit in the stick of the cane, and it has a 3D accelerometer, a 3D magnetometer, a Teensy module, an RFM22b radio transceiver and a LiPo battery. After local processing, the cane is able to evaluate the number of steps taken and the distance covered, as well as detect falls followed by inactivity. This is then transferred through radio alerts [LAC 16]. A CANet LoRaWAN version is also under study and would also help with accompanying elderly persons outdoors, while checking their location without the use of a GPS.

Figure 4.12. *The connected cane and its dedicated WiNo node*

4.5.2. *WiNoLoRa*

One of the advantages of the WiNo architecture is its ability to develop and test level 2 protocols, and even beyond, on physical layers proposed by the associated transceiver. In order for this development to be carried out, it is important to know the physical layer. In this section, we shall present a performance review of the LoRa PHY layer, in terms of data rate and medium occupation. This study was conducted using the WiNoLoRa prototype.

NOTE.– The LoRa technology is systematically presented as a "dial-up" transmission method. However, what is the order of magnitude? This study, which is carried out from the WiNoLoRa node, provides orders of magnitude in terms of the data rate and temporal occupation of the medium.

In order to carry out this experiment, two WiNoLoRa nodes were configured: the first as a transmitter, and the second as a receiver. The scenario is as follows: the transmitter forms frames of a payload of random length, while the receiver ensures the proper reception of these messages. The time on the channel is measured on both sides, and the equality of the obtained values is verified. The scenario is executed for three different configurations of the LoRa PHY, defined through variations in the Bandwidth (BW), Coding Rate (CR) and Spreading Factor (SF) parameters:

– BW = 125 kHz, CR = 4/5, SF = 7 (128 bits of spreading code);

– BW = 125 kHz, CR = 4/8, SF = 12 (4,096 bits);

– BW = 31.25 kHz, CR = 4/8, SF = 9 (512 bits).

The results shown in Figure 4.13 indicate that, according to expectations, the data rate increases with the payload length (PPDU), which is explained by the presence of a native protocol load (header, CRC) of the physical-level protocol. This load is "profitable" on messages of long length. While the first scenario achieves an effective rate of nearly 5 kbit/s, the two other settings can reach a rate of 150 and 250 bit/s, respectively, with regard to payloads of 150 bytes. It should be noted that these data rates are to be considered, taking into account the time on the channel, which can be more than seven seconds in scenario 2, for a payload of 150 bytes (Figure 4.14). Actually, regulations require a utilization rate (duty cycle) that is limited per unit time.

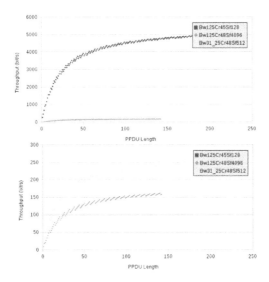

Figure 4.13. *Data rates of a link using a LoRa PHY layer according to PHY parameters. For a color version of this figure, see www.iste.co.uk/saleh/challenges.zip*

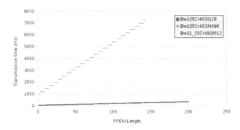

Figure 4.14. *Time on the medium according to PHY parameters. For a color version of this figure, see www.iste.co.uk/saleh/challenges.zip*

Our current research focuses mainly on the joint use of several complementary technologies dedicated to the IoT, including LoRa [GON 16].

4.5.3. *DecaWiNo*

The DecaDuino library is accompanied by known protocol implementations such as TWR and SDS-TWR. These two ranging protocols are often compared in terms of robustness with respect to the quality of the clocks, and more precisely in terms of skew. The SDS-TWR protocol in particular has been highlighted in [IEE 07] for its ability to mitigate the deleterious effects of the difference between transmitter and receiver clocks on propagation time estimates. Unfortunately, SDS-TWR requires a large number of transmitted frames compared to TWR.

From the delayed transmission feature provided by our library, we proposed the 2M-TWR ranging protocol, which is more efficient in terms of overhead.

Figure 4.15 shows the ranging error obtained with 2M-TWR compared to the TWR classic version in a LOS (line of sight) situation. As can be seen, the average error remains within 20 cm. However, the delayed transmission feature causes significant discrepancies between measurements, which we are currently studying and compensating for with a specific protocol.

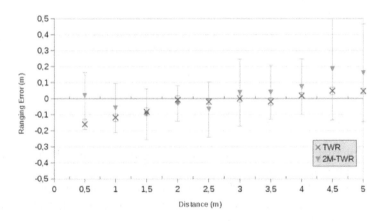

Figure 4.15. *Performance of the 2M-TWR protocol compared to the TWR classic version. For a color version of this figure, see www.iste.co.uk/saleh/challenges.zip*

4.5.4. Summary and comparative analysis

One of the driving forces behind the development of the prototyping platforms presented in this chapter is the reconciliation between the review of theoretical performances and the reality in the field. In order to integrate with different projects and approaches, and besides having a rich control interface, testbeds must be flexible and modular: the cost of switching from one physical layer to another must be reasonable.

The WiNo node family addresses this issue by presenting a standardized interface to the Data Link layer. Research teams wishing to conduct experiments in a real environment just have to make their choice using the indications in Table 4.5.

	TeensyWiNo/WiNoRF22	WiNoLoRa	DecaWiNo
Radio range	100 m indoors (GFSK modulation)	30 km line of sight	20 m line of sight
Supported flow rate	0.123 to 256 kbit/s	0.3 to 20 kbit/s	110, 850 and 6,800 kbit/s
Frequency band	433/470/868/915MHz (ISM)	868 MHz	3.5 GHz to 6.5 GHz
Available resources	API: reception/transmission of radio messages; transceiver configuration		
Applications	Remote monitoring Large-scale multi-hop networks	Remote monitoring Large-scale mono-hop networks	Distance measurement by propagation time Broadband exchange between neighbor nodes

Table 4.5. *Technical features and application recommendations*

4.6. Conclusion and outlook

The Internet of Things covers various aspects of collaboration between different networks in terms of services, size and communication technologies. This heterogeneity is assumed although it introduces requirements for the study of the collection network of the Internet of Connected Objects, now commonly called DL-IoT, short for Device-Layer-IoT. In fact, since various physical layers exist, it is necessary to implement means through which the study of their adequacy in terms of intrinsic capabilities and cohesion with the upper layers, as well as the interoperability/coexistence among them, becomes feasible. The results presented in this chapter aim to meet this need: the WiNo platform was designed in compliance with the principles of the open source ecosystem, from both the hardware and software points of view. Being open and generic, our platform accelerates the support of innovative physical layers through the use of an abstraction layer. If this model was adopted and is being used in cross-cutting research projects, the long-term goal is to grant various laboratories the ability to create their own testbeds at affordable prices. In order to attain this objective, we still have a few steps to go through, such as offering various MAC layers in addition to those currently available (CSMA/CA, TDMA, etc.), proposing middleware and applications to graph the results in order to finely analyze the performance achieved, and making our testbed remotely accessible. These steps are under way in the Ophelia project, sponsored by the Occitanie region. Our goal is also to use this testbed in pedagogical activities, like a SPOC associated with the MOOC [MOO 17] on connected objects in which we are involved, especially on the programming of protocols dedicated to connected objects for IoT.

4.7. Acknowledgments

The authors would like to thank Snootlab.com, a partner in the Ophelia project, and the Midi-Pyrénées/Occitanie region for the co-financing of part of the research work presented in this chapter.

4.8. References

[ABD 17] ABDELGAWAD A., YELAMARTHI K., "Internet of Things (IoT) platform for structure health monitoring", *Wireless Communications and Mobile Computing*, vol. 1, Article ID 6560797, 2017.

[ACC 17] ACCESSMAN, Pictocom, available at: www.access-man.com/en/products /pictocom, 2017.

[BOC 16] BOCCA M.-L., "Evaluation et optimisation d'une aide à la communication chez des patients en situation de handicap (handicap et aide à la communication)", *Conférence handicap 2016*, Paris, June 2016.

[BOR 16] BOR M., VIDLER J.E., ROEDIG U., "LoRa for the Internet of Things", *EWSN '16 Proceedings of the 2016 International Conference on Embedded Wireless Systems and Networks*, pp. 361–366, Junction Publishing, February 2016.

[BOU 16] BOUGEOIS E., DUCHIER J., VELLA F. *et al.*, "Post-test perceptions of digital tools by the elderly in an ambient environment", *International Conference on Smart Homes and Health Telematics (ICOST 2016)*, Wuhan, May 2016.

[BRO 17] BROADLINK, RM Pro+, available at: http://www.broadlink.com.cn/en /rmPro+/, 2017.

[CAO 08] CAO Q., ABDELZAHER T., STANKOVIC J. *et al.*, "The LiteOS operating system: towards unix like abstraction for wireless sensor networks", *Proceedings of the 7th International Conference on Information Processing in Sensor Networks (IPSN 2008)*, 2008.

[DAL 15] DALCÉ R., VAN DEN BOSSCHE A., VAL T., "Reducing localisation overhead: a ranging protocol and an enhanced algorithm for UWB-based WSNs", *IEEE Vehicular Technology Conference (VTC 2015)*, Glasgow, May 2015.

[DOM 17] DOMODEP, HouseMate Control Pro, available at: http://www.do-modep.com/produits/controle-environnement.html/housematecontrol.html, 2017.

[DUC 15] DUCHIER J., VIGOUROUX N., BOUGEOIS E. *et al.*, "Preliminary study of human interactions during entertainment by a facilitator using a cognitive stimulation medium (Mémoire-RED) in a nursing-home setting", *Non-pharmacological Therapies in Dementia*, Nova Science Publishers, vol. 3, no. 2, pp. 181–186, 2015.

[DUN 04] DUNKELS A., GRONVALL B., VOIGT T., "Contiki – a lightweight and flexible operating system for tiny networked sensors", *Proceedings of the 9th Annual IEEE International Conference on Local Computer Networks*, pp. 455–462, Washington, 2004.

[FIE 17] FIESTA-IoT, IoT testbeds, available at: http://fiesta-iot.eu/index.php /fiesta-testbeds/, 2017.

[FLE 15] FLEURY E., MITTON N., NOEL T. *et al.*, "FIT IoT-LAB: the largest IoT open experimental testbed", *ERCIM News*, 2015.

[FOF 16] FOFANA N.I., VAN DEN BOSSCHE A., DALCÉ R. *et al.*, "An original correction method for indoor ultra wide band ranging-based localisation system", *International Conference on Ad Hoc Networks and Wireless (AdHoc-Now 2016)*, Springer International Publishing, Lille, July 2016.

[GON 16] GONZALEZ N., VAN DEN BOSSCHE A., VAL T., "Hybrid wireless protocols for the Internet of Things", *IFIP/IEEE International Conference on Performance Evaluation and Modeling in Wired and Wireless Networks (PEMWN 2016)*, Paris, November 2016.

[IEE 07] IEEE COMPUTER SOCIETY, Specific requirements Part 15.4: Wireless Medium Access Control (MAC) and Physical Layer (PHY) Specifications for Low-Rate Wireless Personal Area Networks (WPANs) Amendment 1: Add Alternate PHYs, IEEE standard for information technology telecommunications and information exchange between systems, 2007.

[IND 17] INDUSTRIAL INTERNET CONSORTIUM, Testbeds, available at: http://www.iiconsortium.org/test-beds.htm, 2017.

[IOT 17] IOT IUT-BLAGNAC, available at: https://iot.iut-blagnac.fr/, 2017.

[JAE 14] JAEWOO K., JAIYONG L., JAEHO K. *et al.*, "M2M service platforms: survey, issues, and enabling technologies", *IEEE Communications Surveys & Tutorials*, vol. 16, no. 1, pp. 61–76, 2014.

[KER 14] KERANIDIS S., GIATSIOS D., KORAKIS T. *et al.*, "Experimentation on end-to-end performance aware algorithms in the federated environment of the heterogeneous PlanetLab and NITOS testbeds", *Computer Networks*, vol. 63, pp. 48–67, 2014.

[LAC 16] LACHTAR A., VAL T., KACHOURI A., "3DCane: a monitoring system for the elderly using a connected walking stick", *International Journal of Computer Science and Information Security*, vol. 14, no. 8, pp. 1–8, August 2016.

[LEE 16] LEE H.-H., KWON J.-H., KIM E.-J., "FS-IIoTSim: a flexible and scalable simulation framework for performance evaluation of industrial Internet of Things systems", *The Journal of Supercomputing*, pp. 1–18, November 2016.

[MAI 17] MAISON INTELLIGENTE, Présentation MI, available at: http://mi.iut-blagnac.fr, 2017.

[MOO 17] MOOC, Objets connectés : des radiofréquences aux réseaux, Université de Toulouse, available at: https://www.fun-mooc.fr/courses/univ-toulouse /101003/session01/about and http://eformation.univ-tlse3.fr/oc/, 2017.

[NS3 17] NS-3, Network Simulator 3: simulator resources, available at: https://www.nsnam.org, 2017.

[ORB 17] ORBIT, Open-Access Research Testbed for Next-Generation Wireless Networks, available at: http://www.orbit-lab.org, 2017.

[PJR 17] PJRC, Teensy USB Development Board, available at: http://www.pjrc.com /teensy, 2017.

[RIO 17] RIOT, The friendly Operating System for the Internet of Things, available at: http://riot-os.org, 2017.

[SÁN 13] SÁNCHEZ L., GUTIÉRREZ V., GALACHE J.A. *et al.*, "SmartSantander: experimentation and service provision in the smart city", *16th International Symposium on Wireless Personal Multimedia Communications (WPMC)*, pp. 1–6, Atlantic City, 2013.

[SHA 17] SHAH A.A., HABIB M., SAJJAD T. *et al.*, "Applications and challenges faced by Internet of Things – a survey", in FERREIRA J., ALAM M. (eds), *Future Intelligent Vehicular Technologies*, Springer, Cham, 2017.

[SHI 17] SHIRRIFF K., Arduino-IRremote, GitHub project, available at: http://github.com/z3t0/Arduino-IRremote, 2017.

[SUR 12] SURYADEVARA N.K., GADDAM A., RAYUDU R.K. *et al.*, "Wireless sensors network based safe home to care elderly people: behaviour detection", *Sensors and Actuators A: Physical*, vol. 186, pp. 277–283, 2012.

[VAN 16a] VAN DEN BOSSCHE A., BLANC MACHADO M., VAL T. *et al.*, "Utilisation des noeuds WiNoIR pour connecter tous les équipements domotiques d'un habitat intelligent", *Journée Nationale de l'Internet des Objets – Nouveaux défis de l'Internet des Objets: Interaction Homme-Machine et Facteurs Humains*, Paris-Saclay, November 2016.

[VAN 16b] VAN DEN BOSSCHE A., CAMPO E., DUCHIER J. *et al.*, "Multidimensional observation methodology for the elderly in an ambient digital environment", *International Conference on Computers Helping People with Special Needs (ICCHP 2016)*, Linz, July 2016.

[VAN 16c] VAN DEN BOSSCHE A., DALCÉ R., FOFANA N.I. *et al.*, "DecaDuino: an open framework for wireless time-of-flight ranging systems", *IFIP Wireless Days (WD 2016)*, Toulouse, March 2016.

[VEL 13] VELLA F., VIGOUROUX N., BOUDET B. *et al.*, "Usage de technologies d'interaction par des personnes âgées atteintes d'une maladie d'Alzheimer", *Workshop – Alzheimer, Approche pluridisciplinaire – De la recherche clinique aux avancées technologiques*, pp. 123–134, IRIT, Toulouse, January 2013.

[VEL 15] VELLA F., SAUZIN D., TRUILLET P. *et al.*, "Codesign of the Medical Assistive and Transactional Technologies system", *Recherche en Imagerie et Technologies pour la Santé (RITS 2015)*, pp. 122–123, IEEE French Section, Dourdan, March 2015.

[VIG 15] VIGOUROUX N., RUMEAU P., BOUDET B. *et al.*, "Wellfar-e-link®: true life lab testing of a homecare communication tool", *Non-pharmacological Therapies in Dementia*, Nova Science Publishers, vol. 3, no. 2, pp. 133–142, 2015.

[VIT 17] VITAL, The future of Smart Cities, available at: http://vital-iot.eu/, 2017.

[WIN 17] WiNo, available at: http://wino.cc, 2017.

[WU 08] WU W., "The SmartCane system: an assistive device for geriatrics", *BodyNets'08, ICST 3rd International Conference on Body Area Networks*, no. 2, Tempe, March 2008.

Multi-standard Receiver for Medical IoT Sensor Networks

5.1. Introduction

The IEEE 802.15.6 standard [IEE 12a] is dedicated to wireless communications with very low energy consumption and coverage (range of 3 m) operating close to the human body to provide, in particular, reliable medical services such as the measurement of vital parameters and non-medical services such as entertainment in real time.

Unlike the UWB mode of the 802.15.6 standard, the narrow band mode [LEE 09] aims to become the Internet of Things (IoT) reference standard for the medical industry [CHE 15]. It is for this reason, and differently from research by [LEE 09, CHO 10, MAT 15, MAT 14, LIA 13], that this chapter focuses on this mode. Nevertheless, the narrow band mode of the IEEE 802.15.6 standard must coexist in the 2.4 GHz ISM band with large competitors such as the IEEE 802.11a/b/g/n (WiFi) [IEE 12b], IEEE 802.15.1 (Bluetooth) [IEE 05] and IEEE 802.15.4 (ZigBee) [IEE 15].

In order to promote the development of the narrow band mode of the IEEE 802.15.6 standard, we propose an OFDM receiver like [MIC 01] (with multiple orthogonal subcarriers) that can, for example, be used by a

Chapter written by Tarak ARBI and Benoit GELLER.

conventional WiFi receiver, and which would then serve as a multi-standard receiver.

This chapter is structured as follows: in section 5.2, we shall revisit the general context and describe the characteristics of various WiFi standards 802.11a/n/ac. Section 5.3 shall revisit the specificities of the WBAN standard signal. Section 5.4 details the physical layer design proposed for the 802.15.6 standard in narrow band mode. Section 5.5 discusses simulation results. Finally, various conclusions shall be presented.

5.2. General context

5.2.1. OFDM

Multi-carrier techniques were invented in 1957 [DOE 57]. The basic idea was to devise the spectrum of the signal to be transmitted in N_c sub-channels in order to simplify the equalization and to take advantage of frequency diversity.

Consider a sequence of N_c symbols $c_0, c_1, \dots c_{N_c-1}$, where c_k is a real or complex symbol. The modulation principle is to transmit each symbol c_k on a carrier f_k. The modulated signal can therefore be written:

$$s(t) = \sum_{k=0}^{N_c-1} c_k e^{j2\pi f_k t}. \tag{5.1}$$

Unfortunately, the complexity of modulators/demodulators made the method difficult to apply. It took 20 years for the processing circuits to be capable of performing orthogonal multi-carrier techniques thanks to the discovery of the discrete Fourier transform [WEI 71].

Note that the multiplexing [5.1] is orthogonal if the space between the frequencies is $\Delta_f = \frac{1}{T_s}$, where T_s is the symbol period.

The modulated signal thus becomes:

$$s(t) = e^{j2\pi f_0 t} \sum_{k=0}^{N_c-1} c_k e^{j2\pi\left(\frac{k}{T_s}\right)t}, \qquad [5.2]$$

where f_0 is the central frequency.

It is easy to notice that the second term of [5.2] is bandlimited and its maximum frequency is $F_{max} = \frac{N}{2T_{FFT}}$. We can therefore sample it at times $t_n = \frac{nT_{FFT}}{N_c}$. These samples can be written as follows:

$$s(t_n) = s(n) = \sum_{k=0}^{N_c-1} c_k e^{2\pi k\left(\frac{n}{N}\right)}. \qquad [5.3]$$

[5.3] shows that the samples of the signal to be transmitted are only the inverse Fourier transform of the sequence $c_0, c_1, \dots c_{N_c-1}$.

The sampling instants $t_n = \frac{nT_{FFT}}{N_c}, n = 0, \dots, N_c - 1$ of the received signal in the absence of noise are thus written:

$$z(t_n) = z(n) = \sum_{k=0}^{N_c-1} c_k H_k e^{2\pi k\left(\frac{n}{N}\right)} \qquad [5.4]$$

where H_k is the gain of the channel on the carrier n°k.

Therefore, we have to just make the Fourier transform of the sequence $z_0, z_1, \dots, z_{N_c-1}$ and equalize it to get the sequence $c_0, c_1, \dots c_{N_c-1}$.

This modulation/demodulation technique is widely used in WiFi.

5.2.2. Characteristics of IEEE 802.11a/b/g/n/ac standards

The IEEE 802.11 standard initially defined three types of FHSS, DSSS and IR physical layers. This standard has not remained unchanged. In fact, over the years, several revisions have been made by the 802.11a/b/g/n/ac standards. Table 5.1 summarizes the characteristics of the first standards, which appeared chronologically.

Standards	Transmission	Frequency band	Maximum throughput	Modulation
802.11a	OFDM	5 GHz	54 Mbps	DBPSK, DQPSK, 16-QAM, 64-QAM
802.11b	DSSS	2.4 GHz	11 Mbps	DBPSK, DQPSK
802.11g	OFDM	2.4 GHz	54 Mbps	DBPSK, DQPSK, 16-QAM, 64-QAM

Table 5.1. *Characteristics of 802.11a/b/g standards*

The OFDM waveform is based on IFFT with a length of 64. In order to reduce the effect of adjacent channel leakage, only 52 of 64 carriers are used. Table 5.2 specifies the OFDM parameters for both IEEE 802.11a/g standards.

Parameters	Values
N_{SD}: Number of data subcarriers	48
N_{SP}: Number of pilot subcarriers	4
N_{ST}: Number of subcarriers in total	52
Δ_F: Frequency spacing of subcarriers	0.3125 MHz
T_{FFT}: FFT/IFFT period	3.2 µs
T_{SIGNAL}: OFDM symbol duration	4 µs
T_{GI}: Duration of the guard interval	0.8 µs
Occupied Bandwidth	16.6 MHz
Total bandwidth	20 MHz

Table 5.2. *OFDM parameters for IEEE 802.11a/g*

The IEEE 802.11n standard improves 802.11a/g standards by using the MIMO system (multiple inputs, multiple outputs) to provide a throughput that can theoretically reach 540 Mbps. The IEEE 802.11ac standard further improves the throughput and facilitates transmission for multiple users. This standard supports two different frequency bands, namely 2.4 GHz and 5 GHz.

All of the OFDM-based 802.11a/g/n/ac standard frames consist of the following fields:

Figure 5.1. *Structure of the 802.11a/n/ac frame. For a color version of this figure, see www.iste.co.uk/saleh/challenges.zip*

Part of the preamble in the 802.11a standards includes the L-STF (legacy-short training field) and the L-LTF (legacy-long training field). For more advanced standards, like 802.11n/ac which uses MIMO technology, there is also a second part of the preamble, including X-STF and X-LTF, where the letter X represents HT (high throughput) for 802.11n or VHT (very high throughput) for 802.11ac. The first part of the legacy preamble differentiates the 802.11 standard from other standards in the same band and marks the beginning of all 802.11a/n/ac generations. L-STF contains 10 repetitions of a short sequence of 0.8 µs for receivers to find the header, control the gain (AGC-automatic gain control) and estimate the frequency offset (CFO-carrier frequency offset). The following L-LTF field contains 2.5 repetitions of a 3.2 µs long sequence and allows for functions such as fine frame synchronization and channel estimation. The L-GIS (legacy signaling) field contains information about 802.11a data modulation and coding parameters. For 802.11n/ac, the X-SIG field contains specific data modulation and coding information.

5.3. The IEEE 802.15.6 standard

Medical networks meet very specific needs. At the base, nodes that support sensors are often disposable, hence the importance of having low complexity and low energy consumption communication. In addition, objects can interact with the human body, for example, the case of the insulin pump. The reliability of communications is therefore a primary need, and sometimes even vital because these sensors are likely to transmit crucial information in case of emergency. Finally, personal medical data must remain strictly private which entails strong security constraints; in particular, the interfacing of a wireless gateway to the Internet.

Conventional personal area networks (PANs), WiFi and Bluetooth have not been developed and do not natively meet all of these requirements. The IEEE 802.15 group therefore developed a specific working group to standardize the two lower layers of the OSI model (the physical layer and the data link layer). This research resulted in the IEEE 802.15.6 standard. By extension, other specifications were developed for user cases close to medical needs, such as physical activity, sports and gaming.

The WBAN standard offers a wide range of throughput and therefore tolerates several applications. This standard operates over several frequency bands as shown in Figure 5.2. It operates worldwide on the ISM band (industrial, scientific and medical), thus coexisting with several standards including WiFi.

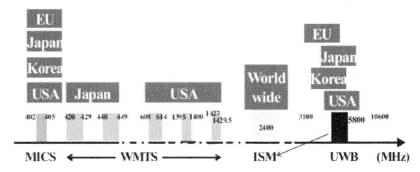

Figure 5.2. *WBAN frequency bands. For a color version of this figure, see www.iste.co.uk/saleh/challenges.zip*

5.3.1. *The WBAN frame*

Figure 5.3 presents the frame structure of the IEEE 802.15.6 standard. It is composed of three fields, namely the Physical Layer Convergence Protocol (PLCP) preamble, PLCP Header and Physical Layer Service Data

Unit (PSDU). The last two forms are called the Physical Layer Protocol Data Unit (PPDU).

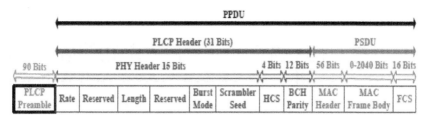

Figure 5.3. *Structure of the WBAN frame. For a color version of this figure, see www.iste.co.uk/saleh/challenges.zip*

The first PLCP preamble field is a receiver-known training sequence required for several baseband processings such as frame synchronization, time synchronization and frequency synchronization. For narrowband mode, two preambles are defined in order to reduce false alarms caused by the use of adjacent channels by the network. Each sequence is obtained by concatenating 63 bits with the following 27 bits 010101010101101101101101101. This field uses $\pi/2$-DBPSK as modulation and contains exactly 90 complex symbols. The second field of the PLCP header frame consists of 31 bits and contains information on transmission such as the modulation and coding parameters. Since this field also uses $\pi/2$-DBPSK as modulation, it contains 31 complex symbols. The last frame field called PSDU contains useful information.

5.3.2. *Specificities of the WBAN physical layer*

The PLCP header fields and the PSDU are coded with the BCH (31,19) and BCH (63,51) algebraic codes, respectively. In fact, the BCH (31,19) code is a shortened version of the BCH code (63,51) obtained by adding 32 zeros to the word to be encoded as shown in Figure 5.4.

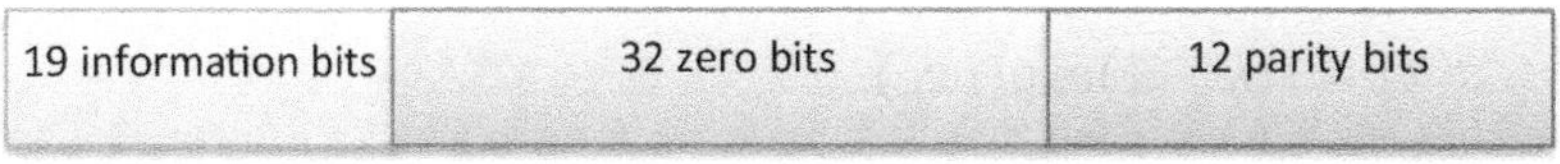

| 19 information bits | 32 zero bits | 12 parity bits |

Figure 5.4. *BCH (31,19)*

After coding, these fields are interlaced in order to increase the diversity [SZC 15], before being scrambled with the generator $g(x) = 1 + x^2 + x^{12} + x^{13} + x^{14}$.

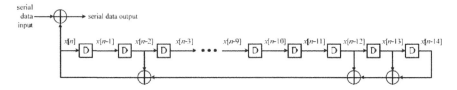

Figure 5.5. *WBN scrambler*

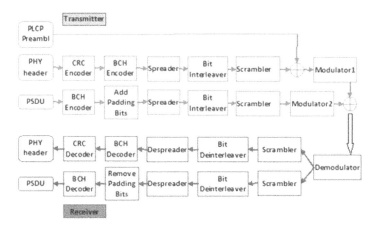

Figure 5.6. *WBAN communication system. For a color version of this figure, see www.iste.co.uk/saleh/challenges.zip*

For the narrowband mode, the binary sequence of this field is modulated by one of the following three differential modulations: $\pi/2$ -DBPSK, $\pi/4$-DQPSK or $\pi/8$-D8PSK.

For each of these modulations, the bit stream is transformed into a sequence of symbols $s(k), k = 0, 1, \cdots, (N/log_2(M)) - 1$ as follows:

$$s(k) = s(k - 1)\exp(j\varphi_k),$$ [5.5]

where M is the modulation order and $s(-1) = \exp(j\pi/2)$ is used as reference for the first preamble symbol. The transition values between the symbols φ_k are given in Tables 5.3, 5.4 and 5.5 for $\pi/2$-DBPSK, $\pi/4$-DQPSK and $\pi/8$-D8PSK, respectively.

$b(k)$	φ_k
0	$\pi/2$
1	$-\pi/2$

Table 5.3. $\pi/2\text{-}DBPSK$

$b(2k), b(2k+1)$	φ_k
0,0	$\pi/4$
0,1	$3\pi/4$
1,0	$7\pi/4$
1,1	$5\pi/4$

Table 5.4. $\pi/4\text{-}DQPSK$

$b(2k), b(2k+1), b(2k+3)$	φ_k
0, 0, 0	$\pi/8$
0, 0, 1	$3\pi/8$
0, 1, 0	$7\pi/8$
0, 1, 1	$5\pi/8$
1, 0, 0	$15\pi/8$
1, 0, 1	$13\pi/8$
1, 1, 0	$9\pi/8$
1, 1, 1	$11\pi/8$

Table 5.5. $\pi/8\text{-}D8PSK$

Owing to low coverage and transmission rate, the channel can be considered as a non-selective slow fading channel. Therefore, the received signal can be modeled by:

$$r(t) = h \sum_n s_n u(t - nT_{symb}) + w(t), \qquad [5.6]$$

where $u(t)$ is a root-raised cosine filter and h is the channel attenuation. It can be considered constant during the transmission of a packet.

Receiver-side baseband signal processing would have to include frame synchronization, frequency synchronization and time synchronization before performing symbol detection. In an IoT context for which simplicity and energy conservation are important factors, there are traditional algorithms for this narrow band synchronization [NAS 16, GEL 16]. Nevertheless, it should be noted that with these modulations, phase synchronization is not necessary due to the nature of the differential detection of symbols.

5.4. Physical layer design

This section details the algorithms proposed for frame synchronization, frequency synchronization and time synchronization in a multi-standard receiver OFDM context.

5.4.1. *Frame synchronization*

Since the IEEE 802.15.6 system is a packet transmission system, locating the start of the packet (SOF) should be the first task to perform before any other baseband processing. Therefore, this task should tolerate several imperfections such as bad sampling, frequency offset and additive noise.

In order to achieve a robust frame synchronization using the sampled received signal with frequency $f_{samp} = 2f_{symb}$, the following algorithm is proposed:

$$\hat{n}_{SOF} = arg \left\{ max_n \left\{ \sum_{l=1}^{L} \left\| \sum_{p=0}^{89-l} r\left(n + p + l\frac{T_{symb}}{T_{samp}}\right) r^*(n + p) * \right. \right. \right.$$
$$\left. \left. \left. \prod_{q=0}^{l} exp\left(-j\tilde{\varphi}_{p+q}\right) \right\| \right\} \right\}, \qquad [5.7]$$

where $\hat{n}_{SOF}$ is the estimated start of the frame, $r(n)$ is the n-th observation of the received signal, $T_{symb} = 1/f_{symb}$ is the symbol period and $\tilde{\varphi}_n$ is the phase transition between the symbols $s(n-1)$ and $s(n)$.

Two points should be noted: first, the correlation term $r\left(n + l\frac{T_{symb}}{T_{samp}}\right)r^*(n)$ reduces the impact of the frequency offset and, second, the index l indicates that the correlation is evaluated not only between the consecutive symbols but also between symbols spaced apart in time, thus increasing the robustness of the algorithm.

We propose to take $L = 2$; which is enough to locate the start of the frame with a frequency offset (CFO) $f_{CFO} = 0.1f_{symb}$ and a signal-to-noise ratio (SNR) $SNR = -1\ dB$.

5.4.2. Frequency synchronization

Frequency synchronization is the second task to perform. It has a significant impact on time synchronization and the final symbol detection. Our synchronization algorithm, developed to compensate for the frequency offset between the transmitter and the receiver, is broken down into two stages: the first has to do a coarse frequency synchronization, while the second deals with fine frequency synchronization.

Coarse frequency synchronization is performed as follows:

1) Transform each N_{FFT}^{CFO} received signal observation in the frequency domain by FFT. These observations in the frequency domain are denoted by $\tilde{R}(k)$, k = 0, 1, ..., N_{FFT}^{CFO}-1.

2) Transform $N_{FFT}^{CFO}/2$ preamble symbols in the frequency domain by FFT. These observations in the frequency domain are denoted by $\tilde{P}(k)$, k = 0, 1, ..., $N_{FFT}^{CFO}/2$-1.

3) Locate the maximum correlation between the two sequences in the frequency domain as follows:

$$\hat{n}_{coarse}^{CFO} = \arg\{\max_n\{\|A_n + B_n\|\}\}, \tag{5.8}$$

where

$$A_n = \sum_{p=0}^{\frac{N_{FFT}^{CFO}}{4}-1} \tilde{R}\left((p+n) mod N_{FFT}^{CFO}\right) \tilde{P}^*(p),$$ [5.9]

and

$$B_n = \sum_{p=\frac{N_{FFT}^{CFO}}{4}}^{\frac{N_{FFT}^{CFO}}{2}-1} \tilde{R}\left(\left(p + \frac{N_{FFT}^{CFO}}{2} + n\right) mod N_{FFT}^{CFO}\right) \tilde{P}^*(p).$$ [5.10]

4) Compensate the frequency offset $\hat{f}_{coarse}^{CFO}$.

It should be noted that the value estimated by the coarse synchronization has an accuracy in the range of f_{samp}/N_{FFT}^{CFO}. The size of the FFT therefore determines the efficiency of the algorithm: the larger the FFT size, the better the exactitude of the algorithm.

We propose to take $N_{FFT}^{CFO} = 128$. Therefore, for each packet containing 90 preamble symbols, there are two partially correlated estimated values.

After the compensation of the value estimated by the algorithm of the coarse frequency-offset synchronization, the fine frequency synchronization is carried out as follows:

$$\hat{f}_{fine}^{CFO} = \frac{1}{2\pi L T_{symb}} *$$
$$tan^{-1}\left(\sum_{l=1}^{L} \frac{1}{(90-l)l} \sum_{p=0}^{89-l} \tilde{r}(n+l)\tilde{r}^*(p) \prod_{q=0}^{l} exp(-j\tilde{\varphi}_{p+q})\right).$$ [5.11]

In order to reduce the complexity of the system, the fine estimate of the frequency offset is performed as follows:

$$\hat{f}_{fine}^{CFO} = \frac{1}{\pi T_{symb}} tan^{-1}\left(\hat{V}_{fine}^{CFO}\right),$$ [5.12]

where $\hat{V}_{fine}^{CFO}$ is obtained by a simple infinite impulse response (IIR) filter of the first order:

$$\hat{V}_{fine}^{CFO} = (1-\alpha)\hat{V}_{fine}^{CFO} + \frac{\alpha}{l}\tilde{r}(p+l) * \tilde{r}^*(p) \prod_{q=0}^{l} exp(-j\tilde{\varphi}_{p+q}).$$ [5.13]

In the simulations of section 5.5, we propose to take L=2 and $\alpha = 0.01$.

5.4.3. *Time synchronization*

The objective of this task is to estimate the time gap τ of the received signal, where:

$$r(t - \tau) = h \sum_n s_n u(t - nT_{symb} - \tau) + w(t - \tau).$$ [5.14]

Unlike conventional time synchronization, usually consisting of two blocks, namely symbol interpolator and timing error detector (TED), the proposed algorithm tends to estimate the global impulse response of the channel $hu(t - nT_{symb} - \tau)$. Therefore, time synchronization comprises two blocks: channel estimation and channel equalization.

The purpose of the channel estimator is to estimate the frequency transfer function of the channel as follows:

1) Transform each N_{FFT}^{TR} received signal observation in the frequency domain by FFT. These observations in the frequency domain are denoted by $\tilde{R}(k)$, $k = 0, 1, ..., N_{FFT}^{TR}$-1.

2) Insert 1 zero between each pair of symbols in the preamble. Then transform each N_{FFT}^{TR} points of the sequence obtained in the frequency domain by FFT; observations in the frequency domain are denoted by $\tilde{P}(k)$, $k = 0, 1, ..., N_{FFT}^{TR}$-1.

3) As with the conventional channel estimator of the OFDM system, the frequency response of the channel can be estimated by: $\hat{H}(k) = \tilde{R}(k)/\tilde{P}(k)$.

4) Linearly interpolate the frequency response of the channel between each pair of consecutive values of $\hat{H}(k)$. As a result, we obtain a new channel transfer function $\hat{H}_I(k)$ that has $2N_{FFT}^{TR}$ points.

Then, the channel equalizer triggers the overlap-save (OLS) method [PRO 07] to perform the frequency equalization of oversampled received signal observations after frequency compensation. It must:

1) take the N_{FFT}^{TR} observations from the previous OLS block;

2) take the N_{FFT}^{TR} new observations to equalize;

3) transform $2N_{FFT}^{TR}$ observations into the frequency domain – the corresponding points are denoted by $R(k)$;

4) perform the equalization: $\widehat{D}(k) = R(k)/\widehat{H}_I(k)$;

5) transform the samples of $\widehat{D}(k)$ in the time domain;

6) extract the last N_{FFT}^{TR} sampled points. The first of each pair of samples provides the DMPSK symbol. This makes it possible to measure the bit error rate (BER) in section 5.5.

We propose to take $N_{FFT}^{TR} = 64$.

5.5. Simulation results

In this section, the performance of the proposed system for $\pi/2$-DBPSK (Figure 5.7), $\pi/4$-DQPSK (Figure 5.8) and $\pi/8$-D8PSK (Figure 5.9) modulations is evaluated in terms of bit error rate (BER) for two scenarios: the first is the simulation with a random time offset $\tau \in \left[-T_{symb}/2, T_{symb}/2\right]$ (see the curves indicated by RTO sim); not only does the other scenario include a random time offset, it also includes a significant frequency offset $f_{CFO} = 0.1 f_{symb}$ (see the curves indicated by RTO + 10% CFO sim). In these simulations, all the previous baseband-processing blocks are enabled (frame synchronization, frequency synchronization and time synchronization). The best performances that can be obtained on an additive white Gaussian noise channel are the theoretical performances (see curves indicated by "theory") [XIO 06, PRO 08], which are obtained by assuming a perfect synchronization between the transmitter and the receiver. These theoretical curves act as absolute reference for us to compare the results of our proposal.

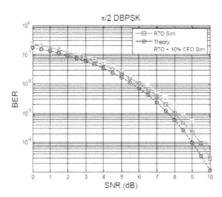

Figure 5.7. *Performance of the proposed system for $\pi/2$-DBPSK. For a color version of this figure, see www.iste.co.uk/saleh/challenges.zip*

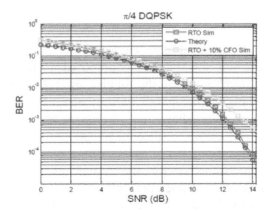

Figure 5.8. *Performance of the proposed system for π/4-DQPSK. For a color version of this figure, see www.iste.co.uk/saleh/challenges.zip*

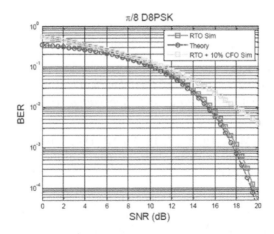

Figure 5.9. *Performance of the proposed system for π/8-D8PSK. For a color version of this figure, see www.iste.co.uk/saleh/challenges.zip*

Figures 5.7, 5.8, and 5.9 show that the curves of the bit error rate (BER) of the proposed system remain very close to the optimal theoretical performance with only a random time offset (RTO). Moreover, it is noteworthy that, under very difficult conditions of synchronization, and considering additional degradation with a significant frequency offset, the proposed algorithms remain robust for $\pi/2$-DBPSK and $\pi/4$-DQPSK modulations.

5.6. Conclusion

In this chapter, a physical layer algorithm design for the narrow band mode of the IEEE 802.15.6 standard is proposed. Unlike the conventional design of the physical layer of the single-carrier receiver, the proposed processing algorithms can be directly used by an OFDM system, such as on WiFi. Simulation results show that the performances of the studied algorithms are very close to theoretical performances with a perfect synchronization on a Gaussian channel with a random time offset. This makes this design attractive for the design of a multi-standard and multi-channel receiver, including applications for medical IoT. Subsequently in our study, we would like to include a soft decoder in our multi-standard receiver [VAN 08] and a cross-layer design that can be used for localization.

5.7. References

[CHE 15] CHEN W., GELLER B., HU F. *et al.*, "Wireless body area network", *Special Issue of China Communications*, vol. 12, no. 2, February 2015.

[CHO 10] CHOI B., KIM B., LEE S. *et al.*, "Narrowband physical layer design for WBAN system", *Proceedings of First International Conference on Pervasive Computing Signal Processing and Application (PCSPA)*, Harbin, China, pp. 154–157, 2010.

[DOE 57] DOELZ M.L., HEALD E.T., MARTI D.L., "Binary data transmission techniques for linear systems", *Proceedings of the IRE*, vol. 45, no. 5, pp. 656–666, May 1957.

[GEL 16] GELLER B., "Advanced synchronizing techniques for the internet of things", *8th International Symposium on Signal Image Video and Communications*, IEEE ISIVC, Tunis, Tunisia, November 2016.

[IEE 05] IEEE Standard for Local and Metropolitan Area Networks. Part15.1: Wireless Medium Access Control (MAC) and Physical Layer (PHY) Specification for Wireless Personal Networks (WPANs), 2005.

[IEE 12a] IEEE Standard for Local and Metropolitan Area Network. Part 15.6: Wireless Area Body Network, 2012.

[IEE 12b] IEEE Standard for Local and Metropolitan Area Networks. Part 11: Wireless LAN Medium Access Control (MAC) and Physical Layer (PHY) Specification, 2012.

[IEE 15] IEEE Standard for Low-Rate Wireless Networks 802.15.4-2015, 2015.

[LEE 09] LEE C., KIM J., LEE H.S. *et al.*, "Physical layer designs for WBAN systems in IEEE 802.15.6 proposals", *Proceedings of 9th International Symposium on Communications and Information Technology, ISCIT 2009*, Icheon, South Korea, pp. 841–844, 2009.

[LIA 13] LIANG Y., ZHOU Y., LU Y., "The design and implementation of IEEE 802.15.6 Baseband on FPGA", *Proceedings of International Conference on Health Informatics, IFMBE Proceedings*, Barcelona, Spain, vol. 42, pp. 231–235, November 2013.

[MAT 14] MATHEW P., AUGUSTINE L., KUSHWAHA D. *et al.*, "Hardware implementation of NB PHY baseband transceiver for IEEE 802.15.6 WBAN", *International Conference on Medical Imaging, m-Health and Emerging Communication Systems, MedCom 2014*, Greater Noida, India, November 2014.

[MAT 15] MATHEW P., AUGUSTINE L., KUSHWAHA D. *et al.*, "Implementation of NB PHY transceiver of IEEE 802.15.6 WBAN on FPGA", *Proceedings of 2015 International Conference on VLSI Systems, Architecture, Technology and Applications, VLSI-SATA*, Bangalore, India, pp. 1–6, 2015.

[MIC 01] MICHEAL S., STEFAN F., GUNNAR F. *et al.*, "Optimum receiver design for OFDM-based broadband transmission", *IEEE Transactions on Communications*, vol. 49, no. 4, April 2001.

[NAS 16] NASR I., GELLER B., ATALLAH L. *et al.*, "Performance study of a near maximum likelihood code aided recovery technique", *IEEE Transactions on Signal Processing*, vol. 64, no. 3, pp. 799–811, 2016.

[PRO 07] PROAKIS J.G., MANOLAKIS D.K., *Digital Signal Processing*, 4th ed., Pearson, 2007.

[PRO 08] PROAKIS J.G., SALEHI M., *Digital Communications*, 5th ed., McGraw Hill, 2008.

[SZC 15] SZCZECINSKI L., ALVARADO A., *Bit-Interleaved Coded Modulation: Fundamentals, Analysis and Design*, John Wiley and Sons, Chichester, 2015.

[VAN 08] VANSTRACEELE C., GELLER B., BARBOT J.P. *et al.*, "A low complexity block turbo decoder architecture", *IEEE Transactions on Communications*, vol. 56, no. 12, pp. 1985–1989, December 2008.

[WEI 71] WEINSTEIN S.B., ELBERT P.M., "Data transmission by frequency division multiplexing", *IEEE Transactions on Communications*, vol. 19, pp. 628–634, October 1971.

[XIO 06] XIONG F., *Digital Modulation Techniques*, 2nd ed., Artech House, Norwood, 2006.

6

Ambient Atoms: a Device for Ambient Information Visualization

Recent decades have seen an explosion of available information. This explosion concerns public as well as private information. From an individual perspective, this phenomenon is largely materialized by the computer system that we constantly carry with us, namely the smartphone. The smartphone provides immediate access to a wealth of information and a multitude of data. All these various data are often delivered to the user by means of the same single output module, that is, the screen (and, episodically, sound or vibrations) of the smartphone. In addition, while the smartphone is an easy way to get access to various different data, it is not always the most practical solution for each category of information, nor in all circumstances. Ambient devices may offer a complementary output useful in certain situations for which the smartphone is not convenient enough to access the required information. Ambient displays deliver effortless, instant access to information at a glance. This paper introduces Ambient Atoms, a new ambient visualization device. Ambient Atoms is a simple and flexible connected object that looks like a frame on which information is symbolically visualized. An application for the visualization of data in the context of an apartment is proposed as a sample application.

6.1. Introduction

In recent years, the amount of both public and private information has tremendously increased. Weather forecasts and traffic information are good examples. Private information is largely derived from the multitude of sensors that monitor our environment and our every move. At the individual level, this wealth of information is greatly materialized by the computer system, which is now part and parcel of us, that is, the smartphone. The smartphone provides quick access to a wealth of information and an

---

Chapter written by Sébastien Crouzy, Stan Borkowski and Sabine Coquillart.

incredibly rich supply of data. All of these data are almost always delivered to the user using the same output module: the screen (and, episodically, sound or vibrations) of the smartphone. The smartphone is a simple means used to access different information, though it is not always the most convenient. It all depends on the type of data or the circumstances of use. In general, using a smartphone requires us to first of all suspend our activity in order to take the smartphone out of the pocket or bag and then launch the desired application or search the Web. Furthermore, the inconvenience is even more significant if this activity is performed with dirty or wet hands. This problem is partially solved by notifications, though not in all cases. In addition, the multiplication of notifications quickly becomes cumbersome and difficult to manage.

Ambient devices can be an alternative to viewing information on the smartphone. Ambient displays provide instant and effortless access to information in a blink of an eye.

This article proposes a new ambient visualization mode that we call Ambient Atoms. Ambient Atoms is a simple and flexible connected object. It has the form of a frame on which information is represented symbolically. An application for visualizing information about data collected by a smart apartment is proposed as a sample application. However, we can imagine many other applications in everyday life, such as visualizing plant needs for water and/or fertilizer, reminders of expiry dates on food products, visualizing weather forecasts in several regions of interest, displaying delays or cancellations of public transport used daily, displaying the agenda of relatives, displaying the results of league matches of our favorite sport, displaying stock market values of one's favorite companies, showing notifications about incoming phone calls, emails or SMSs sent by relatives, etc.

The rest of this article is structured as follows: section 6.2 defines and presents a brief state of the art of ambient display systems, section 6.3 introduces Ambient Atoms from a user point of view, and section 6.4 that follows presents the hardware and software components that make up Ambient Atoms. Finally, section 6.5 describes the first prototype developed for the visualization of various data relating to accommodation such as the temperature of each room, the presence of people, whether doors and windows are open or closed, and electrical and gas consumption.

6.2. Previous research

Pioneering research on ambient displays dates back to the late 1990s. The purpose of ambient displays is to allow users keep an eye on useful but non-central information concerning their activities. This can be done in a simple and discreet way, through an integrated display system in the environment. Pousman and Stasko [POU 06] propose a set of properties to characterize ambient information systems:

– they should display important but not critical information;

– they should be able to move from the periphery to the focus of attention of users, and back again;

– their representation should be tangible in the environment;

– their updates should be discreet and must not distract users;

– they should be aesthetically pleasing and environmentally appropriate.

Many ambient display devices have been proposed. We shall limit ourselves here to visual devices. Among these devices, we can distinguish screen-based systems such as CareNet [CON 04], Infocanvas [MIL 01], Kandinsky [FOG 01], Chumby [CHU 18] and Digital FamilyPortraits [MYN 01] as well as those that do not integrate a screen.

More particularly, we shall focus here on ambient displays that do not integrate a screen.

6.2.1. *Dedicated ambient displays that do not integrate a display screen*

Among ambient displays that do not integrate the screen, most are dedicated to a given application, such as LockDoll [CHO 16], which is a small figurine that, from its movements, discreetly transmits a smartphone's information to its owner; Dangling String [WEI 96], which visualizes the load of a computer network; or Lumitouch [CHA 01] which is a set of two frames with photos that can remotely transmit emotions to a person.

Ambient displays dedicated to an application also often feature the transformation of an object of everyday life, such as an umbrella with

Ambient Umbrella [AMB 09] or a power cord with the Power-Aware Cord [GUS 05]. In some cases, the ambient display is even based on a natural aspect, such as the sky with the Green Cloud [EVA 08].

6.2.2. *Generic ambient displays that do not include a display screen*

One of the best known and the simplest ambient displays that do not integrate a screen is Ambient Orb [AMB 18]. This is a ball-shaped lamp whose color changes according to information updates. Ambient Orb, which displays a single information slot that can take several values (colors), is marketed by Ambiant Devices Inc. An extension of Ambient Orb was proposed by Moores Cloud. Holiday [PES 12] is a garland of LEDs, where each LED can take a different color and can be treated separately. Water Lamp and Pinwheels [DAH 98] are two other examples of generic ambient display systems that do not integrate screens.

6.3. Ambient Atoms: user's point of view

This research is a direct continuation of previous research on Ambient Orb [AMB 18], Holiday by Moores Cloud [PES 12] and Infocanvas [MIL 01]. Ambient Atoms is an extended and surface version of Ambient Orb or Holiday. It can also be considered as a simpler and more modest version of Infocanvas, which does not integrate a screen. Here, the screen is replaced by a low-cost display consisting of a panel and a set of LEDs, which we call atoms, positioned on the frame. Just like Ambient Orb, Holiday or Infocanvas, Ambient Atoms is a generic ambient display. As a result, it is adaptable to a large number of varied applications. The panel base is engraved with static information, especially about the role and meaning of each atom, while LEDs provide dynamic information in real time. In addition to the example of information visualization regarding a connected apartment that is presented in section 6.5, below we show a few other examples of possible applications. Figure 6.1 shows Ambient Atoms alerting about phone calls, SMSs and email messages from relatives.

Figure 6.1. *Calls from relatives*

Similarly, Figure 6.2 shows a simple Ambient Atoms setup used to view the schedule of family members. For each person, there is a presence at home or at work for that day and the following day. The black rings represent atoms, materialized by LEDs whose color, that symbolizes information, is updated in real time.

Agenda	AM home	PM home	AM office/ school	PM office/ school	Tomorrow AM home	Tomorrow PM home	Tomorrow AM office	Tomorrow PM office
Mick	O	O	O	O	O	O	O	O
Jane	O	O	O	O	O	O	O	O
John	O	O	O	O	O	O	O	O

Figure 6.2. *Family schedule*

6.4. Ambient Atoms: hardware and software components

6.4.1. *Hardware: microcontroller*

This section describes Ambient Atoms' first prototype developed using the Equipex Amiqual4Home [AMI 17] prototyping workshops. Our technological choices are just one of many possible approaches to implementing Ambient Atoms. This section particularly focuses on the display of real-time information using LEDs. The panel base will be described in the example described in the following section.

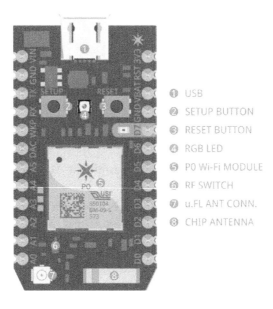

Figure 6.3. *Particle Photon (source: https://www.particle.io/prototype).*
For a color version of this figure, see www.iste.co.uk/saleh/challenges.zip

The first developed prototype integrates the Particle Photon microcontroller, a successor of the Spark Core. The microcontroller, which is powered via USB, has a WiFi connection, 1 MB flash memory, and 128 KB of RAM to run the firmware. The device, when declared and connected to the cloud, can be controlled and monitored in real time through the Particle.io web server. The firmware can be developed online using Particle's web IDE. Particle uses the same development environment as Arduino and is therefore compatible with the code written for Arduino, with little or no modifications. The programming is done in C/C++ or ARM assembly, and the code can be compiled at the web IDE. Particle can also be downloaded directly from the Internet via WiFi connection. For more information, see [PAR 18]. Figure 6.3 presents a picture of Particle Photon.

6.4.2. *Hardware: LEDs*

The first developed prototype integrates a garland of Adafruit WS2801 LEDs connected to the microcontroller (see Figure 6.4). The status of each LED, represented by its color, can be accessed and modified separately from other LEDs. The color of the LEDs provides the user with an abstract representation of the information. Each LED integrates a silicone molded controller. LEDs are connected with a four-conductor cable (5V, earth, data, clock). Data is transmitted from one LED to the other until it reaches the destination LED. The color of each LED is coded on 24 bits representing three values corresponding to the three primary colors (red, green and blue). A value of 0 for each of the three components corresponds to an LED when switched off, while a value of 255 leads to a white LED. The information provided by an LED is given by its color. It can also come from various animation sequences, such as blinking, fading and pulsing. For this purpose, several animation sequence tests have been tried.

Figure 6.4. *Adafruit WS2801 (source: https://www.adafruit.com/products/738). For a color version of this figure, see www.iste.co.uk/saleh/challenges.zip*

6.4.3. *Software*

The development of Ambient Atoms uses several libraries to manage a web server, process JSON chains and communicate with the LED garland.

The developed firmware uses a cJSON library to process JSON messages from POST requests. These messages are formatted as a list of LEDs with their parameters. Many LEDs can be managed separately.

Beyond the change of colors of LEDs, the firmware also integrates several predefined animations that can be activated using a POST request on the web server.

Animations are defined using a structure containing several parameters necessary to play the animation. Among them are: the type of animation (constant, flashing, progressive, random, etc.), the duration of the animation and its frequency.

6.5. Ambient Atoms: prototype applied to the housing information visualization

The first prototype that has been developed makes it possible to view information related to a connected apartment such as the opening/closing of doors and windows, power consumption, water consumption and people's presence in rooms. In this case, the panel base represents the plan of the apartment, and each LED/atom provides information related to consumption, presence, opening/closing of doors or windows, etc. (see Figure 6.5). Hanging Ambient Atoms on the kitchen wall, for example, allows the supervision of the state of the apartment at a glance, in a non-intrusive way.

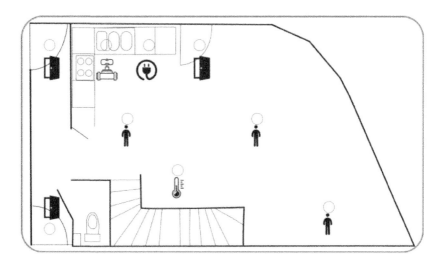

Figure 6.5. *Prototype pattern of Ambient Atoms dedicated to viewing information about a connected apartment. For a color version of this figure, see www.iste.co.uk/saleh/challenges.zip*

The panel base, which would be different for each application, is a plywood piece engraved with a numerically-controlled laser. The plan of the apartment, as well as symbols to identify information provided by each LED, are engraved on the base. Holes that enable the positioning of LEDs/atoms are made simultaneously with engraving and laser.

Nine LEDs are integrated in Ambient Atoms and are used to display temperature, the state of doors (open/closed), people's presence in rooms, as well as power and gas consumption. This is a smart apartment with many sensors. Atoms represent the status of sensors, materialized by the color and/or animation of LEDs. For example, temperature display is done using the standard color gradient from blue to red. Consumptions are also visualized this same way. The opening of doors is visualized by a fixed color, in this case, the green color, while the presence information is communicated by blinking of the atoms. The microcontroller and cables are hidden behind the panel base (see Figure 6.6 for more details). The picture is taken from the entrance to the room with Ambient Atoms placed on the kitchen cabinet, to the left of the picture. The door seen on the left being closed, it is represented be the green atom located on the top right. Similarly, the presence of a person in the room is indicated by the red atom located on the top center and on the right (as animations could not be provided, a green or red code was chosen to represent the presence). The sensor is attached to the ceiling, above the table and near the lamp. The entrance door (atom at the bottom right) and the garage access door (atom at the top left), both of them being closed (they are not visible in the picture) are represented by two green atoms. The two atoms at the top, between the door state atoms, indicate power and water consumption. The two green atoms in the room correspond to two other presence atoms. They are green because nobody is present nearby. Finally, the blue atom (bottom middle) indicates temperature.

The smart apartment that served as a test for the first prototype of Ambient Atoms is an apartment set up as part of the Equipex Amiqual4Home project [AMI 17]. All of the systems within the apartment are managed by OpenHAB [OPE 18], an open source home automation software. The apartment is fully instrumented with various sensors. It is used to test prototypes and new services in full scale. The apartment integrates a multitude of sensors of all kinds, ranging from water consumption, electricity and gas meters, to door and window state detectors, etc. A dismountable floor and ceiling enable the addition of sensors at will.

Figure 6.6. *(a) Picture of the apartment with Ambient Atoms placed on the kitchen cabinet, on the left; (b) zoom on Ambient Atoms. Take note of somebody's presence symbolized by a red LED, and the closed door symbolized by a green LED. For a color version of this figure, see www.iste.co.uk/saleh/challenges.zip*

OpenHAB makes it easy and reliable to add, control, configure, and read sensors or actuators. It also facilitates the processing and storage of information from sensors. OpenHAB also makes it possible to unify the management of sensors or actuators using different communication protocols thanks to the concept of the *eventbus*. Whenever the status of a device changes, a notification is sent on the eventbus (see Figure 6.7).

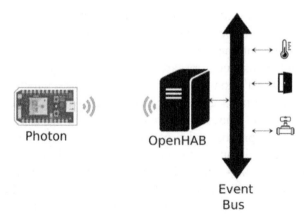

Figure 6.7. *Communication between Photon, OpenHAB and sensors*

OpenHAB Designer is software for configuring different items and their connections. EventBus commands and updates can trigger rules defined in OpenHAB Designer. For example, a temperature sensor can be declared in OpenHAB as a Number item, which is then connected to its real equivalent, which in this case is a temperature sensor. Whenever the sensor status changes, a notification is sent on the eventbus, and rules can be written in reaction to this new status. For example, we can define a rule to illuminate an LED on a spectrum from blue to red to visualize the temperature emitted by the sensor.

These rules are also used to send commands to items or perform more complex operations. These operations range from sending HTTP requests to formatting received sensor values and transforming them into usable data. Several rules to send HTTP POST requests to the Photon in order to update the status of the LED were setup, so as to allow the display of information from the sensors of the connected apartment on Ambient Atoms. POST requests are built in OpenHAB based on sensor values.

6.6. Future research and conclusion

This chapter introduces Ambient Atoms, a new connected object for ambient visualization. This device is generic and can therefore be adapted for various applications. A first prototype was developed for an ambient visualization application of various types of information relating to a smart apartment. This first prototype made it possible to integrate Ambient Atoms in an existing home automation system. It also allowed promising early tests to be carried out. Subsequent research will aim to carry out a more formal evaluation of Ambient Atoms in a specific case of use, which could be that of the connected apartment, as well as other cases. During these evaluations, different visualization modes (colors/animations) can be tested in different contexts in order to propose rules of use. The current prototype integrates nine atoms, though this number is not linked to a technical limit. Ambient atoms of different sizes and with more atoms can therefore also be considered in order to define a possible ergonomic limit to the amount of retrieved information. This first prototype allowed us to better understand the issues to reflect on. Among them, the question that arises is that of making the user a stakeholder of the design of their Ambient Atoms. For example, to facilitate the customization of the shape and behavior of the device, we might wonder whether an IFTTT-based solution would be acceptable or whether a specific programming language would be more suitable.

6.7. Acknowledgments

This project was carried out as part of Equipex Amiqual4Home [AMI 17] ANR-11-EQPX-0002. The authors would like to thank Nicolas Bonnefond and Rémi Pincent, for their help with prototyping tools, and OpenHAB services [OPE 18]. Many thanks also to James Crowley, director of Amiqual4Home, for making this project a success.

6.8. References

[AMB 09] AMBIENT UMBRELLA, available at: http://www.geeky-gadgets.com/the -ambient-umbrella-30-12-2009, 2009.

[AMB 18] AMBIENT, available at: http://www.ambientdevices.com, 2018.

[AMI 17] AMIQUAL4HOME, available at: https://amiqual4home.inria.fr/home/, 2017.

[CHA 01] CHANG A., RESNER B., KOERNER B., "LumiTouch: an emotional communication device", *Proceedings of the CHI 2001*, pp. 313–314, 2001.

[CHO 16] CHOI S., JEONG H., KO M. *et al.*, "LockDoll: providing ambient feedback of smartphone usage within social interaction", *Proceedings of the CHI 2016*, pp. 1165–1172, 2016.

[CHU 18] CHUMBY, available at: http://www.chumby.com/, 2018.

[CON 04] CONSOLVO S., ROESSLER P., SHELTON B.E., "The CareNet display: lessons learned from an in home evaluation of an ambient display", *UbiComp 2004 – Ubiquitous Computing, 6th International Conference*, pp. 1–17, 2004.

[DAH 98] DAHLEY A., WISNESKI C., ISHII H., "Water lamp and pinwheels: ambient projection of digital information into architectural space", *Proceedings of the CHI 1998*, pp. 269–270, 1998.

[EVA 08] EVANS H., HANSEN H., NuageVert, available at: http://hehe.org.free.fr /hehe/texte/nv/index.html, 2008.

[FOG 01] FOGARTY J., FORLIZZI J., HUDSON S., "Aesthetic information collages: generating decorative displays that contain information", *Proceedings of the UIST 2001*, pp. 141–150, 2001.

[GUS 05] GUSTAFSSON A., GYLLENSWÄRD M., "The power-aware cord: energy awareness through ambient information display", *Proceedings of the CHI 2005*, pp. 1423–1426, 2005.

[MIL 01] MILLER T., STASKO J., "The InfoCanvas: information conveyance through personalized, expressive art", *Proceedings of the CHI 2001*, pp. 305–306, 2001.

[MYN 01] MYNATT E.D., ROWAN J., JACOBS A. *et al.*, "Digital family portraits: supporting peace of mind for extended family members", *Proceedings of the CHI 2001*, pp. 333–340, 2001.

[OPE 18] OPENHAB, available at: http://www.openhab.org/, 2018.

[PAR 18] PARTICLE.IO, available at: https://www.particle.io/, 2018.

[PES 12] PESCE M., Holiday, available at: http://MooresCloud.com (accessed 2014), 2012.

[POU 06] POUSMAN Z., STASK J., "A taxonomy of ambient information systems: four patterns of design", *Proceedings of the AVI 2006*, pp. 67–74, 2006.

[WEI 96] WEISER M., BROWN J.S., "Designing calm technology", *PowerGrid Journal*, vol. 1.01, available at: http://powergrid.electriciti.com, 1996.

7

New Robust Protocol for IoV Communications

ABSTRACT.– First, this chapter presents some definitions of vehicle networks, application areas, communication technologies and barriers that disrupt communications and deteriorate quality of service (QoS) in the Internet of Vehicles (IoV). Then, it introduces our proposition aiming to detect and bypass disconnection zones through a new routing protocol based on (1) the estimation of the contact time between a vehicle and its neighbors, (2) the data load to be transferred and (3) logs of communication errors. The objective is to ensure the availability, the reliability and the robustness of inter-vehicle communications by taking these three criteria into account in a data routing algorithm.

7.1. Introduction

The new era of the Internet of Things (IoT) has spurred the evolution of classic ad hoc vehicular networks (VANETs) toward the paradigm of the Internet of Vehicles (IoV). This type of network is formed mainly of on-board units (OBUs) installed in vehicles and terminals installed along roads (Road Side Units, or RSUs). The types of communication in vehicular networks are called "V2X", where X refers to a vehicle (V2V), an infrastructure (V2I), a person (V2P) or any other connected object (V2O). Because of its characteristics, the IoV is considered as a part of the IoT, where the objects are vehicles, enabling the creation of a

Chapter written by Lylia ALOUACHE, Nga NGUYEN, Makhlouf ALIOUAT and Rachid CHELOUAH.

multitude of services dedicated to the intelligent transport ecosystem [GER 16, REH 15]. V2V communication is the main component of the IoV, as the majority of data produced must be transmitted from one source to one or more other destinations. To do this, the services offered by the IoV greatly depend on the vehicles in question, which act as transmitters, relays and receivers. Vehicles carry out their own communications but simultaneously serve as information relays for communication between other vehicles as well.

The issue here consists of studying the availability, reliability and robustness of communications between IoV agents. The dynamic nature of the IoV imposes constraints on communication, specifically frequent disconnections liable to hinder the execution of applications aboard a vehicle; in fact, some vehicles find themselves isolated and unable to transmit or receive for indefinite periods of time. The objective of this work is to provide drivers and passengers with uninterrupted, impeccably up-to-date access to new, easily available and reliable operational data, in order to respond to the ever-rising demand for quality of service in the IoV environment. We attempt to improve existing solutions and propose a solution to the problem, thus ensuring the availability of services, the reliability of communications and data, and the robustness of the IoV.

The rest of this chapter will be structured as follows: section 7.2 describes the latest developments in vehicular networks, the axes of research concerning the layered architecture of the IoV, obstacles that may negatively affect the quality of communication within the network layer and an overview of the work being conducted pertaining to multi-hop and reactive routing protocols. Section 7.3 gives a detailed explanation of our routing protocol for IoV communications. It is made up of three different phases: the estimation of contact duration and load balancing, the use and updating of communication anomaly logs and hop-by-hop routing calculation. Section 7.4 concludes the chapter with the potential outcomes of our work.

7.2. Latest developments

7.2.1. *Architecture of the IoV*

From a network perspective, an IoV system is made up of three layers [HUA 13, REH 13, FAN 15]: application, network and perception.

The application layer includes security, traffic management and comfort applications, as well as the human–machine interface. The network layer represents various communication technologies, while the perception layer is composed of all types of sensors and means of data collection. Here we will focus on the network layer (communication system), and using three axes of research, we will exploit:

– quality of service: determining the metrics of service quality (reliability, availability and robustness);

– routing: transporting information within inter-vehicular networks without interruption;

– applications, collaboration and collective intelligence: achieving a complete integration of the human/vehicle/object/environment network via IoV applications.

7.2.2. Communication obstacles

The IoV is an emerging technology that studies inter-vehicle communication differently than the traditional Internet network [SIL 17], posing new challenges due to the specific characteristics of the deployment environment and the composition of the network. These characteristics manifest themselves as communication obstacles that may cause disconnections in the IoV, such as:

– high mobility of vehicles, high speed of movement and rapid change in network topology;

– variation in the density of vehicles within urban areas, on highways, and in open countryside, and lack of RSU terminals;

– utilization of limited-coverage cellular networks for communication;

– black hole attacks to which communication networks may be subjected;

– distributed denial of service attacks;

– network surcharges due to a high number of agents communicating on the IoV and limited bandwidth;

– distributed architecture and remote access to services offered by the IoV;

– heterogeneity of entities constituting the IoV;

– lack of cooperation between IoV agents and certain infrastructures that may act as communication relays (due to the requirements of differing security levels, for example);

– the complexity and density of the outside environment (forests, buildings, etc.);

– egotism of some mobile agents;

– competing access to communication channels;

– a full-duplex communication mode [RII 17] between network entities.

7.2.3. Related work

The services offered by deploying the IoV gravitate and evolve around data traffic in real time or offline [COS 12]. Various modes, strategies and routing protocols exist for the transportation of data.

Some work attempts to take advantage of the mobility of vehicles by relying on V2I communication. RSU terminals act as replication servers for the dissemination of content and try to guarantee maximum network coverage. A vehicle leaves the coverage zone of one terminal A and enters the coverage zone of another terminal B. The object of the work carried out in this axis is thus to minimize the number of RSUs deployed while maximizing network performance during road planning.

This opportunistic deployment strategy is costly, so the authors [SIL 17] begin by developing a performance metric that measures the rate of data dissemination (defined in terms of probability of V2I contact and duration of V2I contact). The second part consists of using this metric to identify the best placement of RSU terminals in order to adequately support the exchange of data content, with each item of content requiring a specific level of performance. Although the reliance of the IoV on V2I communications has many advantages, particularly in terms of the overall network view, the very nature of this network, and notably the movement speed of vehicles, does not guarantee stability of communication; therefore, solutions based on V2I mode do not mitigate the obstacles cited in section 7.2.2.

The next part of this chapter examines the routing layer of IoV architecture. We present a study of routing protocols dedicated to vehicular networks. Among the protocols studied, we cite multi-hop and reactive routing [IND 14]. According to these characteristics, the latter proves well suited to mobile networks, ensuring better performance than data source-oriented routing (in terms of the overall results of packet delivery and end-to-end delay). Consequently, it is used by most wireless ad hoc routing protocols in mobile environments. Figure 7.1 presents a taxonomy of existing routing protocols in vehicular networks, grouped according to different operating modes. Routing algorithms dedicated to mobile networks are often multi-criterion protocols and may belong to more than one of the categories cited in Figure 7.1.

The AODV (Ad hoc On Demand Distance Vector) routing protocol [GHA 15] supports unicast and multicast routing on demand, using a sequence number for each of the routes. Because it is reactive, AODV responds to connection failure in the network. Its principal disadvantage is that this type of network may decide on a route that is not necessarily the optimal one. An improved version of AODV, SD-AOMDV (Ad hoc On-demand Multipath Distance Vector Routing), is proposed in [MAO 12] to process the characteristics of VANET. SD-AOMDV adds new factors (speed and direction) to the field that determines the next hop during the process of route discovery and construction. The AODV protocol and its variant are linked to a process of route discovery before the start of transmission, which is their main disadvantage. It calculates multiple complete routes from the source to the destination, and it becomes reactive in the event of a communication problem or a broken link in order to construct another route. This type of source-oriented protocol seems inadequate for highly dynamic networks such as VANETs. Moreover, the calculation of multiple routes causes an increase in the protocol's end-to-end delay.

Figure 7.1. *Taxonomy of vehicular network routing protocols*

The authors of [ZHA 08] propose the VADD (Vehicle-Assisted Data Delivery) protocol, which utilizes the "store and forwarding" technique, in which a moving vehicle carries a packet, calculates the next link able to reduce delivery delay using a transport delay model and then sends the packet via this link. Unlike other solutions, this protocol relies on the anticipated mobility of vehicles, delineated and reframed by an existing traffic model and by route structure. The authors propose variants of VADD, which determine which link guarantees the shortest delivery period. The choice of the next link is based on the location in the first variant

(Location VADD) and on the direction in the other variant (Direction VADD). The authors also combined the two selection criteria in Hybrid VADD. Their experimental results show that of the VADD protocols proposed, Hybrid VADD performs more effectively than Location VADD and Direction VADD [CHE 15]. They also prove that the VADD protocols proposed surpass the Epidemic and GPSR (Greedy Perimeter Stateless Routing) with buffer and Dynamic Source Routing (DSR) protocols in terms of packet delivery ratio, delivery time and protocol overhead.

Another protocol based on road structure information is the RBVT-R (Road Based Vehicular Traffic Reactive Protocol) [NZO 09], a reactive protocol that uses real-time road traffic to create routes via the so-called "connected" road segments; that is, segments with a high probability of network connectivity. It then makes a distributed choice of the next hop based on a multi-criterion prioritization function, such as the density of neighboring vehicles [KAR 00].

The GPSR routing protocol [CHE 15, KAR 00, SHR 12] (Greedy Perimeter Stateless Routing for wireless networks) is based on geographical position, which makes it well suited to VANETs. A node chooses the next relay based on position information it receives periodically from these neighbors and from the destination. Its defining characteristic is that it can recover information from neighboring vehicles using GPS positioning equipment, rather than obtaining a large amount of routing information and maintaining both a list of neighbors and a routing table. The transmission strategy combines a greedy conveyance strategy with a perimetric conveyance strategy. An improved version of GPSR, the I-GPSR (Improved GPSR) protocol, was proposed in [KAU 16], which adds movement speed and vehicle orientation as a decision-making criterion. The I-EGRP protocol [KAR 00] is well suited to low-output environments because it dynamically changes its routing decisions with the aid of each RSU terminal detected. The disadvantage of this protocol is that its choice is determined as a function of the presence of a fixed infrastructure.

Like other multi-criterion routing protocols, the MUDDS (Multi-metric Unicast Data Dissemination Scheme) protocol proposed in [CHA 12] is a unicast data propagation strategy. It determines its choice of the next relay using two metrics calculated locally: packet reception rate (PRR) and link availability (LA). It operates in two phases. During its first phase, it adapts its transmission range to guarantee a maximum PRR according to the network status in terms of congestion and communication density. Next, the transmission of messages takes place based on the LA metric. The use of the PRR guarantees reliable message transfer, and the choice of relay based on LA reduces the number of hops and avoids network fragmentation.

The MA-DSDV [HAR 14] (Multi Agent Destination-Sequenced Distance Vector routing) protocol is an improvement on the distance vector routing protocol, modeled as a multi-agent system. It supplies the route with the smallest number of relay agents. The multi-agent aspect makes it possible to autonomously act in the event of a breakdown and to communicate the information necessary for resumption of routing to all its neighbors between agents.

The GVGrid [SUN 06, NZO 09] protocol is quality of service (QoS) oriented and constructs a route on demand from a source toward vehicles positioned in a predetermined geographic region. It divides the geographical map into several grids on which it highlights the links between nodes. The choice of relay nodes is made according to the number of disconnections from the link connecting it to the transmitter. The objective of GVGrid is to maintain a robust route resistant to vehicle mobility. Experimental results have shown that GVGrid is able to supply itineraries with a longer life span compared to other routing protocols for VANETs. Its principal disadvantage is that it offers no guarantee of optimal delay, which is a required service quality metric in VANETs.

The additional characteristic contributed by the IoV compared to traditional VANET networks is the strong probability of having a network and connected objects that are completely heterogeneous. In addition to the classic problems of homogeneous routing, the use of heterogeneous networks results in additional "handover" time, which represents the time of passage from one network access technology to another. The authors of [SHA 11] propose a shared strategy of vertical transfer of one communication technology to another, called Optimal Vertical Handoff [SHA 11].

In a heterogeneous large-scale network, the idea of clustering is much sought after by the community. When nodes are grouped together and each cluster chooses its cluster Head, the question remaining for a source node is to choose which vehicle will act as proxy, that is, as a pathway toward the infrastructure of another communication technology [KAR 00]. A selection strategy proposed in [LAB 12] prioritizes available technologies. For example, the authors opt for Long Term Evolution-Advanced (or LTE-Advanced technology, a fourth-generation telephone network standard) as a second wireless interface, which directly links the source to the infrastructure. With an eye to improving communication costs, the authors have also designed a distributed, adaptive and multi-criterion algorithm for the selection of a pathway from one network to another, called QoS based Gateway Selection. This algorithm has proven to work better than the deterministic approach using the cluster Head as a pathway.

Finally, the authors of [LI 12] propose a strategy that consists of selecting a portion of the vehicles as mobile pathways to link the various components of the heterogeneous network. Coalitions of nodes are created based on game theory, which stimulates the nodes to choose the best coalition in order to move from one pathway to another and to join coalitions which can most effectively maximize data outflow.

The works analyzed show that in order to fulfill communication requirements in highly dynamic networks, a routing strategy must take into account multiple criteria, no matter the category to which it belongs. We note that each protocol attempts to balance a certain number of parameters, which depend on the protocol proposed and the mode of communication, with the principal objective of optimizing three metrics: routing reliability, end-to-end conveyance delay and packet delivery ratio.

The V2V and V2I modes of communication are complementary. In order to mitigate the communication obstacles cited in section 7.2.2, a hybrid communication strategy is preferable for a better communication performance.

7.3. Multi-criterion routing protocol

We need well defined routing protocols in order to solve the problems caused by the large-scale nature and heterogeneity of the IoV. It would be optimal to switch between communication technologies when a problem arises, as this approach theoretically offers better performances. However, this has issues of stability and many other constraints (material, legal, etc.).

Our focus is on the algorithmic part of the subject, in which the principal object is to contribute effective, reliable, robust methods optimized for the secure transmission of data packets according to the evolution of the network's topology and mobility. This means guaranteeing network connectivity despite mobility. Movement by the vehicles in the network, even minimal, can thus cause the physical fragmentation of the network into multiple sub-networks. The movement of a vehicle on a routing path alters the routing possibilities available to this vehicle. Previously contactable neighbors may become unreachable, while other, previously unknown ones can now be reached. The movement of vehicles thus simultaneously causes both the elimination and the creation of possible routing paths which must be taken into account when routing choices are made. Knowledge of inter-vehicle contact duration is thus an important and useful parameter for vehicles [ALS 16] as it allows for the proactive avoidance and anticipation of premature disconnections. In addition, it represents one of the input parameters in the conveyance process as it makes it possible to select the next optimal hop as well as the local and proactive construction of a robust route for data transmission. However, due to the high mobility of the vehicles and the complexity of mobility models, the estimation of link duration in mobile networks and vehicular networks remains an open research topic.

Based on these observations, we have proposed a routing algorithm that first makes use of the estimation of contact durations to construct packet routing paths. It anticipates as far as possible the routing and relay agent choices on each hop locally. In addition to the estimation of contact durations, we add a second input item to the process of selecting the next relay, which is the load-balancing parameter. The vehicle itself transmits its load in the number of packets to be relayed, as a variable. Finally, before choosing a relay, we confirm that this relay has no connectivity problems.

7.3.1. *Applications and services*

Vehicular networks consume a large amount of data, which they use to enhance performance in various types of applications, such as the following:

1) road safety: information on weather conditions, obstacles on the road, avoidance of a dangerous vehicle, or location of a stolen vehicle;

2) management of road traffic: information on traffic jams, the choice of route, the adjustment of speed according to traffic lights, and stoplights where pedestrians are present;

3) access to multimedia content via Internet hotspots passing from one car to another up to the closest access point: video streaming, mp3 files, etc.;

4) transfer and control of applications from mobile terminals to vehicle screens for shared use in real or staggered time (online games) [ALS 16];

5) downloading and sharing of content and services onboard the vehicle for future use;

6) monitoring of merchandise transport vehicles: synchronization of convoys, buses, taxis, etc.

Although these applications have different objectives, they are all subject to the same constraints in terms of communication networks. They must be able to be supplied continually by their users, by the entities in the vehicular network or by RSUs. There are two distinct types of communication:

Forward communication: When a vehicle moves, it acquires a history of events on the section of a road traveled, which it wishes to share with vehicles entering this section in order to capitalize on it. In this case, this information is distributed to vehicles in the traveled section (the information is moving in the opposite direction to the vehicle's movement) so that users can make use of it. This type of communication is event-based. Figure 7.2 illustrates this type of communication.

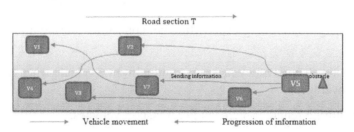

Figure 7.2. *An example of forward communication. For a color version of this figure, see www.iste.co.uk/saleh/challenges.zip*

Request/reply communication: These are communications in which a vehicle transmits an access request to a web service, for example, and then re-enters a dead zone. The response to its request is then transferred via V2V. The first vehicle that begins transfer of the response has an Internet connection. Initially, we are assumed to know the IP address of the vehicle to which the information must be transmitted (the destination) and of the first relay vehicle that has an Internet connection. This case is illustrated in Figure 7.3.

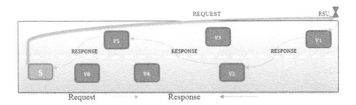

Figure 7.3. *An example of request/reply communication. For a color version of this figure, see www.iste.co.uk/saleh/challenges.zip*

Our work is aimed to guarantee data conveyance toward a specific vehicle or even an RSU infrastructure and ensure communication between a source and a destination, thus improving the performances of the types of applications mentioned previously. Our algorithm is generic and can be applied to various types of applications, such as:

– sharing a breakdown diagnosis with a nearby service station, the geographic location of which is known via V2V;

– supplying input to a fixed weather station in real time via V2V;

– downloading multimedia content from a fixed access point via V2V;

– enjoying a stable, high-speed Internet connection during a journey, via V2V;

– relaying an emergency message coming from a vehicle when there is no cellular coverage;

– monitoring rental or merchandise transport vehicles;

The goal of our work is to find a solution for one-to-one communications between a mobile source and a fixed or a mobile source, via intermediary vehicles, as part of the application of the IoV on a one-dimensional plane.

7.3.2. *Multi-criterion routing protocols in IoV communications*

The aim of our approach is to minimize disconnections during communications and thus to reduce the costs of troubleshooting and repetition of certain system messages. When vehicles enter into contact, for example, to supply input to a traffic management application, warn of an obstacle, transmit information in real time to a weather station, or even to transmit data retrieved from the Internet network (P2P), communication links are maintained for short periods of time. These opportunistic communications limit the volume of data exchanged over a connection and reduce the reliability of transmission. In order to optimize data packet conveyance, we must previously estimate the durations of contact between the entities of the IoV and take these into account in the process of distribution. Consider a road section T delineated by two intersections, where an intersection is defined by a traffic control signal, a highway entrance or any other obstacle causing a change in the movement system. Figure 7.4 illustrates an example of a data exchange scenario on a highway, in which we can see how the concept of neighbors is redefined, and how to select one relay out of several.

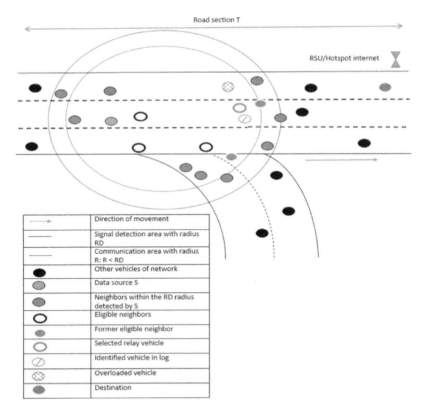

Figure 7.4. *An example of the execution of our best-neighbor choice strategy. For a color version of this figure, see www.iste.co.uk/saleh/challenges.zip*

Here, V is all of the vehicles in the network, while V_1 is a vehicle transmitting a need to communicate with another vehicle in order to transmit data to it, or to enrich an application distributed or stored on a remote server with new information. To do this, the vehicle relies on V2V communications. As long as V_1 has the need to communicate, it executes our geographic routing interval at a time interval t_{me} (given by formula [7.4]). The parameter t_{me} is linked to the last estimated contact duration, influenced by the communication reliability rate of the previously chosen relay.

Each vehicle selected as a relay will execute the routing algorithm in its turn to choose its own next relay. The process of routing and the execution of the routing algorithm end when the packets reach their final destination. Our general algorithm is composed of three phases.

7.3.2.1. Phase 1: estimate duration of contact

The objective of this stage is to estimate the durations of contact between vehicles in a neighborhood.

Hypotheses

Each vehicle knows its geographical coordinates (GPS) and has access to a wireless communication interface. A small Beacon message, $V_2 <x_2, y_2, v_2, \overrightarrow{dir}, C_2, id_2>$, is sent beforehand and at regular intervals by a vehicle to its neighbors within a signal detection radius RD, to transmit its local information. This relatively small message can be combined with another type of control message to reduce the cost of the messages exchanged. The variables x, y represent the geographical coordinates of the mobile agent; v is the travel speed, the vector $\overrightarrow{dir}$ gives the direction of travel, c represents the free load of the vehicle in the number of packets and id is the agent identifier, in this case its IP address. These messages thus exchanged give us a quasi-overall view of the network for each vehicle.

Description

Using the information from the Beacon messages, we develop a distributed algorithm, which estimates windows of connection time, during which a communication is or will be available and reliable for a pair of vehicles.

Let $V_1 <x_1, y_1, v_1, \overrightarrow{dir}, C_1, id_1>$ and $V_2 <x_2, y_2, v_2, \overrightarrow{dir}, C_2, id_2>$ for two entities in a vehicular network driving on a road section T. To estimate the duration of contact between V_1 and V_2, the distance between the two entities must be less than or equal to the transmission radius R of the radio equipment on-board the vehicles. This condition is given by the following inequality, where R is the radius of a circle, which represents the maximum communication area covered by the radio communication technology used by a vehicle:

$$\sqrt{(x_2-x_1)^2 + (y_2-y_1)^2} \le R \qquad\qquad [7.1]$$

Given that vehicle speeds are never constant in practice, we will not use the travel speed of the vehicle in relation to the road, but rather the relative speed of each vehicle in relation to another vehicle. If two vehicles are moving at the same speed $v_1 = v_2$, their duration of contact (DDC) is equal to the ratio of the distance over the travel speed of one of the vehicles. In the opposite case, the contact duration time is given by the following expression:

$$\frac{\sqrt{(x_2-x_1)^2 + (y_2-y_1)^2}}{|v_2-v_1|} \text{ with } v_2 \ne v_1 \qquad\qquad [7.2]$$

which implies that the duration of contact DDC between a pair of vehicles V_1 and V_2 belongs to the interval:

$$\left[0, \frac{R}{|v_2-v_1|} \right]$$

After having calculated this duration of contact, a vehicle V_1 will have as a result a group of potential neighbors with the information $<Id_i, v_i, \overrightarrow{dir_i}, C_i, DDC_i>$ corresponding to each of them. We redefine the concept of neighborhood in this algorithm. A vehicle V_i is considered the neighbor of a vehicle V_1 if and only if:

– it detects its signal;

– it is traveling in the same direction of displacement and in the same traveling direction as the other vehicle;

– it has a Euclidian distance $d(V_i, V_1)$ less than the radius R.

After the estimation of the durations of contact of a vehicle with its neighbors, it communicates this list of potential neighbors ordered according to the needs of our strategy.

In our work we take, on road section T, a fixed point of origin O, to which the coordinates (x_i, y_i) will be referenced and which will serve to determine the direction of displacement of the vehicles. With regard to the direction of travel dir_i, which we need for the selection of relays, we take the neighbor vehicles V_i which respond to the following equation:

$$\overrightarrow{dir_{v_i}} = k\, \overrightarrow{dir_{v_1}} \text{ with } k > 0 \qquad\qquad [7.3]$$

In our proposal, we have decided not to specify the communication technology. The importance of communication technology for our contribution lies in the parameters it offers, in this case, the transmission range (radius R), as well as the length of the data segment it carries. We consider packet data units of fixed size, which require, depending on the speed offered by the communication technology, a direct transmission time Tp from a vehicle V_1 to a vehicle V_2.

The Algorithm for Estimation of Duration of Contact (AEDC) is executed for each vehicle in order to redefine its neighborhood according to our communication needs and to estimate the durations of contact with each neighbor. It then sends back a collection of "Neighbors" with "Beacon_DDC" information. The pseudo-code of the AEDC function is illustrated in Figure 7.5. The Beacon_DDC object groups information relative to each eligible neighbor such as the Identifier ID of the vehicle transmitting the object, its travel direction, travel speed, available load and duration of contact.

```
Object Beacon_DDC
      String id;
      Integer dir;
      Real v;
      Integer C;
      Real DDC;
End Object


Function AEDC (V1: Vehicle): Beacon_DDC
Integer i;
Beacon_DDC Neighbors [ ];
Begin
    For all (Vehicle Vᵢ ∈ V) do // Vᵢ ∈ neighbors of V₁
        Receive (xᵢ, yᵢ, vᵢ, dirᵢ, Cᵢ idᵢ); // Extract Vᵢ's Beacon
            If (√ ((xᵢ − x₁)² + (yᵢ − y₁)²) ≤R ∧ (dirᵢ = dir_Destination)) then // formula [3]
                    Neighbors[i].id← idᵢ;
                    Neighbors[i].x← xᵢ;
                    Neighbors[i].y← yᵢ
                    Neighbors[i].dir← dirᵢ;
                    Neighbors[i].v← vᵢ;
                    If (Neighbors[i].v ≠ v₁) then // different speed values of V₁ and Vᵢ
                            Neighbors[i].DDC ← (√ ((xᵢ − x₁)² + (yᵢ − y₁)²)/| vᵢ . v₁ |);
                    Else
                            Neighbors[i].DDC ← (√ ((xᵢ − x₁)² + (yᵢ − y₁)²)/ v₁);
                    End if;
            End if;
        End for;
    Return (Neighbors); // Beacon_DDC is the type of Neighbors []
End.
```

Figure 7.5. *Algorithm for estimation of durations of contact between V₁ and its neighborhood*

7.3.2.2. *Phase 2: updating communication anomaly logs*

On a road section T, we use logs distributed over each vehicle, which will be accessible for writing and reading by the vehicle safeguarding them and as read-only by the other vehicles.

Exploitation of logs

When a vehicle encounters a communication anomaly with another vehicle, such as a disconnection, its log file is updated with information concerning the anomaly detected. The primary items of information are the vehicle(s) concerned, time and/or duration of disconnection, non-covered area, density of vehicles in this area and possibly the cause of disconnection. This phase will detect dead zones and enable vehicles to act accordingly when choosing the intermediary vehicles by which data will be conveyed. Dead zones are inventoried in the log of each vehicle and updated either by the vehicle itself if it is able to do so or by direct neighbors via partial distribution of their logs.

The detection of V_1 communication anomalies by neighboring vehicles V_i is done either by:

– premature disruption of a communication link;

– non-receipt of acknowledgment of messages sent; or

– random variations in Beacon messages from a vehicle sensed to be a neighbor.

We present the pseudo-code of the updating procedure for communication anomaly logs, executed by each vehicle, in Figure 7.6.

```
Procedure UpdateLog (V₁)
Begin
        Switch (Error):
                case (Weakened Signal (Vᵢ) or Broken Link (Vᵢ, V₁)):
                        Log. Add (Vᵢ: Position Vᵢ, date/hour, Broken_Link);
                        break;
                case (Random Reception of Beacon (Vᵢ)):
                        Log. Add (Vᵢ: Position Vᵢ, date/hour, Delete_Neighbors (Vᵢ));
                        break;
                case (NoAcK from last selected node relay (Vᵢ)): // Vᵢ is previous relay node
                        Log. Add (Vᵢ: date/hour, NoAcK (Vᵢ)); // we can't have its position
                        break;
                default:
                        AddLog.wait ();
        End Switch
End.
```

Figure 7.6. *Updating strategy for communication anomaly logs*

7.3.2.3. *Phase 3: determining geographical routing*

At a lower level than the standard communication level, the network layer enables us to combine IP routing and geographical routing. Our protocol is reactive and adaptive, that is, the transition path of packets from a source to a destination is constructed as the message travels. The principal metrics that enable us to determine a routing strategy are the premature disruption of a communication, distance, communication density, belonging to a cluster, and the speed and status of connections. Our strategy adds two other decision-making metrics, specifically the duration of contact and the rate of referencing in the communication anomaly log.

Hypotheses

– Each vehicle is cooperative and has access to a communication interface.

– The neighbor localization tables [ATE 10] of vehicles are improved by Beacon messages.

– The direction of the final destination and its identifier are known beforehand.

Description

In order to have a complete system, we use a communicating interface to integrate the results of estimation of durations of contact with our routing algorithm, as even though they are separate modules, they remain complementary. To add to the objectives fixed at the outset, the results of phase 1 and phase 2 will contribute to the decision of the next relay for packet conveyance. To better manage the consequences of frequent disconnections, we choose to orient our protocol toward a local and progressive approach. The data relaying path is constructed as we move forward, respecting the temporal and real limitations of the vehicle.

When a vehicle is a transmitter or receives packets to be retransmitted, it exploits the results of the preceding phases to choose the relay that has the lightest load and an optimal contact duration from among its neighborhood, and which is not shown in the communication anomaly log. This strategy is applicable when a link disconnection occurs as well, or when a vehicle is notified by an anomaly recorded in a log file concerning a vehicle with which it is currently communicating.

Each log file contains a data structure that records the vehicles responsible for communication anomalies. During the construction of vehicle communication links, it:

– retrieves the list of potential neighbors;

– compares the load balancing variables C_i;

– consults the communication anomaly log.

Using C_i, we will choose the relays so as to balance the load among neighbors and minimize packet loss due to the overload of certain relays. Using the DDC of the chosen relay, and at the time of transmission of a packet Tp, influenced by other events and possibly log notifications, we determine as a function of parameter α, the average time t_{me} of the next re-execution of our contact duration estimation algorithm, which is given by the following equation, where the parameter α determines the time elapsed before an anomaly arises:

$$t_{me} = t_0 + DDC_i - \alpha \text{ with } \alpha \in R \qquad [7.4]$$

The principal algorithm GRFDC (Geographic Routing with Free Load Duration of Contact and Log) (Figure 7.8) uses the Max_Min function (Figure 7.7), which enables us to list eligible neighbors in a decreasing order, according to the number of packets NB that can be sent to each of these neighbors. This number of packets to be sent must respect the free load of the vehicle and come close to the number of packets to be sent during the calculated DDC.

For each vehicle, the Max_Min function is used with the "Neighbors" list as a parameter. It returns a "Max_Min_Neighbors" list sorted in a decreasing order of their load receiving capacity.

Each "Eligible_Neighbor" object groups the identifier (id) and the "min" calculated value of each eligible neighbor.

```
Objet Eligible_Neighbor
        String id;
        Integer min;
End objet

Function Max_Min (Neighbors [ ]: Beacon_DDC): Eligible_Neighbor[ ]
Eligible_Neighbor Max_Min_Neighbors [ ];
Begin
    For all (Vehicle Vᵢ ∈ Neighbors) do
    End for;
        Extract  (Idᵢ, Cᵢ, DDCᵢ);
        Eligible_Neighbor Eligible_Vᵢ ;
        Eligible_Vᵢ.min ← Min(Cᵢ, DDCᵢ /Tp);
        Eligible_Vᵢ.id ← idᵢ;
        Max_Min_Neighbors[i] = Eligible_Vᵢ;
    End for;
    Sort (Max_Min_Neighbors) by min's value;
    Return Max_Min_Neighbors [ ];
End.
```

Figure 7.7. *Max_Min function, which returns an ordered list of eligible vehicles*

```
Algorithm RGDCL (V₁, log)
Boolean Choice ← false;
Begin
    Beacon_DDC Neighbors [ ];
    Eligible_Neighbor Max_Min_Neighbors [ ];
    Neighbors [ ] ← AEDC (V₁);                          // DDC estimation (V₁, Vᵢ)
    Max_Min_Neighbors [ ] ← Max_Min (Neighbors);        //order neighbors with Max_Min ()
    While (Choice = false) do
        If (Max_Min_Neighbors [i].id ∉ log) then
            Choice← true;
            NextRelay ← Max_Min_Neighbors [i].id;        // send data to Vᵢ
            Max_Min_Neighbors [NextRelay].C ← Max_Min_Neighbors [NextRelay].C +
                                               Max_Min_Neighbors [NextRelay].min;
            Send (Ack);                                  // send Ack to previous relay node
            If (Vᵢ ≠ idDestination) then
                Route← Route+ RGDCL (NextRelay);         // next Relay execute the same functions
            Else
                Send (FinalAck);
            End if;
        End if;
        i ← i+1;
    End while;
End.
```

Figure 7.8. *GRFDC multi-criterion geographic routing algorithm*

The GRFDC algorithm uses the AEDC function and the Max_Min function to select the next relay according to the Log. It then acknowledges to its transmitter that it has received the packets the transmitter just relayed and awaits the receipt of the next relay selected. The concept of acknowledgment mentioned in the GRFDC enables the communication anomaly log to be updated.

Table 7.1 provides an example of the values of V_i, $i \in [1, 8]$, the new neighbors of vehicle V_0, defined according to our strategy. For each V_i, we calculate the number of packets that on V_0 can transmit to it as a function of:

– duration of contact: $NBd = DDC(V_0, V_i) / T_p$ [7.5]

– free load C_i which gives us the number of packets that V_i is capable of receiving from V_0.

In order to avoid disconnections during communications, the loss of packets, and the overloading of certain relays, the Max_Min function determines the number of packets to be sent over each connection (V_0, V_i). Of all these connections, we choose the one that enables the largest number of packets NB to be sent. This choice is expressed by the formula below:

$$Max \left\{ NBi / NB \in Min(Ci, \frac{DDCi}{Tp}) \right\} \quad \text{with } i \in [1, n] \qquad [7.6]$$

So, the algorithm will group the neighbors in order $(V_7, V_6, V_1, V_4, V_5, V_2, V_3, V_8)$, and their presence in the anomaly log file will be verified in order to choose the next eligible element:

Neighbor of V_0	V_1	V_2	V_3	V_4	V_5	V_6	V_7	V_8
NB (packets)	15	8	25	9	11	14	21	12
C (packets)	10	9	5	16	8	13	22	0
NB = Min (NBd, C)	10	8	5	9	8	13	21	0

Table 7.1. *An example of a neighborhood*

7.4. Conclusion and perspectives

Communication and the exchange of content is a key characteristic for the updating of the Internet of Vehicles. In these types of networks, vehicles act as cooperative mobile sensors, constantly exchanging messages with other vehicles, the cellular network and infrastructures [SIL 17] as part of comfort applications, road safety services or road traffic management. However, the task of supplying content in such a dynamic network is far from being easy to execute.

In order to convey the large amount of data generated by the IoV, we need a reliable data dissemination process and impeccable connectivity. Our objective is to ensure the reliability and robustness of communications in vehicular networks, as these networks are sporadic due to the mobility and speed of vehicles or the presence of obstacles. The conveyance of information is entirely dependent on the reliability of these communications.

With the aim of satisfying the requirements of this system and working around communication constraints, one solution consists of implementing a distributed, reactive and adaptive communication strategy, one that relies on the vehicles themselves. To communicate with one another, vehicles must define a routing that will enable them to manage the frequent disruptions that characterize this type of network.

In our proposal, we begin by quantifying the durations of contact between vehicles. To do this, we propose an analytical model for the duration of contact between a vehicle and each neighbor, on the transmission radius R, based on a uniform distribution of vehicle flow entering a highway zone during a given period of the day.

We then implement this model on a flow of vehicles, with a Jade Multi-Agent System (MAS) [FAB 07] in which "vehicle" agents evolve dynamically and autonomously in their environment. MASs enable an agent to have a specific "behavior" that can be programmed; an agent can also communicate with other agents, thanks to ACL communications specific to the SMAs. Thanks to these two characteristics, Jade allows us to program our vehicle agents to execute hop routing and to make the best choice of next relay agent at each iteration.

The role of the MAS is to create our own small-scale simulator and recreate the following scenario:

– A group of vehicle agents evolve on a highway road section, move in a linear fashion and calculate their future positions with respect to travel speeds and previous positions.

– Agents within reach (i.e. whose new positions are less than the transmission radius R) receive one of the periodic Beacon messages.

– Thanks to these exchanges of messages, each agent possesses a list of agents able to execute the protocol.

– Two agents at either end of the road section attempt a message exchange via multiple intermediary agents.

– The initiator chooses the best agent from the list available to it; it then relays the message to this agent and continues the process of travel on the road section.

– The agent selected takes on the role of an initiator and executes the best relay selection protocol in its turn. This procedure continues until the intended recipient agent is reached.

Communication between agents on the Jade platform, as well as the different types of offered messages possible, makes it possible to assign an agent to each vehicle, which enables us to execute a simulation of the scenario described in section 7.3.2.1. At the conclusion of this simulation, the principal measurable metric is message conveyance time.

Subsequently, we test and validate our work on an NS2 network simulator [GAJ 13] and a VanetMobiSim road traffic simulator [HAR 09]. The resulting durations of contact will be used in the geographic routing protocol. Along with the load balancing variable and the communication anomaly log, they are a determining factor in the choice of a relay entity. In addition to the contribution of important information to the routing algorithm, we also provide a system of acknowledgment between two agents. A vehicle V_1 receives n packets from a transmitting vehicle V_0. When V_1 has conveyed these n packets to its own relay V_2, V_1 sends an acknowledgment to V_0 and awaits the acknowledgment of V_2. This local acknowledgment between two nodes contributes to the updating of communication anomaly logs and allows the reliability of a vehicle to be verified. Finally, to make our strategy robust and able to manage mobility and connectivity problems in high-mobility networks, we add a final global acknowledgment. To provide perspective, we will broaden the scope of our work to other communication scenarios and to multicast and broadcast modes. In addition, in our approach, we consider an execution scenario lacking RSU terminals; consequently, the V2I mode of communication is not taken into consideration, in order to obtain better performance. A hybrid mode of communication is envisioned for updating logs, in particular.

7.5. References

[ALS 16] ALSHARIF N., ALDUBAIKHY K., SHEN X.S., "Link duration estimation using neural networks based mobility prediction in vehicular networks", *Electrical and Computer Engineering (CCECE), 2016 IEEE Canadian Conference*, Vancouver, Canada, pp. 1–4, 2016.

[ATE 10] ATECHIAN T., Protocole de routage géo-multipoint hybride et mécanisme d'acheminement de données pour les réseaux ad hoc de véhicules (VANETs), PhD thesis, INSA Lyon, September 24, 2010.

[CHA 12] CHAKROUN O., CHERKAOUI S., REZGUI J., "MUDDS: Multi-metric Unicast Data Dissemination Scheme for 802.11p VANETs", *8th International Wireless Communications and Mobile Computing Conference, IWCMC*, Cyprus, pp. 1074–1079, 2012.

[CHE 15] CHENG J., CHENG J., ZHOU M. *et al.*, "Routing in internet of vehicles: a review", *IEEE Transactions on Intelligent Transportation Systems*, vol. 16, no. 5, pp. 2339–2352, 2015.

[COS 12] COSTA-MONTENEGRO E., QUINOY-GARCIA F., GONZALEZ-CASTANO F. *et al.*, "Vehicular Entertainment Systems: Mobile Application Enhancement in Networked Infrastructures", *IEEE Vehicular Technology Magazine*, vol. 7, no. 3, pp. 73–79, 2012.

[FAB 07] FABIO LUIGI B., CAIRE G., DOMINIC G., *Developing Multi-agent Systems with JADE*, vol. 7, Wiley, 2007.

[FAN 15] FAN L., LI G., YANG J. *et al.*, "The design of IOV overall structure and the research of IOV key technology in intelligent transportation systems", *International Power, Electronics and Materials Engineering Conference*, Dalian, China, pp. 1085–1090, 2015.

[GAJ 13] GAJANANAN K. SONTISIRIKIT S., ZHANG J. *et al.*, "A Cooperative Its Study on Green Light Optimisation Using an Integrated Traffic, Driving, and Communication Simulator", *Proceedings 36th Australasian Transport Research Forum, ATRF*, Brisbane, Australia, pp. 1–13, 2013.

[GER 16] GERLA M., LEE E.K., PAU G. *et al.*, "Internet of vehicles: from intelligent grid to autonomous cars and vehicular clouds", *International Journal of Distributed Sensor Networks*, vol. 12, pp. 241–246, 2016.

[GHA 15] GHANISHTHA N., YOGESH J., "Review on classification of different VANET Protocols based on routing information", *International Journal of Advanced Research in Computer and Communication Engineering*, vol. 4, pp. 388–392, 2015.

[HAR 09] HARRI J., FIORE M., FILALI F., "Vehicular mobility simulation with vanetmobisim", *Simulation*, vol. 87, no. 4, pp. 275–300, 2009.

[HAR 14] HARRABI S., CHAINBI W., GHEDIRA K., "A multi-agent proactive routing protocol for Vehicular Ad-Hoc Networks", *The 2014 International Symposium on Networks, Computers and Communications, ISNCC 2014*, Hammamet, Tunisia, pp. 1–6, 2014.

[HUA 13] HUANG J.M., "Research on internet of vehicles and its application in intelligent transportation", *Applied Mechanics and Materials*, vol. 321, pp. 2818–2821, 2013.

[IND 14] INDRA A., MURALI R., "Routing Protocols for Vehicular Ad-hoc Networks (VANETs): a review", *Journal of Emerging Trends in Computing and Information Science,* vol. 5, pp. 25–43, 2014.

[KAR 00] KARP B., KUNG H.-T., "GPSR: Greedy perimeter stateless routing for wireless networks", *Proceedings of the 6th Annual International Conference on Mobile Computing and Networking*, Boston, MA, pp. 243–254, 2000.

[KAU 16] KAUR S., KAUR K., "An New Improved GPSR (I-GPSR) routing protocol for VANET", *Imperial Journal of Interdisciplinary Research*, vol. 2, no. 7, pp. 1190–1196, 2016.

[LAB 12] LABIOD H., EL MOUNA ZHIOUA G. *et al.*, "An Efficient QoS based gateway selection algorithm for VANET to LTE advanced hybrid cellular network", *Proceedings of the 15th ACM International Conference on Modeling, Analysis and Simulation of Wireless and Mobile Systems*, New York, NY, pp. 353–356, 2012.

[LI 12] LI Y., YING K., CHENG P. *et al.*, "Cooperative data dissemination in cellular-VANET heterogeneous wireless networks", *4th International High Speed Intelligent Communication Forum*, Nanjing, China, pp. 1–4. 2012.

[LIA 15] LIANG W., LI Z., ZHANG H. *et al.*, "Vehicular ad hoc networks: architectures, research issues, methodologies, challenges, and trends", *International Journal of Distributed Sensor Networks*, vol. 11, no. 8, pp. 102–113, 2015.

[MAO 12] MAOWAD H., SHAABAN E., "Enhancing AOMDV routing protocol for V2V communication", *Proceedings of the 6th International Conference on Communications and Information Technology, and Proceedings of the 3rd World Conference on Education and Educational Technologies*, Stevens Point, WI, pp. 20–27, 2012.

[NZO 09] NZOUONTA J., RAJGURE N., WANG, G. *et al.*, "VANET routing on city roads using real-time vehicular traffic information", *IEEE Transactions on Vehicular Technology*, vol. 58, no. 7, pp. 3609–3626, 2009.

[REH 13] REHMAN S., KHAN M.A., ZIA T.A. *et al.*, "Vehicular Ad-Hoc Networks (VANETs) – An overview and challenges", *Journal of Wireless Networking and Communications*, vol. 3, no. 3, pp. 29–38, 2013.

[RII 17] RIIHONEN T., WICHMAN R., "Full-duplex protocol design for 5G networks", in WONG V., SCHOBER R., NG D. *et al.* (eds), *Key Technologies for 5G Wireless Systems*, Cambridge University Press, Cambridge, 2017.

[SHA 11] SHAFIEE K., ATTAR A., LEUNG V.C.M., "Optimal distributed vertical handoff strategies in vehicular heterogeneous networks", *IEEE Journal on Selected Areas in Communications*, vol. 29, no. 3, pp. 534–544, 2011.

[SHR 12] SHRIVASTAVA K., JAIN S.K., "Enhanced greedy perimeter stateless routing protocol (E-Gprs)", *International Journal of Engineering Research and Technology*, vol. 1, no. 10, pp. 1–8, 2012.

[SIL 17] SILVA C.M., SILVA F.A., SARUBBI J.F.M. *et al.*, "Designing mobile content delivery networks for the internet of vehicles", *Vehicular Communications*, vol. 8, pp. 45–55, 2017.

[SUN 06] SUN W., YAMAGUCHI H., YUKIMASA K., "Gvgrid: A QoS routing protocol for vehicular ad hoc networks", *Proceedings of 14th IEEE International Workshop on Quality of Service, IWQoS*, New Haven, CT, pp. 130–139, 2006.

[ZHA 08] ZHAO J., CAO G., "VADD: Vehicle-assisted data delivery in vehicular ad hoc networks", *IEEE Transactions on Vehicular Technology*, vol. 57, no. 3, pp. 1910–1922, 2008.

Interconnected Virtual Space and Theater: A Research–Creation Project on Theatrical Performance Space in the Network Era

8.1. Introduction

Since 2014, we have been conducting experiments based on a multidisciplinary collaboration between theatrical staging specialists and researchers in the field of virtual reality, digital art and video games. This team focused its work on the similarities and differences that exist between real physical actors (actor-performers) and virtual digital actors (avatars).

From this multidisciplinary approach, experimental research–creation projects have emerged, which we have previously described [GAG 15, GAG 17]. These projects rely on a physical actor playing with the image of an avatar, controlled by another physical actor via the intermediary of a low-cost motion-capture system (a mobile inertial motion-capture system, which we describe later).

In the first part of this chapter, we introduce the scenographic design on which our presentation is based and the modifications we have made in relation to our previous work. Next, in the second section, we discuss the impact of augmenting the player's game using an avatar in detail, compared

Chapter written by Georges GAGNERÉ, Cédric PLESSIET and Rémy SOHIER.

to the scenic limitations of the theatrical stage. In part three, we discuss the software-related aspects of the project, focusing on exchanges between the different components of our design and we describe the algorithms that enable us to utilize the real-time movement of a player via various capture devices. To conclude, we examine how our experimental system linking physical actors and avatars profoundly alters the nature of collaboration between directors, actors and digital artists in terms of actor/avatar direction.

8.2. A multidisciplinary experiment involving live performance and digital art

The introduction of an avatar controlled in real time by an actor on a stage mobilizes the transdisciplinary skills of the team in the fields of theater, digital art and video games. It leads to the definition of new terms and functions that have to do with the expressive potentialities explored. The experimental system is continuously evolving in terms of the improvement of the software and motion-capture devices used, eventually resulting in a precise documentation and a permanent adjustment of the concepts and technical solutions necessary for a truly shared experimentation.

8.2.1. *Defining avatar and mocaptor*

First of all, we must define some concepts. While the idea of an avatar itself has been adequately defined [DAM 97, SCH 12], we have yet to define the concept of a mocaptor – a neologism derived from fusing the terms "motion-capture" and "actor". A mocaptor is a physical actor equipped with a motion-capture device, which enables the real-time control of an avatar generated as a synthetic image. While these techniques, frequently used in Hollywood [BAL 09], rely on large teams of computer graphics artists in charge of motion processing, the approach we use, due to its real-time nature, is closer to Patoli's work [PAT 10]. Moreover, our approach is based on a real-time dynamic with little or no cleanup work, that is, there is no correcting of post-production measurement errors or of the noise generated by the capture process. At most, we use basic filters such as the Kalman filter to eliminate major capture errors.

8.2.2. *System description*

For our experiments, we have developed an improvisation system for theater students to use during rehearsals. This system has been successfully used for teaching purposes since the 2016/2017 academic year.

The stage space defined in the project is occupied by several entities (see Figure 8.1):

(A) physical actors, located at the center of the stage;

(B) the mocaptor controlling an avatar;

(C) the digital artist(s) and participant(s) involved within parameters to be defined;

(D) the avatar(s) represented onscreen.

From a performance perspective, a space (E) is reserved for the audience, where the director is usually located as well. We might think at first that scenographic actions only concern the relationship between the physical actors (A) and the avatar (D); however, the avatar is the combined result of the actions of the mocaptor (B), the artist and the digital participants (C). Thus, we have chosen to put the three entities B, C and D in the stage space, leaving it to the viewer to choose to concentrate their gaze on whatever interests them the most. This offers the actors and the director the ability to increase the number of staged interactions among all participants.

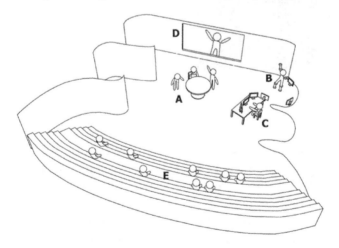

Figure 8.1. *A diagram of staging in practical workshops*

8.2.3. *From Kinect to Perception Neuron: a new mobility*

One development that has occurred since the International Conference Frontières Numériques [GAG 17] is the shift from Kinect to a combination of inertial motion capture called Perception Neuron Mocap. This system is composed of a network of 32 inertial measurement units (IMUs) connected in a hierarchy and communicating with the computer via WiFi connection. This system allows us to capture the accelerations and angular velocities of certain parts of an actor's body (head, shoulders, elbows, hands, fingers, torso, knees and feet), which we then use to recreate the motion captured. This mechanism was originally designed for a low-cost, real-time motion capture for use in video games.

Figure 8.2. *A mocaptor and the avatar reproducing his gestures (left) and the capture device (source: neuronmocap.com, manufacturer's image) (right)*

We have actually observed two significant limitations with Kinect: (1) the skeleton constructed by Kinect depends on a frustrum (see Figure 8.3), which limits the propagation of the body in space; and (2) the mocaptor's orientation is not local; rather, it depends on the orientation of the Kinect. This second point makes it difficult for the mocaptor to execute a 360° rotation without causing display problems.

With Perception Neuron, (1) the area of play becomes much larger, since the mocaptor is no longer limited to the Kinect's capture zone, but rather to the capture zone of the WiFi terminal (see Figure 8.3); and (2) the mocaptor has greater freedom of movement, as the mocaptor is no longer required to act facing the Kinect. Finally, the quality of the motion capture is much higher with Perception Neuron. However, this system must be used with great care so that it does not lose the position of the body, as it functions relative to points of contact on the ground.

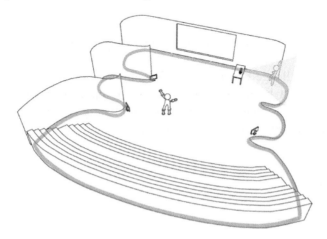

Figure 8.3. *Action zones of the Kinect (blue) and of Perception Neuron (red). For a color version of this figure, see www.iste.co.uk/saleh/challenges.zip*

The possible juxtaposition of the mocaptor's performance space to that of the physical actors allows for a stimulating triangulation between physical space and digital space. An actor can actually have a double presence: a digital one on the screen and a physical one on the stage. However, this triangulation assumes the specific organization of a double interaction: that of the mocaptor directly with the physical actors and that of the mocaptor with the physical actors via the intermediary of the avatar. Faced with this complexity, we chose to begin our experimentations by confining the performance space of the mocaptor to a delineated area outside the stage space of the physical actors (see the upper right corner of Figure 8.1). However, compared to our previous experimentations with Kinect, the mocaptor equipped with Perception Neuron can cover a larger space by turning back on itself. On the other hand, the question of returns is still significant, which explains the positioning of three screens around the mocaptor.

8.3. Acting relationship between the mocaptor and the avatar

The end purpose of the avatar is to construct an acting situation with a physical person. To do this, it must occupy a digital space that is linked to the physical performance space of the actor. The reciprocal positions of the two entities in their respective spaces impose a field of limitation within which to build what we call the spatial disposition of a character (physical or digital), that is, the place toward which it projects a scenic (in-performance) action.

8.3.1. *Controlling the avatar's spatial disposition*

The first challenge consists of positioning the developing avatar in a 3D space but it must be present in the physical space via a two-dimensional image projected on a video projection screen facing the audience behind the physical actors (see Figure 8.4, Orientation N°1).

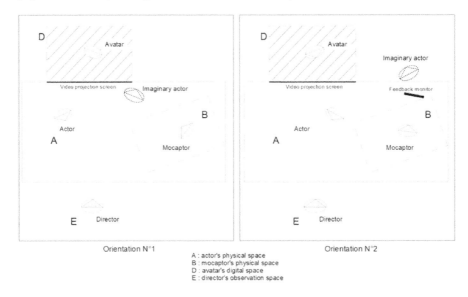

Orientation N°1   Orientation N°2

A : actor's physical space
B : mocaptor's physical space
D : avatar's digital space
E : director's observation space

Figure 8.4. *Controlling the avatar's spatial disposition via mocaptor movement*

If the viewer is located at the center of the audience, where the director usually sits (space E), they have a completely different perception from that of the mocaptor located in the lateral space (space B) due to the effects of perspective. Thus, the mocaptor cannot base their movements on the feedback they see on the video projection screen to orient their avatar in relation to the actor. They must follow the director's instructions and must incorporate a "bias" against their own perception into their actions. We have already noted this limitation in our previous experiences with Kinect [GAG 17], and we have solved it for the time being by finding a fixed orientation for the mocaptor facing the Kinect and the video projection screen at the same time, which enables the mocaptor to have a lateral perception of the actor's physical performance space and to learn the biases "necessary" for establishing the avatar's contact with its lateral partner according to the directions of the director positioned among the audience members. The constraint of being positioned facing the Kinect (see Figure 8.5) has made it possible to set limits on the "biases" to be internalized that are acceptable for the mocaptor, who is now able to ensure that their own performance space corresponds with the digital space of the avatar in relation to the actor acting in front of the screen.

8.3.2. *The mocaptor's reference space: the Ninja Theory example*

We must address the complex question of articulation among three performance spaces in order to better understand the limitations on the mocaptor's acting. This performs in the physical performance space (B), which allows the mocaptor to exist in a digital performance space by controlling the figure of the avatar (D), which must position itself in its turn in relation to the acting of the actor evolving in a third space (A). To better understand the specific characteristics of our system, we compare it to the pioneering work of Ninja Theory and Epic Game on the cutting edge of video games and computer-generated 3D film [SIG 16]. The demonstration offered by Ninja Theory consists of constructing a trailer for the video game Hellblade in real time and in a condensed production pipeline.

Figure 8.5. *The real-time capture device used by Ninja Theory and Epic Game*

A mocaptor is equipped with a double system of facial and body motion capture which enables a realistic real-time rendering, thanks to specially designed motion retargeting rigs. In front of a mirror, the avatar Senua speaks to her double, located in another world. Senua and her double are two independent characters. A cameraman (Figure 8.5, left) uses a rendering camera and a rig to determine the camera position that creates the scene in the video game engine in real time (Figure 8.5, right). The first take consists of filming the mocaptor's first performance; she plays the role of the specular double, who speaks into the mirror to the true Senua. Then, the double walks forward to pass through the mirror and continues talking to Senua while moving in a half-circle around her. The performance is done by the mocaptor using pre-set marks on the floor and internalizing the overall temporalities of the dialogue. The take is recorded in the game engine and can be replayed with various effects used as desired on the character and the performance space. Next, a second take is shot to incorporate the character, Senua (see Figure 8.5, right), which shows the juxtaposition of the two characters although only one is captured). The cameraman specifies key positions to the mocaptor, particularly at the point when her double passes through the mirror and at the moment when she goes through the mirror herself to enter her double's world. The previous sequence begins with the character of the double, which has just been recorded, and the mocaptor acts as the role of the true Senua in real time and reacts to the double's actions, saying her parts of the dialogue in the spaces of silence left during the first take. The cameraman adjusts the camera angle in real time according to the relationship between the two characters, and this is where artistic and technical prowess comes into play. The cameraman can actually compose shots as if they were filming two real film actors, even though they are "only" virtual avatars.

This experiment demonstrates a promising view of future real-time pre-visualization. In this context, the avatar's digital space mingles directly with the mocaptor's performance space. The mocaptor projects herself emotionally into a character with whose realistic expressive potentialities she understands. For the first take, she imagines that she is facing the other character, whom she will play during the second take and whose marks on the floor she can make note of. Then, during the second take, her scene partner, though invisible to her, is visible to the audience and the cameraman. The third performance space of the physical partner also blends with the two other ones. It is the responsibility of the cameraman-filmmaker to give positioning directions to adjust the control of the avatar according to the pre-recorded game path. The precise superimposition of the three performance spaces thus facilitates the mocaptor's acting.

8.3.3. *A closer look at the articulation of the reference spaces*

In our theatrical trial, the three spaces are sharply separate, which causes difficulty for the mocaptor's acting. The digital performance space of the avatar (D) is represented via a flat image, giving the impression of another physical space contiguous to that of the actor (A) (see Figure 8.4). In order to correctly interact with the physical partner, located in front of the video-projected image of the avatar's space (video projection screen), the mocaptor must mentally transpose their partner's movements in relation to the digital space of the avatar in their own performance space (B). If we assume that the mocaptor is angled towards the video projection screen and orients themself correctly with their avatar, with the help of the director (located in space E), in order for the avatar to interact with the actor, it is the responsibility of the mocaptor to imagine that they are looking at an imaginary actor located at the same distance from the as the real actor in relation to the avatar. Thus, if the actor moves in the space and takes up a new position (see Figure 8.4, Orientation N°2), the mocaptor needs to imagine the same movement and must position themself accordingly so that their avatar will also be correctly positioned. This results in the mocaptor being no longer able to see the video projection screen, and a feedback monitor must be installed so that they can continue to have contact with the image of their avatar.

In practice, this imaginary transposition of the real actor's movements is, of course, impossible for the mocaptor to accomplish; they would have to do geometric calculations in their head regarding movements taking place more or less behind them. The practical solution used in our platform consists of turning once again to the director, who indicates the correct movements to the mocaptor, who can memorize key positions, which they connect to the positions taken by the avatar, with which they maintain visual contact via the feedback monitor, and they must empirically construct the own course of movement as an echo to the actor's movements, which they observe on the physical stage A.

8.3.4. *Mobility of the mocaptor in their performance space*

In order to make the mocaptor's work simpler, we have developed a second method inspired by video game motion retargeting techniques. Instead of asking the mocaptor to move, we play on the position in space B of the mocaptor's acting, by applying the necessary rotation to it so that the avatar is correctly positioned in relation to the actor in space A (see Figure 8.6).

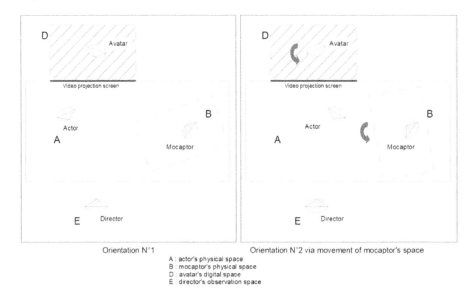

Orientation N°1   Orientation N°2 via movement of mocaptor's space

A : actor's physical space
B : mocaptor's physical space
D : avatar's digital space
E : director's observation space

Figure 8.6. *Controlling the avatar's spatial disposition via rotation of space B*

In reality, this rotation of space B is only an image manifesting an algorithmic operation we carry out on the avatar in space D, and which we will discuss in detail in section 8.4. One clear advantage is immediately noticeable: the manipulation enables the mocaptor to maintain contact with the video projection screen. However, as it turns out, it is necessary for the mocaptor to retain freedom of movement and to orient their body in positions that cause them to lose visual contact with the video projection screen. Thus, we have placed monitors in performance space B that augment the yield of the video projection screen and allow the mocaptor to maintain a relationship with the final avatar (see Figure 8.1, space B). This requirement for a feedback is similar to an opera singer's requirement, where the singer is always able to see the orchestra conductor. This is why, in an operatic production, several monitors are arranged around the performance space and the audience space, in order to give the singer the required freedom of movement to follow the director's instructions. This enables the singer to be able to expressively perform without losing the lifeline to the orchestra conductor, which guarantees musical cohesiveness between the singer and the orchestra.

The introduction of digital manipulations to the mocaptor's motion-capture information will have significant consequences for the creative potentialities of the system and the relationships among the various artistic collaborators, several aspects of which we analyze in the last part of this chapter.

8.4. From mocaptor to avatar from a technical perspective

In this section, we give a more detailed description of the control conditions of the avatar (D) by the mocaptor (B) in the context of a staged interaction of this avatar with physical actors (see section 8.3). In reality, we need to deal with three major issues as follows:

– the transfer of a real actor's movement to a virtual character while taking into account differences in size and morphology that may be encountered in mocaptors and virtual avatars;

– the combination of multiple control sources (mocaptor and digital technician) to manipulate and change the avatar;

– the necessity of doing all of this in real time in an adaptable evolutive architecture.

8.4.1. *Two-stage motion retargeting*

To understand the necessity of effective motion retargeting, we can see that a difference in morphology, or body type, between two people causes numerous differences in gestures (though these may be technically identical) (see Figure 8.7). Because we may have mocaptors and avatars with different body types, we have developed a two-stage processing procedure that allows us to transfer a mocaptor's movement onto a complex avatar, with the help of a third party: the puppeter.

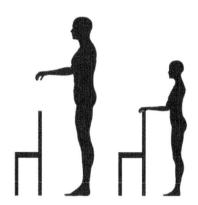

Figure 8.7. *Adapting an action to the actor's morphology*

The concept of a puppeter is closely related to the original definition of the term *puppeteer*, but goes well beyond this definition, which we explain as follows:

1) The mocaptor manipulates the motion-capture device (Perception Neuron, Kinect, etc.), which sends data via WiFi to the computer, and the data sent by the motion-capture device is applied to a neutral character. This allows us to have formalized values; the neutral character is not visible to viewers.

2) The puppeter executes a second motion retargeting on complex avatars that often do not have a much more evolved architecture in terms of positioning or number of joints.

It is important to understand that the puppeter is not a marionettist/puppeteer manipulating the different parts of the avatar's body, but rather a "blender" of motion sources for these different parts, which the puppeter can then combine and rearrange according to the motion retargeting issue, but also dynamically or even in terms of behavior. This area has already been explored in an on-set pre-visualization tool intended for a film, called the OutilNum project [PLE 15] which uses the concept of "behavior reproduction", which will eventually be incorporated into the new architecture.

The act of executing motion retargeting in two stages has several advantages. First, the neutral character acts as an initial filter able to eliminate excess data, delete unnecessary data and make data uniform, no matter what motion-capture device is used. In addition, using a neutral character with a well-established morphology allows us to retain and reuse animations for future use. Profound differences may exist in the architectures of a complex character created on an *ad hoc* basis. Because the architecture of the character's joints is not homogeneous, it is impossible to transfer the movements of one complex character to another character. By animating for the neutral avatar and by using the puppeter, we can make the most possible use of animations. Finally, the fact that the source movements are all applied to the same character enables us to combine them with each other in order to obtain unique animations.

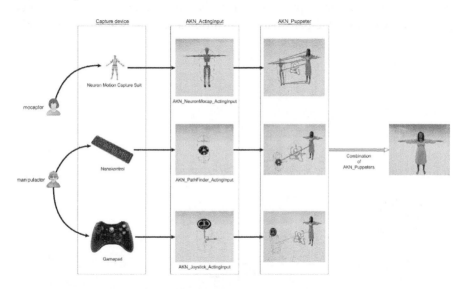

Figure 8.8. *The two phases of motion retargeting with three capture devices*

8.4.2. *Avatar movement: combination of multiple sources*

The operation of positioning within the mocaptor's reference space mentioned at the end of section 8.3 is carried out as follows. The NeuronMocap data is collected in the AKN_NeuronMocap_ActingInput tool, which is used to animate the neutral character. The AKN_NeuronMocap_ActingInput tool then serves to control the complex avatar using the Puppeter object.

However, we can also use other information to control the avatar, generated by a gamepad, for example. We then use the AKN_RefMove_ActingInput tool to recover the information from the gamepad device and use it to modify the mocaptor's space B, which goes back to combining this new data with the data from the AKN_NeuronMocap_ActingInput tool using a second puppeter working on the complex avatar. Figure 8.9, shows the possibility offered by the architecture of combining NeuronMocap_ActingInput with two different mocaptors to control the final complex avatar. Also, note the presence of a Joystick_Input tool, which can be used to change the avatar's position with a gamepad. While the NeuronMocap_ActingInput data is produced by what we have called the mocaptor, we have chosen here to refer to the digital participant who uses the gamepad to position the avatar as a "manipulactor".

Figure 8.9. *NeuronMocap_actingInput, joystick_input and puppeter in action. For a color version of this figure, see www.iste.co.uk/saleh/challenges.zip*

The devices used by a manipulactor can include the gamepad, which is used to control the position and movement of the final avatar, as in a video game, as well as a midi controller such as the Korg NanoKontrol2, which is useful to trigger effects using potentiometers, cursors and on-off buttons (see Figure 8.8). Keyboards and mice may also be used, as well as any other controllers that allow an ergonomic relationship between the human body and the machine producing digital parameters.

8.4.3. *Combination with independent behavior: pathfinding*

The manipulactor may choose to use pathfinding functionalities to facilitate the mocaptor's performance in the avatar's digital space. Our pathfinding algorithm is based on classic shortest-route algorithms that have been used for many years in video games. A navigation mesh (navmesh) is generated according to the topology of the stage and the obstacles placed on it, and we use an A* algorithm to traverse the graph, using the distance between the character's position and the navigation points attached to the navmesh as a heuristic function [CUI 11]. The AKN_Pathfinder_ActingInput tool, combined with a puppeter, is used to guide the complex avatar independently in the digital space D, helping it to avoid any possible obstacles. Our practical experiments have in fact led to the use of a digital game space for the avatar that is much more capacious than the mocaptor's performative space. The pathfinding functionality enables us to organize intelligent movement for the avatar, independent of the mocaptor's movements.

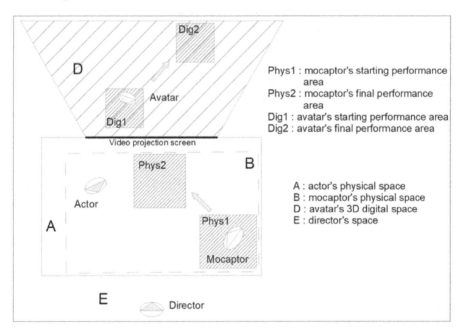

Figure 8.10. *A scenario in which pathfinding is used to guide an avatar*

The taking-over of control from the mocaptor is decided upon by the manipulactor, who initiates the independent movement of the complex avatar. Then, control is released and the mocaptor once again has the total control of the avatar. At the moment of release, the manipulactor must be careful to ensure that the complex avatar is correctly positioned in the new performance location and will possibly use a gamepad to reposition the complex avatar. It should be specified that the mocaptor retains control of the avatar's limbs during the pathfinding phases. This involves good coordination with the manipulactor to choose the timing of control-taking and disengagement.

A second use of pathfinding has proven necessary in situations where the mocaptor performs in the physical space A of the actor. The stage direction concept was to duplicate on the video projection screen, in a specific digital space, the actions of the mocaptor-actor performing in the physical performance space representing another space. Figure 8.10 represents the superimposition of the actor's space A with the mocaptor's space B. The mocaptor thus plays a double role; they simultaneously act and control an avatar. The avatar's position is represented in the cross-hatched virtual digital space D. Space D is shown approximately in perspective according to the point of view of the director, located in the viewer observation space E. For staging reasons, there is no 1:1 scale homothety between the two performance spaces B and D; therefore, it is not possible to make the mocaptor's performance space correspond to that of the avatar. It has thus been decided to choose specific action zones in each of the two spaces of a few square meters each in size and to move from one zone to the other using the pathfinding function in the digital space. The mocaptor moves from zone Phys1 to Phys2 in their physical space B, while the pathfinder transports the avatar from zone Dig1 to Dig2 in the digital space, under the control of the manipulactor. Note that the manipulactor must reorient the avatar's final position based on that of the mocaptor so that the avatar maintains the spatial disposition desired by the director. This means that it is necessary to construct a final location for the avatar, which is implemented by the manipulactor at the moment when the pathfinder releases control of the avatar, using a preset system utilizing the AKN_Event tool (see section 8.4.4), which allows the coordination of avatar control information circulation.

We would like to specify our reasons for choosing a combination of the terms "manipulator" and "actor" to describe the function of the mocaptor's partner, who extends the mocaptor's movements in the final complex avatar.

We believe that the manipulactor must draw on the theatrical expressiveness of an actor's performance to successfully embellish the mocaptor's movements. It is a matter of initiating transformations in physical appearance that will be interpreted by a partner actor and the audience. Similar to how the actor-marionettist pulls the strings of their marionettes in keeping with the art of dramatic acting, the manipulactor must embellish the mocaptor's performance. We look at the consequences of the emergence of these two roles in section 8.5.

8.4.4. *An architecture oriented toward interconnected objects*

The current software architecture is descended from a development library that begun in 2002, called Taupistool [PLE 07]. It was actually necessary for us to carry out simultaneous studies of artificial intelligence for visual effects in films, and interactions with virtual reality devices for sound detection and image analysis for artistic installations and effect systems for live performances as well as pedagogical support. This library, programmed in C++, was interconnected with multiple 3D platforms (Maya, Virtools, Motion Builder, Ogre and a real-time 3D engine developed internally) and enabled the digital artist to reuse developments, either for real-time or for precalculated movements. This architecture subsequently evolved and was redubbed AKeNe (dandelion pollen) to mark both its creation within the INREV EA4010 EDESTA Paris VIII team (with a homage to its founders Michel Bret, Edmond Couchot, and Marie-Hélène Tramus, who recreated the interactive work "Dandelions" in 2005) and its capacity to disseminate itself. This adaptable framework was then deployed in the previously mentioned OutilNum project, as well as in a number of systems mixing theater and virtual reality [GAG 15]. Finally, it was restructured as a network so that it could be shared on multiple machines, creating different workstations.

It has also been our intention to improve communication among the various control stations at events (keyboard entry, midi controller, etc.). This relies on a system of simple discrete events (SDEs) which are non-centralized and have no waiting queue [CAS 08], which we have called AKN_Event_Manager. We assume that there is little or no delay between the transmitter of the event and its recipients. Likewise, it is highly probable that we will have to rethink this mechanism if the network output among the various stations is too low. This is possible, as the transmitted information is very small in size (less than 10 ko) and, except for data generated by the combination of motion captures, is intermittent. The transmitted message relies on an archetypal boxing/unboxing system [LER 97] able to transmit simple data (float, string, etc.) as well as more complex data (objects and other types).

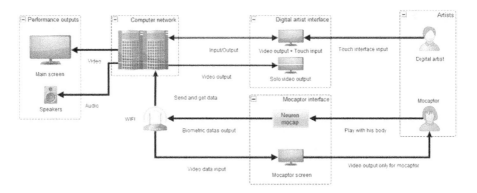

Figure 8.11. *Diagram of input and output according to a local network and WiFi. For a color version of this figure, see www.iste.co.uk/saleh/challenges.zip*

Though the mocaptor uses their body to send information via WiFi, the modifications made by the digital artist and the manipulactor are made directly on the computer (see Figure 8.11) by means of the keyboard, mouse and various other devices (joystick, midi controller). Each of these workstations has one or more feedback screens to help with understanding actions taking place on the virtual stage D. The interface currently used by the digital artist has a number of screens showing various parameters that can be adjusted in real time. Thus, there are two categories of tools: those meant for use by all of the people present and those meant to be used exclusively by the manipulactor(s) and mocaptor(s). The first category of tools is used to transmit aesthetic information to the computer and then to the main screen for the purposes of modifying the virtual representation. The second category of tools communicates past and future information in order to aid with directing. Though we have already put some basic tools in place, our intention is to create ergonomic communication systems between the mocaptor, manipulactor, director and actors.

8.5. A practical application that raises new questions

Our experimentations have raised several questions from a theatrical, technical and game design perspective. Firstly, we examine those having to do with the appearance of new protagonists on the stage; we then address questions raised by the staging of virtual decor for the augmented stage, as well as the new role that could be played by digital artists in the theater.

8.5.1. *New experimentation spaces for actors, directors and digital artists*

The potentialities created by taking into account the human body's movements via a capture device transmitting via WiFi open up many stimulating, creative perspectives for directors, but they also pose challenges in terms of ergonomics and team management. We have seen that the mocaptor projects rotations of parts of their body into the avatar, but the final control of the avatar is also in the hands of the manipulactor, who can influence certain parameters including the rotation and translation of the avatar, or its overall position, via pathfinding. The mocaptor can move in a given direction while their avatar goes in another direction, determined by the manipulactor depending on constraints having to do with the physical stage space, notably the position of the actors with whom the avatar is interacting (see section 8.3).

The mobility gained by the mocaptor and the tools developed to insert their movements into a hybrid physical/digital scene through the intermediary of the manipulactor make it possible to create new combinations of movements in collaboration with the digital artist and the director. By acting to organize the performance space in relation to the digital space of the avatar, the mocaptor can thus plan to interact while playing two roles: that of the avatar's controller and that of the physical actor, in direct contact with the other physical actors in the system. This latter scenario would be of great interest for a more in-depth study in order to explore what the rules might be for a bodily connected user in relation to avatars which this user could manipulate in mixed reality to interact in other spaces.

Another creative route consists of enabling the mocaptor to control multiple avatars simultaneously. Each avatar makes the same movement as the mocaptor, but its spatial orientation is controllable. In this way, we might recreate a classical-era theatrical choir or a crowd of individuals with a single actor. As another example, the director might wish to have an avatar perform while aloft. The mocaptor could be asked to act as if they are taking flight, and then the manipulactor would take over by raising the avatar into the air, with the mocaptor acting as if they were levitating.

However, the fact that the avatar's movement is the result of the combined control of the digital artist, the mocaptor, the manipulactor and the director makes it necessary to create dialogue tools so that everyone can communicate. This leads more broadly to a redefinition of their collaboration in the context of an augmented scene, notably with regard to the challenges of "avatar direction", which, in traditional theater, corresponds to actor direction.

8.5.2. *The problem of visual composition for augmented scenes*

The visual composition of an image is vital to ensuring its communicability [MAT 10], but also to allow aesthetic expression [KAT 91]. However, as we have seen in the previous sections, the visual composition of a virtual scene with avatars can change in many ways: the avatar turns and moves in an environment in which the architecture can evolve, with a camera and lights which may also be in a continuous state of change. These different parameters raise the question of real-time virtual composition, for augmented scenes in particular.

The case of video games is already clear in this respect: visual composition is essential in these games for the ergonomic experience of the player, but must also guarantee pleasant reading of the image [SOL 12]. Thus, it is common in game design to ensure the "three Cs" – Camera, Controls, Character [ALB 15]. Real-time visual composition for video games is therefore planned to ensure that the player will have an optimal experience. Yet, we can see a significant difference between composition for video games and film. While, in the first case, the composition may be interactive because of the unpredictability of the player's actions while guaranteeing clarity of information in the image, in the second case, the composition is designed upstream and is frozen on film, never to be changed upon viewing. In the case of visual composition for real time, the question is raised of the use of expressive tools which can enter into conflict with the unpredictability of a performer's actions.

The case of video games is also already very clear concerning this issue, but it is even more so in the case of augmented scenes, in which new factors come into play. In our case study, the avatar is piloted by an actor on stage via motion capture, and the actors can interact with one another and create unforeseen situations. A digital artist or the director may decide to draw attention to details of the virtual stage, and the image projected onscreen is not necessarily designed ergonomically as in the case of video games and can extend itself toward an exploitation of cinematic tools that is more complete, but also has all the complexity of the unpredictable evolution of the avatar. The visual composition of the augmented scene is thus based on a set of unpredictable actions involving multiple human actors. Composing an augmented scene requires the upstream provision, therefore, ways to modify the composition.

Before defining a free-interaction space for visual composition, we can define two forms of compositions that we have used: fixed composition and manipulated composition. The difference between these two types of composition is the extent of intervention by a person through tools, enabling the transformation of the visual composition onscreen. The idea of every person on the stage having the ability to participate in composition enables the delegation of tasks, as well as the creation of expressive situations related to their roles. For example, it has been planned that the gestures of the mocaptor have an effect on elements of the scene and thus potentially on the camera or lighting. The manipulactor takes charge of the avatar's position and can also be responsible for the manipulation of other digital elements.

In this sense, in a fixed composition, the camera, lights or elements of decor remain in a fixed position so as to guarantee readability of the image in the context of an onscreen projection. This composition relies above all on cinematographic camerawork, and only the avatars can evolve freely. However, the parameters of a manipulated composition evolve with the actions of the different people in the scene. Thus, the camera, lights or onscreen elements are in motion and involve new visual composition as each event takes place. Table 8.1 sums up the strengths and weaknesses of compositions currently used.

	Strengths	**Weaknesses**
Fixed composition	+ Use of a well-established photographic/cinematographic language + Control of plan	− Little freedom of improvisation − Loss of interactive power
Manipulated composition	+ Great capacity for improvisation and expression + Digital artist can perform rather than being a simple technician	− Precision is difficult − Significant camera presence (temporality of camera placement)

Table 8.1. *Strengths and weaknesses of the two types of compositions used for augmented scenes in our system*

In our study of visual composition for staging a scene, we have attempted a fixed composition in order to exploit cinematic tools as far as possible (see Figure 8.12). While the camera and lights are placed in specific spots, the composition is fixed, and any modification will result in a new form of composition. The explanation we are seeking to give through this example allows us to emphasize the expressive responsibility of the tools we are developing for augmented scenes.

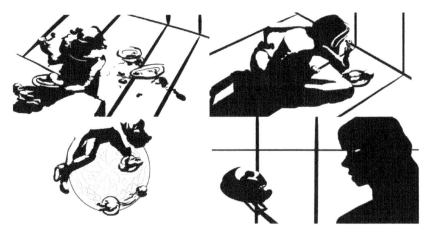

Figure 8.12. *Studies of visual compositions for cannibalism*

Our initial method will consist of hybridizing the traveling and storytelling techniques of film with the camera-movement tools used in video game development. A fixed composition would strip any interest in interacting with the image, but manipulated composition could lead to imprecision on the part of the person executing the action. Hypothetically speaking, to delineate the field of intervention in a visual composition, one possibility would be to use rails and intelligent camera observations.

8.5.3. *Redefining the role of the digital artist*

It is necessary to specify a few things with regard to the role of the digital artist in the experimentation process. While this individual is not a physical actor or a mocaptor, they are nevertheless involved in all the digital parameters of the manipulated visual composition, which they can then make available to the manipulactor: screen display, virtual cameras, virtual objects, avatar movement constraints, etc. They have an important power of action which the must continuously put in dialogue with the actors and the director; they can, for example, make it possible to change the virtual camerawork and lighting to accentuate the avatar's expressions. They can also provide new movement potentialities to the neutral avatar via the mocaptor's body language.

As we have seen, there was a lack of common vocabulary available for use in terminological discussions of actor augmentation. This shortcoming is related to the crisis of indexicality invoked by Auslander concerning the relationship between the actor producing digital mocapture data and the avatar onto which this data is transferred [AUS 17]. In the context of 3D film animation, Auslander indicates that the transformation of motion-capture data by the digital artist in order to produce an avatar makes it difficult to assess the quality of the interpretation by the physical actor producing digital data.

In a theatrical context, we recognize that an actor's performance has to do not only with their quality of interpretation alone but also with the instructions given by the director. The director's influence is not problematic – on the contrary. We believe, therefore, that the digital artist must be placed at the heart of the direction of the avatar, and a new avatar direction paradigm must be constructed that integrates new augmentation writing tools into a close and equal collaboration with these protagonists: the mocaptor, the manipulactor, the director and the digital artists.

8.6. Conclusion

This chapter has described the impact of the use of a new portable motion-capture device in an ongoing theatrical experiment in which physical actors and digital avatars interact onstage. The new mocap system resembles a sort of tagging of the human body, which makes it possible to transcribe a hybridization between physical and digital space in real time via the intervention of an avatar manipulated by a mocaptor. We propose a method that enables the digital artist to articulate the data produced by the mocaptor in the digital avatar's frame of reference with the aim of producing a creative augmentation of gestures improvised live. This method relies on a highly adjustable software architecture, where the characteristics of which we have described are concerned by the challenges of motion capture and information exchange.

The real-time production of the avatar requires a close dialogue between the digital artist, the manipulactor, the mocaptor and the director, which involves utilizing various types of feedback on the digital elements produced; we have described those already in use. The simplicity of using the new mocap system has greatly stimulated mocaptors and directors, which has led to requests for avatar augmentation, requiring extensive expertise on the part of digital artists. The result of this is that new challenges related to avatar direction must now be considered in an overlapping distribution of roles among all the protagonists involved.

Our next experimental prospective studies will lead us toward the production and documentation of communication interfaces for this distribution of roles, which will enable the creation of a lexicon and a vocabulary for the interactions in play.

8.7. References

[ALB 15] ALBINET M., *Concevoir un jeu vidéo : les méthodes et les outils des professionnels expliqués à tous*, FYP éditions, 2015.

[AUS 17] AUSLANDER P., "Le jeu cinématographique et la capture d'interprétation : l'index en crise", *L'Entretemps International Conference*, 2017.

[BAL 09] BALCERZAK S., "Andy Serkis as actor, body and gorilla: motion capture and the presence of performance", in BALCERZAK S., SPERB J. (eds), *The Age of Digital Reproduction: Film, Pleasure and Digital Culture*, vol. 1, 2009.

[CAS 08] CASSANDRAS C.G., LAFORTUNE S., *Introduction to Discrete Event Systems*, Springer, 2008.

[CUI 11] CUI X., SHI H., "A*-based pathfinding in modern computer games", *International Journal of Computer Science and Network Security*, vol. 11, no. 1, pp. 125–130, 2011.

[DAM 97] DAMER B., JUDSON J., DOVE J., *Avatars! Exploring and Building Virtual Worlds on the Internet*, Peachpit Press, 1997.

[GAG 15] GAGNERÉ G., PLESSIET C., "Traversées Des Frontières", in HACHOUR H., BOUHAÏ N., SALEH I. (eds), *Frontières Numériques & Artéfacts*, pp. 9–35, L'Harmattan, 2015.

[GAG 17] GAGNERÉ G., PLESSIET C., "Perceptions (Théâtrales) de l'augmentation numérique", in HACHOUR H., BOUHAÏ N., NAPPIER O. (eds), *Proceedings of the International Conference Frontières Numériques – Perceptions*, Toulon, France, 2017.

[KAT 91] KATZ S., *Film Directing Shot by Shot: Visualizing from Concept to Screen*, Focal Press, 1991.

[LER 97] LEROY X., "The effectiveness of type-based unboxing", *Workshop on Types in Compilation*, vol. 97, 1997.

[MAT 10] MATEU-MESTRE M., *Framed Ink: Drawing and Composition for Visual Storytellers*, Design Studio Press, 2010.

[PAT 10] PATOLI M.Z., GKION M., NEWBURY P. *et al.*, "Real time online motion capture for entertainment applications", *Third IEEE International Conference on Digital Game and Intelligent Toy Enhanced Learning (DIGITEL)*, IEEE, pp. 139–145, 2010.

[PLE 07] PLESSIET C., Artiste, ordinateur et spectateur : pour l'émergence d'une création interactive et autonome en art numérique, PhD thesis, Université de Paris VIII Saint Denis, 2007.

[PLE 15] PLESSIET C., CHAABANE S., KHEMIRI G., "Autonomous and interactive virtual actor, cooperative virtual environment for immersive previsualisation tool oriented to movies", *Proceedings of the 2015 Virtual Reality International Conference*, Laval, France, 2015.

[SCH 12] SCHROEDER R., *The Social Life of Avatars: Presence and Interaction in Shared Virtual Environments*, Springer Science & Business Media, 2012.

[SIG 16] SIGGRAPH Conferences, Ninja Theory and Epic Games Talk Hellblade and the Future of Real-Time, available at: http://blog.siggraph.org/2016/10/ninja-theory-epic-games-talk-hellblade-future-real-time.html, 2016.

[SOL 12] SOLARSKI C., *Drawing Basics and Video Game Art: Classic to Cutting-Edge Art Techniques for Winning Video Game Design*, Watson-Guptill, New York, 2012.

Mobile Telephones and Mobile Health: a Societal Question Under Debate in the Public Domain

9.1. Introduction

One feature of the Internet of Things (IoT) is that it broadens the Internet network to include objects and places in the physical environment. The IoT is the source of a considerable increase in the quantities of data generated by the new usages associated with it, thus contributing to the supply of Big Data. An issue falling at the crossroads of technical dimensions and social usages, this has led to its definition as:

> "...a network of networks which makes it possible, via standardized and unified electronic identification systems and wireless mobile devices, to identify digital entities and physical objects directly and unambiguously, and thus to be able to collect, store, transfer, and process the data attached to these entities and objects with no discontinuity between the physical and virtual worlds" [BEN 09, pp. 15–23].

In this chapter, we focus our attention on the social, political, economic and regulatory challenges of the IoT; these lie in the exponentially increased modes of access to information characteristic of "ubiquitous computing" [GRE 06], in the creation of new services, and in data exploitation conducted by means of algorithms. In its social usages, the IoT is embodied in the Web

Chapter written by Brigitte JUANALS.

of Objects, which refers to connected objects, particularly telephones but a wide variety of other objects as well. It brings out the complexity of information and communications technologies in terms of their interoperability and the preservation of the security and reliability of data. The Web of Objects offers unforeseen possibilities in matters of communication between people and objects, direct communication between objects, and connections to centralized servers and networks of servers. However, the large amounts of data collected and the associated processing, carried out by public or private actors, raise questions of human traceability in information systems and the protection of the personal data of users of these sociotechnical systems [JUA 09, JUA 14].

Belonging to the field of Information and Communication Sciences, this chapter addresses the sociopolitical challenges and mobile information access systems encompassing the production of and access to online content and services via a portable computer terminal, focusing on mobile telephones (smartphones). The IoT's challenges are addressed in mobile health usages and sociotechnical systems, which have destabilized the traditional health system.

Within these political and social challenges, changes in the systems of production, distribution and exchange of information generated by this "Internet of the future"[1] once again raise ethical questions concerning open access to information and to cultures in their diversity, in tandem with the protection of private life and liberties (as in the first days of the Internet's opening to the public in the early 1990s). In this constantly evolving field, in which new equipment and techniques emerge regularly, the objective targeted is to construct an analytical framework in order to understand the policies and strategies of actors in relation to the artifacts and systems of information and mediation they implement.

We begin by presenting the specific characteristics of the hybrid field of mobile health and the social science approaches taken in studying it. The theoretical framework that joins the analysis of artifacts and innovative forms of sociotechnical mediation to the socioeconomic strategies of actors will then be discussed. Next, the strategies and socioeconomic models of the industrial actors active in the field of mobile telephony will be studied in correlation with the consequences of the changes observed in modes of

---

1 European Future Internet Portal: http://www.future-internet.eu.

access to information, particularly in the field of mobile health. We examine the way in which new forms of publication[2] and communication, centered on new modes of production, presentation, organization and distribution/circulation of information or knowledge, affect the production of and mobile access to content in detail. As we show, these access systems are the result of interrelations between technical innovations, socioeconomic models and modes of regulation still in development.

9.2. An interdisciplinary activity sector and field of research: between connected health and connected well-being

The uses of the terms "eHealth", "telehealth" and "telemedicine" lend themselves to confusion, as revealed by the *Haute Autorité de Sante* (French National Authority for Health) in 2016 [HAU 16]. In actuality, the lines blur in the field of connected health; it is difficult to make a clear distinction between connected objects and the applications utilized in the field of well-being, of health, and in the exercise of medicine (telemedicine)[3]. However, the regulation of mobile health requires that its different components be defined and the regulated activities identified. Dating from the period of rapid technological development in the early 2000s, the term "eHealth" refers to a new international industrial sector combining health with information and communication technologies. The World Health Organization defines eHealth as "the use of information and communication technologies (ICT) for health" [WHO 17]. The term "mHealth", referring to "mobile health", was introduced in 2000 by Robert S.H. Istepanian, a researcher in electronic and electrical engineering in the context of unwired medicine (e-med), an expression which refers to "the next generation of wireless and internetable telemedicine" [IST 00]. He defined mHealth as follows in 2003:

---

2 In the book publishing field, the term "publication" has to do with the activities of the publisher responsible for the publication and sale of a printed material. Recently, it has come to include digital, audiovisual and multimedia content on electronic artifacts as well.

3 In France, telemedicine is defined by the law and by the regulatory framework set out by the decree of October 19, 2010. This text describes the five acts that constitute telemedicine: teleconsultation, tele-expertise, medical telemonitoring, medical tele-assistance and the medical response made within the context of medical regulation.

"In general terms, m-Health can be defined as mobile computing, medical sensor, and communications technologies for health care" [IST 00, p. 405].

With mHealth gaining international scope, the World Health Organization has redefined this term by linking the technical dimension to the social uses that go along with it and to the prospective advantages they are likely to contribute:

"mHealth: use of mobile wireless technologies for public health", reflecting the increasing importance of this resource for health services delivery and public health, given their ease of use, broad reach and wide acceptance. "mHealth" or mobile health has been shown to increase access to health information, services and skills, as well as promote positive changes in health behaviors and manage diseases [WHO 16, p. 1].

More specifically, the usages and technical systems falling under the category of mobile health include "medical and public health practices relying on mobile devices such as portable telephones, patient monitoring systems, personal digital assistants, and other wireless devices" [WHO 11, p. 6]. The technological solutions provided by mobile health "enable in particular the measurement of vital signs such as heart rhythm, blood sugar, blood pressure, body temperature, and brainwave activity". Its applications include "communication, information, and motivation tools such as devices that remind people to take their medication and others that make recommendations regarding diet and exercise" [EUR 14, p. 3]. With a view to conducting a global analysis, the WHO has grouped mobile health services into 14 categories ranging from call centers to decision-making assistance systems, including access to information, observance assistance, appointment reminders and mobile telehealth. Its last study of 114 countries shows that mobile telemedicine, understood from the angle of communication among health professionals, belongs, along with call centers, to the four types of programs most frequently implemented in most of the nations studied. It should also be noted that the WHO's definition includes the concept of patient monitoring [WHO 11].

Mobile health can be seen as a market and an industry [BUT 16] that raises complex issues in terms of security of information [HAN 16] and legal regulation connected to modes of utilization and data protection [THI 16]. It constitutes a hybrid domain bringing together different types of actors with the same motivations; public authorities see it as an opportunity for preventive usage [CAM 16], improved accessibility of health services (via telemedicine) and reduced public health expenditures, while health-care professions are experimenting with mobile tele-assistance and remote medical monitoring (particularly with chronic illnesses). In addition, public participation in the compiling of health data can be seen as belonging to increased autonomization, empowerment and health-related democracy. Numerous recent international studies, inventoried by the Haute Autorité de Santé, focus on the assessment of mobile health applications for smartphones. Conducted using a variety of disciplinary and thematic approaches, these have focused notably on the public and end goals (preventive medicine, medical monitoring, tele-assistance, observation, well-being, etc.), data security and management, health-related content, technical systems, utilization and use [HAU 16, pp. 8–13, 56–59]. Studies have also focused on "mobinauts" (members of the public and health-care professionals) who use and do not use these mobile applications, examining them in terms of knowledge, perceptions, uses, expectations and needs [CNO 15, pp. 15–16]. Target audiences go beyond the field of eHealth and its medical solutions with regard to the monitoring of chronic diseases and the observation or caretaking of dependents. They include users wishing to gain a better understanding and mastery of their health and well-being. Comprehensive approaches are interested in the "quantified self" in "digital self-measurement rituals" [ARR 13] and the "self-quantification" associated with sharing within communities [PHA 13].

The digital informational ecosystem continues to contribute to the destabilization of the health-care industry. Websites, forums and social networks have already caused evolutions and tensions resulting from ubiquitous information, the opening up of access to medical information and modes of communication ushering in growing public participation. The loading of health-care applications on to mobile terminals introduces specific issues connected to sociotechnical systems and new facets of intermediation, information and communication.

9.3. "Boundary objects", socioeconomic strategies and innovative forms of sociotechnical mediation in equipped mobility

Innovations – that is, long social processes by which inventions travel along their path to users of sociotechnical objects [ALT 00] – are common in communication-related industries. By opening up remote access to the Internet in mobility situations via connected objects, computer and electronic artifacts have progressively evolved interrelationally with the public's technological and communicational practices. The characteristics of these portable, miniaturized items of hardware combine multiple functions of electronic scheduling and communication[4], Internet navigation via web browsers for mobile devices, file exchanges, listening and reading. Multimedia functions (text, sound, image and video) are broadened with the addition of digital reading software, MP3 audio readers, video and digital cameras. The integration of social platforms (Twitter, Facebook) has encouraged exchanges within online social networks.

Innovations occupy a central place in the highly competitive area of communication industries. The proliferation of mobile objects and interfaces has now multiplied the technical points of entry available and thus information mediation. The concept of the boundary object helps us to understand these technical, hybrid and multitasking objects that combine functions of telephony, mobile Internet and multimedia reading devices while also giving access to information. This concept has been evoked in reference to:

> "concrete or abstract objects, the structure of which is sufficiently common to multiple social worlds that it ensures a minimum intersection identity while being flexible enough to adapt to the specific needs and constraints of each of these worlds" [TRO 09, p. 8].

These "boundary objects" are widely distributed in the form of netbook computers which are being progressively supplanted by smartphones and PC tablets – computer tablets equipped with touchscreens. In mobile health, a wide variety of connected objects (bathroom scales, pillboxes, watches,

---

4 Functions of agenda (address book, time management, dictaphone, notepad, calculator, clock), word processor and spreadsheet, and electronic communication (e-mail).

eyeglasses, clothing) constitute hybrid objects that fall at the intersection of multiple universes.

The social dimension of communication technologies has led to the questioning of "sociotechnical mediation" [AKR 93, JOU 93, LAT 93] and the social appropriation of connected objects, analyzed in the informational systems and practices of private or professional life. Beyond conformity to international norms and standards having to do with the "usability" of hardware and applications, the forms of sociotechnical mediation reveal that sociotechnical innovations (manufacturers of hardware and software), by joining together with new publishing practices (those who offer services and content) as well as information practices (users), are contributing to the construction of a technical and media-friendly culture. The "sociotechnical framework" [FLI 95] comes within the scope of reflection on the structuring of technical and social dimensions. Thus, the artifact becomes "a mediator, a social actor, an agent, an asset that is part of an 'action plan' composed of social relationships and relationships of power, law, and morality...". Artifacts are considered as "social relationships continued by other means" [LAT 93, pp. 44–45]. Falling within the paradigm of innovation and translation theory, studies of the sociology of innovation show the social dimension of technical innovation and bring up to date the interactions and negotiations – going so far as to become confrontations – of the various actors, including the agents, that participate in it [CAL 86, LAT 89]. A digital culture is created, at the intersection of changes in the publishing practices of publishers of software and services, socioeconomic models of actors in the communication industry and the informational practices of users of the new tools and services offered [JUA 15].

In the same movement, digital technologies, by modifying the conditions of access to content, have destabilized socioeconomic balances and modes of organization in the publication of information in the health-care sector. Actors in the communications and Internet industries are playing an increasingly important role in the hybrid domain of mobile health. Intermediation focuses attention on the introduction of new actors, their status and the role they play in the mediation of information and knowledge. In the international context of the Internet of Things, the media and communications industries constitute a hybrid category that combines electronic media and technologies (the hardware industry, which includes computers, portable music players and mobile telephones), services having to do with telecommunications (the Internet, the Web and the digital services associated with it) and content in digital formats that deals with health on mobile terminals. In their relations with content publishers, hardware and software manufacturers are developing socioeconomic strategies and models, resulting in new tools and services being offered to users. We show how the socioeconomic strategies and models of these industry members are connected to cases of intervention via national and European regulations, with the whole contributing to the structuring of systems of access to information and services.

9.4. Mobile health-care service access systems: toward intermediation or disintermediation?

The scientist and futurist Joël de Rosnay, in a 2016 interview with the economic and financial newspaper *La Tribune*, emphasized the unforeseen possibilities opened up by digital technology and the use of sensors in personalization and personalized prevention in the health-care domain. He stated that:

> "Disintermediation is underway, and it will spare neither big pharmaceutical companies, nor drugstores, nor even doctors. To what can this uberisation be credited? To the fact that small organizations are capable of creating algorithms and software, particularly on the Internet, which link supply and demand, and it is from this that they draw their shares and pay themselves. It is Uber with taxis, Airbnb with hotels, BlaBlaCar with rental cars, and Alibaba in China with business. Yet Uber owns no taxis, Airbnb owns no hotels, Alibaba has no stock. The uberisation of health care may be just as extensive and just as fast. All that is required is to lay down, atop the large and costly production and distribution systems, a thin human- and software-based structural layer and to link products and services directly with clients via proactive software. Would you resist, if you could access products and services that were cheaper, faster, less administrative, and less complicated?"[5]

5 Joël de Rosnay, 24/02/2016, "Les défis de la santé pour demain, vers le patient augmenté", La Tribune.fr, http://www.latribune.fr/opinions/tribunes/les-defis-de-la-sante-pour-demain-vers-le-patient-augmente-552732.html.

The question of intermediation and disintermediation is now being raised for the mobile health market, which is one of the markets developing due to the generalization of mobile Internet access via smartphones and health-care services based on equipped mobility. Firstly, the evolution of the fixed Internet toward the development of mobile access is having an increasingly significant effect on access to information. Mobile computing technology (hybrid connected devices combining mobile telephones and pocket organizers, as well as tablets and "ultra-portable" laptops) has flooded these markets [MED 17][6]. The success of smartphones has contributed to the development of new uses, and the number of people connecting more frequently to websites, portals and mobile applications is on the rise. This trend has gone along with access to wireless telecommunications (WiFi and Bluetooth technology; the Apple iBeacon), the use of electronic identification systems (RFID chips) and high-speed Internet. Secondly, the mobile health market is in the midst of booming growth, according to the annual report by Research 2 Guidance, a mobile application market analyst: at the end of 2015, there were 7,900 mobile health applications (mHealth apps) available worldwide (55% of these in Europe, 28% in the United States, 2% in Africa, 2% in South America and 13% in the APAC [Asia-Pacific] region), with 2,600 health practitioners using them. This market, worth more than 5 billion dollars in 2015, should reach 26 billion dollars in 2017 and 31 billion dollars by 2020, thanks mainly to the provision of services linked to applications [RES 16, p. 2, 10]. It is predominantly a European and North American industry.

However, an organization cannot communicate about a health-care product, a medication or a health-care application in the same way it communicates about a car, a hotel service or a mass market commodity. The modes of communication in terms of practices, regulation and discourse are specific to this sector[7]. However, new industrial actors from the information technology and Internet fields are investing heavily in the health-care field,

---

6 Médiamétrie, 02/15/2017, "L'Audience Internet Mobile en France en décembre 2016". 40% of the population visited at least one family practice commercial application via mobile device in December. In December 2016, 22.1 million individuals visited sites and applications belonging to the subcategory "family practitioner commercial site" via a mobile device, or two out of five French citizens. Women between 25 and 49 years old and young people aged 15–24 were particularly heavy users of family practitioner commercial sites, 62% and 55.7% of them, respectively, visiting one of these sites or applications at least once during the month of December.

7 See section 9.5.

considering it as a market liable to bring substantial profits rather than a scientific domain with ethical and health-related challenges.

In these large-scale industrial, strategic and technological reconfigurations, new actors in the IT and communications industry have established themselves in the mobile health market through their products and services, socioeconomic models, and business strategies. In 2015, 23% of companies publishing mobile health-care applications were IT/TECH companies; 27% were computer software developers and 5% were specialists in telehealth. On the other hand, historic health-care sector actors are a minority in the field of mobile health (7% in medical devices, 6% in the pharmaceutical sector, 4% in health insurance and 4% in hospitals) so dominated by new arrivals [RES 16, p. 1].

What are the links between the socioeconomic models used and the technological choices – in terms of both hardware and software – made by industrial actors? What are the consequences for systems of access to information? In this innovative field, material and technical aspects are very important for the user's ability to access information. The possibilities opened up by equipped mobility and the expansion of telecommunication networks may imply that they facilitate the circulation of information to a large extent; however, the choices made, exploiting the plasticity of the informational process as they do, belong as much to strategies of opening up information as to those of access control.

On the international market, competition is quite intense among manufacturers of electronics and computer hardware and software. These companies add value to their technological innovations by associating them with the brand identity of their products. Windows Mobile, iPhone OS and Android are the principal operating systems for mobiles that share the smartphone market, while Apple Safari, Android Chrome and Microsoft IE are the major web browsers. Many of the most well-known hardware brands (Samsung, Nokia, Acer, Sony Ericsson, LG, HTC, Motorola) function on the Google Android or Microsoft Windows Phone operating systems (with a mobile Office suite in the case of the latter). Devices with keyboards or touchpads functioning on the Blackberry system by the Canadian manufacturer of the same name, whose niche strategy was aimed at a top-of-the-line business market, no longer include telephones, which ceased to be manufactured in September 2016. The various generations of Apple iPhones and iPad tablets (using the iPhone OS system) rely on the elegance of the object itself, its multimedia functions and a highly intuitive touchscreen interface, which is itself in keen competition with Google Android. The tablet market continues to attract Google and Microsoft, actors which are also opportunistically testing the market for portable connected objects designed for frequent use, following the example of Nokia, which purchased the French company Withings and is offering an innovative connected wristwatch linked to the dedicated application Withings Health Mate via smartphones. However, despite its media success, this market still lacks maturity; a number of its products often give rise to a "gadget effect", are expensive and have problems of interoperability; moreover, their autonomy and life spans have been deemed inadequate (e.g. the withdrawal from the market of Google Glass, or the criticisms aimed at the Apple Watch, which was considered overpriced and lacking in autonomy).

In the end, three American multinational corporations (Apple, Google and Microsoft) occupy the majority of this international IT market, which is highly competitive and relies on innovative technologies. They are among the major actors of the Internet industry, often collectively nicknamed GAFA (Google, Apple, Facebook, Amazon), which, with Microsoft, represent the five largest market capitalizations whose activities rely partially on the exploitation of user data; these users are obligated to use equipped mobility hardware and software in order to access mobile health information and services.

With regard to publishers of mobile health applications, because their content is linked to software, they must comply with the norms set out by these dominant actors, which have established themselves as new intermediaries for the development and downloading of applications. Yet, an application developed for iPhone is not directly usable on Android, and *vice versa*. The development languages used (Objective C for Apple; Java for Android) are not the same, and differences can be seen between Java interfaces and Objective C protocols. Multiplatform publication on Android and iOS is the norm for mobile health-care publishers; 75% of them produce applications for both platforms. Non-exclusive usages of platforms are distributed among Android (88%), iOS (84%), Windows Phone (16%) and HTML5 (29%) [RES 16, p. 2].

The major Internet and communications actors, like the "boundary objects" they publish, can be characterized as "boundary organizations"; they are situated at the intersection of multiple industrial worlds and activities while still relying on their IT specialization, on the Internet and on electronic hardware. Google, renamed Alphabet, is simultaneously a search engine, an Internet access provider, an advertising agency, a publisher of resources and services (in areas of activity as wide-ranging as health and culture) as well as office suites, an online storefront, an investment fund, a health researcher and an artificial intelligence. Likewise, Apple is simultaneously a manufacturer of electronic hardware, a software publisher, a content publisher, an online storefront, an artificial intelligence researcher (voice recognition), and more. These organizations are characterized by their financial power, their established presence in multiple sectors of activity, and their high capacity for technical innovation and the absorption of innovative actors. In a highly competitive and unstable market, they deploy various development strategies which their competitive situation leads them to cause to evolve and adapt according to their competitors' initiatives.

From a concentration-based approach, the strategy used by Apple in terms of its competitors' practices illustrates how controlling hardware and software in mobile access enables it to cordon off access to information and services while at the same time making it necessary to purchase its devices. These limitations apply as much to mobile device application developers as to publishers of applications and users of portable devices. This "cordoning-off" or "locking" approach is applied first to developers. Since 2010, beginning with the arrival of the iPhone OS 4.0, Apple has modified its conditions of use for developers by imposing a development platform and programming language (Objective C) required for applications to function on iOS and for their authorization to be included in application sale software (the Apple Store). This situation is unprecedented in the history of information technology, as no operating system publisher has ever before insisted upon a software programming language. Conversely, Microsoft's strategy for conquering the PC market was to allow developers the freedom to write applications, on the condition that they would be executable only under Windows and incompatible with other operating systems. Apple's strategy seems to consist of attempting to prevent a competitor from imposing one multiplatform standard on the mobile market. The blocking of the Adobe company's Flash software in applications and the Safari mobile web browser shows how Apple blocks its competitors and imposes its own operating system, iPhone OS[8]. The company thus capitalizes on its dominant position in different segments of the market on smartphones, particularly in eHealth, and on the success of the iPad tablet to impose its own operating system in these segments.

Because users wishing to access Apple applications for iPhone OS, or to use those applications already purchased, must buy or replace an Apple device, the company's sales have increased all the more. The last stage of this locking-off is the diffusion, with the subtraction of a £30 commission, of subscriptions to various types of products generated via the online store (since 2011). Apple is positioned within a specific type of organizational convergence, vertical integration, in which the company controls every stage of the production line using technical lock-offs. From a proprietary perspective, it retains power through the fact that it manufactures the hardware, develops the operating system and develops or controls access to applications via its Apple Store software.

Google has made a different choice instead, playing the "open product" card. This is a horizontal concentration, not through the absorption of competitors, but via the positioning in multiple markets in the software industry and more recently in the mobile access field as well. This major industrial actor specializes in the field of software (originally its search engine) and manufactures neither tablets nor mobile telephones. It has established its place in the mobile Internet software market via an operating system for mobile telephones (Android), which is a free and open software that does not depend on a telephone. These technical characteristics mean that any mobile telephone manufacturer can use the Android system and develop applications for it in whatever technical manner they desire. Control is exercised downstream, in terms of the diffusion channel imposed via the Android Market online store. Its web browser for mobile devices, Google Chrome, is the second most-used software on mobile telephones and exceeds Apple Safari in terms of the number of users.

An analysis of the development strategies of these Internet, information technology and Web "boundary organizations" shows the methods of controlling the mobile Internet and the data collection markets they

8 Numerama.com, Réfléchir le numérique, 04/12/2010, Champeau G., "Pourquoi Apple rend obligatoire les langages C, C++ ou Objective-C sur l'iPhone", http://www.numerama.com/magazine/15480-pourquoi-apple-rend-obligatoire-les-langages-c-c-ou-objective-c-sur-l-iphone.html.

implement. These are composed of several key elements that must be controlled: the computer hardware that enables mobile access, the operating systems that pilot the mode of operation of this hardware, the mobile web browsers used for Internet access, the system of diffusion of applications that opens up access to them (according to an economic model to be defined) and the smartphone applications used by the public to access content. The locking off of modes of electronic intermediation and interoperability is central to controlling the diffusion of content and services.

The role of communication service operators, insurers and health-care professionals remains to be defined in the new intersectoral environment of mobile health. Partnerships with health-care actors such as hospitals and pharmaceutical laboratories are aimed at generating innovative projects in mobile and connected health, in which the participants would be partners. The public is participating in emerging practices such as "ubimedicine", which is "a medical practice based on the receipt and analysis of health-care data collected on the users' initiative at multiple times and places" outside the usual medical settings such as doctors' offices or hospital rooms [CNO 15, p. 12]. Concerns have arisen with regard to certain partnerships, however, particularly those between insurance companies and Internet actors.

9.5. Forms of regulation of mobile health-care access: a legal, technical and sociopolitical issue under debate

Several types of organizations are involved in the development of regulations for the protection of personal data. These organizations may be institutional or technical (national, European or international): regulatory agencies, industrial interest groups or industrial stakeholders. The texts generated include public legislative acts and modes of secondary regulation consisting of technical or management norms and standards, with the whole evolving as new innovations in information and communication technology emerge [JUA 14]. Public authorities and professional health-care organizations circulate legal and regulatory provisions pertaining to hosting, the sharing of information and the processing of personal data:

> "when data processed by the App/OC concerns an individual who is or can be identified, directly or indirectly [...]

Health-related data[9], especially sensitive data, is subject to enhanced security measures"[10] [HAU 16, p. 12].

In the field of mobile health, as specified by the *Haute Autorité de Santé*, the design and use of connected objects and health-related data must "conform to existing national and European legal regulations, particularly in matters of medical devices, exchange of information, and the processing of personal health-related data". Applications liable to be qualified as medical devices are taken from article L. 5211-1 of the code of public health, in addition to those specified by the *Agence nationale de sécurité du médicament et des produits de santé* (French National Agency for Medicines and Health Products), or ANSM. The hosting of personal health-related data on behalf of individuals or corporations for the production or collection of said data or on behalf of the patient him/herself must comply with article L. 1111-8 of the Code of Public Health [HAU 16, p. 13]. At the European level, the 2014 Green Paper on mobile health [EUR 14] applies to medical and public health practices that make use of mobile devices.

However, it appears that mobile access is problematic with regard to the protection of personal data. Via the intermediary of applications downloaded on telephones, user information is gathered and sold for marketing purposes to advertising agencies. Data may concern the location of a telephone user, the telephone's unique identifier (the confidentiality of which is not protected) or data about the user's identity (age, gender, etc.). The problem stems in part from the non-obligation of application designers (downloaded via online stores such as the Apple Store or Android Market) to provide confidentiality rules regarding the manner in which personal data is used and protected. Let us also emphasize the fact that the economic model of free web browsers for mobile devices relies on user data collected by their designers, which is then relayed to advertisers.

---

9 "Data of a personal nature pertaining to the physical or mental health of an individual, including the provision of health care services, which reveal information on the person's state of health" (European regulation of April 27, 2016).

10 Law no. 78-17 of January 6, 1978 relative to information technology, files and freedoms; Regulation (EU) 2016/679 of the European Parliament of April 27, 2016, relative to the protection of individuals with regard to the processing of data of a personal nature and to the free circulation of this data, and abrogating directive 95/46/CE (this regulation will be applicable to all EU member states from May 25, 2018, with no transposition necessary).

According to a report by the *CSF Santé*[11], or The Industry Strategic Committee for Health [CSF 16], the protection of personal data remains an unresolved question to date for mHealth applications:

> "[...] numerous apps do not respect the confidentiality of data collected for the needs of the application, or even use data contained in the smartphone (calendar, address book). Thus, certain certification programs for mHealth apps initiate processes that ensure the quality of the apps, but it seems that these processes did not include risk control in terms of data protection" [CSF 16, pp. 14–15][12].

The report cites another inquiry [CSF 16, p. 15] conducted in 2015 in the United Kingdom, into applications recommended by the NHS (National Health Service) [HUC 15]. The updating by researchers of the 79 applications certified as medically reliable by the NHS led to the closure of its health-care application library site, the NHS Health Apps Library:

> "Poor information privacy practices have been identified in health apps. Medical app accreditation programs offer a mechanism for assuring the quality of apps; however, little is known about their ability to control information privacy risks. [...] The study revealed that 89% (n = 70/79) of apps transmitted information to online services. No app encrypted personal information stored locally. Furthermore, 66% (23/35) of apps sending identifying information over the Internet did not use encryption and 20% (7/35) did not have a privacy

---

11 Linked to the *Conseil national de l'industrie* (National Council on Industry) (CNI), the *CSF Santé* is an industry strategic committee (or *comité stratégique de filière* (CSF)) concerning health-care industries. In organizational terms, the CNI brings together, under the presidency of the Prime Minister, industry and union organizations from around the nation. The CNI's work is carried out within different CSFs.

12 Group 28 of the *CSF Santé* was created to work on the area of mobile health (mHealth) as a sector of eHealth currently in full growth. The report, published in 2016, presents the conclusions of the work carried out by this group between September 2015 and August 2016. The work group was composed of members of the ministries of health, industry and research, as well as representatives of the relevant industries and of a wider circle of participants, such as the CNIL (*Commission nationale de l'informatique et des libertés*), the ANSM (*Agence nationale de sécurité du médicament et des produits de santé*), the HAS (*Haute Autorité de Santé*), the CNOM (*Conseil national de l'Ordre des médecins*), the CISS (*Collectif Interassociatif Sur la Santé*) and the scholarly society ANTEL (*Association nationale de télémédecine*).

policy. Overall, 67% (53/79) of apps had some form of privacy policy. No app collected or transmitted information that a policy explicitly stated it would not; however, 78% (38/49) of information-transmitting apps with a policy did not describe the nature of personal information included in transmissions. Four apps sent both identifying and health information without encryption. [...] Systematic gaps in compliance with data protection principles in accredited health apps question whether certification programs relying substantially on developer disclosures can provide a trusted resource for patients and clinicians. Accreditation programs should, as a minimum, provide consistent and reliable warnings about possible threats and, ideally, require publishers to rectify vulnerabilities before apps are released" [HUC 15].

Cybersecurity also constitutes a "major problem", with multiple studies proving the existence of security flaws in connected insulin pumps and pacemakers[13] [CSF 16, p. 16].

Moreover, numerous problems have arisen both industrial and technical in nature. These particularly concern the reliability and precision of data collected and its interpretation, as well as the question of sensor quality control. The assessment of the degree of reliability and precision of the measurements they produce is highly complex. Insofar as the applications and connected devices are liable to be part of patient care, the *CSF Santé*[14] has defined a set of prerequisites grouped under the umbrella term of "medical reliability":

"[...] the taking into account of connected objects or apps in the context of care, even if it is only a simple recommendation for use made to a patient by a health-care professional, requires that its harmlessness be ensured, as well as the veracity of the advice given and the measurements taken. [...] Beyond fantasies, it is useful to guarantee that these devices enable the collection of correct and precise data, and that the recommendations made on the basis of the data collected be at least non-harmful. These

13 Kim Zetter, 04/09/2015, "Drug Pump's Security Flaw Lets Hackers Raise Dose Limits", Wired, https://www.wired.com/2015/04/drug-pumps-security-flaw-lets-hackers-raise-dose-limits.
14 See notes 8 and 9.

two concepts are to be grouped under the term 'medical reliability'" [CSF 16, p. 13].

According to these criteria, the CSF notes cases of reliable applications (such as the "Moovcare" application for monitoring patients afflicted with metastatic lung cancer), as well as those that are medically unreliable. The report cites a 2016 study [CSF 16, p. 14] concerning the "Instant Blood Pressure" application, which has been downloaded more than 100,000 times, and whose measurements are imprecise:

"Dr. Timothy Plante, a fellow in general internal medicine at Johns Hopkins, led the study in which a total of 85 participants were recruited to test the accuracy of the Instant Blood Pressure app. Participants had their blood pressure measured by both the app and a validated, standard blood pressure monitor. They found that the difference between the app and the real blood pressure was 12.4 mm Hg for systolic blood pressures and 10.1 for diastolic blood pressures. When looking at individuals with low blood pressure or high blood pressure, they found that the Instant Blood Pressure app gave falsely normal values. In other words, someone with high blood pressure who used the app would be falsely reassured their blood pressure was normal. Perhaps most striking, the sensitivity for high blood pressure was an abysmal 20%"[15].

In addition, the complexity of the technical assessment of artifacts is amplified by the hybrid nature of the sociotechnical system implemented:

"Who will address the weighty question of the legitimacy of applications, devices, sensors? When does a sensor become reliable enough to propose data that makes sense? What happens if the software application you're using is very good, but the telephone you're using is equipped with bad sensors that distort the measurements taken? Who will tell you this? Who is responsible? You, the unaware user? The developer of the application? The manufacturer of the smartphone? Who will the family of a runner who has died of a cardiac arrest because his

15 Satish Misra, MD, 03/02/2016, "Blood pressure app study shows that top health app was highly inaccurate", iMedicalApps. Medpagetoday, https://www.imedicalapps.com/2016/03/instant-blood-pressure-app-study/#.

telephone told him that his heartbeat was optimal, when he was actually in arrhythmia, turn to?"[16].

Despite the numerous problems that have cropped up, new industrial actors are now in a position to manufacture measurement instruments capable of collecting and broadcasting data on the health of users of mobile telephones and miniaturized sensors. This situation raises the question of compliance by industrial actors with standards guaranteeing the reliability of the measurements taken using these artifacts. Health data is becoming a major economic challenge in terms of innovation and the privatization of both its production and access to it. These various aspects raise questions having to do with connected objects and sensors in a rapidly evolving political and social issue. In this context, beyond the establishment of new companies, new perspectives are opening up concerning the participation of the public, which can acquire applications and equip itself with micro-sensors outside the normative context of public policies. The argument invoked, of a democratization of health care made possible by popular access to health services and microsensors, is put under debate due to numerous unresolved technical, legal, scientific and security-related questions.

Faced with the proliferation and heterogeneity of mobile health products, public bodies and professional organizations are publishing, as a complement to legislative and regulatory texts, directional documents on mobile health intended for health-care professionals, patient groups and publishers of applications. These actors are thus sharing their concerns regarding the impact of these new products or services on public health while also contributing to the understanding of users' needs and expectations. They are also focusing on the evolution of practices toward personalized medicine that respects the principles of security of information and the protection of personal data.

In 2016, SNITEM (*Syndicat national de l'industrie des technologies médicales*, or the French National Union of the Medical Technology Industry) inventoried international normalization projects conducted in the field of connected objects and information security, putting two complementary approaches into perspective: "hard law" (legal tools such as

16 Guillaut H, 01/22/2015, "Applications de santé (1/3): que captent les capteurs?", Internet Actu, http://www.internetactu.net/2015/01/22/applications-de-sante-13-que-captent-les-capteurs.

laws, decrees and contracts) and "soft law" (including guidelines, charters, recommendations and norms), particularly a selection of norms in the European regulatory system [CSF 16, p. 63]. These documents also include good-practice reference documents on mobile health application and connected objects; among these are the "good practice reference document on Apps/Cos for developers and assessors (medical scholarly societies, consumer associations, or private businesses)" by the *Haute Autorité de Santé*, published in 2016 [HAU 16]. Likewise, the *Agence française de normalisation* (AFNOR), or French Agency for Normalization, published a certification reference document in September 2016. White papers and analyses of innovation and prospective strategy [CNI 14] have also been published. Several recent studies, conducted since 2013 with mobile health users, have centered on their needs, representations and usages [CNO 15]. These documents guide the practices of health-care professionals according to principles of compliance with regulations, adoption of labels and common evaluation reference documents for the profession, taking ethical considerations into account as well. The same is true at the European and international levels [HAU 16].

9.6. Conclusion and new avenues of research

Mobile access constitutes an intersectoral collective including industrial actors from the computer hardware and software industries, telephony and telecommunications, and health care. As conveyors of diverse professional cultures and socioeconomic models, they compete or join together to conquer areas of a hybrid market, composed of health-related hardware, software, services and content working in an interconnected manner. We have analyzed the mechanisms according to which technical formatting, when corresponding to market rationales, could become unfavorable in terms of access to information. Indeed, they are liable, through an excessive desire for control, to describe and compel their users in an ever more detailed way according to localized, narrow IT patterns.

Challenges having to do with the development of the production of and mobile access to information in the field of mobile health have aspects simultaneously encompassing health, industry, economics and technology. They also have social and political repercussions involving health democracy, the protection of personal data and cybersecurity on portable devices. These have led to debate and studies dealing with mobile access in its relation to communication and the circulation of health-related information and knowledge. By connecting the materiality of sociotechnical devices to modes of producing, communicating, participating in and circulating health data in the public space, it appears that technical resources facilitating the production and diffusion of information are bearers of different and even divergent ideologies which use similar means. For this reason, it is important to discuss their characteristics, the actors that convey them and the relationships of power inherent in the underlying socioeconomic models and their consequences in terms of "medical reliability" [CSF 16, p. 13], cybersecurity and respect for personal data in a critical manner.

The hybrid domain of mobile health, and more broadly the intersectoral meeting of members of the communication industries and health-care industries leading to eHealth, constitutes a vast area of investigation for those desiring to study the collaborations and competitions among its participants and the interests, ideologies and perspectives on information and resources brought out in digital environments. The democratic adaptation of new political economics of information and knowledge – its production, memorizing, processing and diffusion – to changes in informational scales introduced by digital technologies [JUA 10], and the interconnection of telecommunication networks and mobile access to health-related questions have emerged as a challenge facing society.

9.7. References

[AKR 93] AKRICH M., "Les formes de la médiation technique", *Réseaux*, no. 60, 1993.

[ALT 00] ALTER N., *L'innovation ordinaire*, PUF, Paris, 2000.

[ARR 13] ARRUABARRENA B., QUETTIER P., "Des rituels de l'automesure numérique à la fabrique autopoïétique de soi", *Les Cahiers du numérique*, vol. 9, pp. 41–62, 2013.

[BEN 09] BENGHOZI J.-P., BUREAU S., MASSIT FOLLEA F., *L'Internet des objets. Quels enjeux pour l'Europe?*, Éditions de la Maison des sciences de l'homme, Paris, 2009.

[BUT 16] BUTHION A., "Marché unique européen du numérique et politique française de santé", *Annales des Mines-Réalités industrielles*, vol. 2016-3, pp. 61–65, 2016.

[CAL 86] CALLON M., "Eléments pour une sociologie de la traduction, la domestication des coquilles St-Jacques et des marins pêcheurs dans la baie de St-Brieuc", *L'Année Sociologique*, vol. 36, pp. 169–208, 1986.

[CAM 16] CAMBON L., "Objets connectés, mobiles, communicants en prévention: dépasser l'outil, penser l'intervention", *Santé Publique*, vol. 28, pp. 5–6, 2016.

[CNI 14] CNIL, "Le corps, nouvel objet connecté", *Cahiers IP. Innovation et prospective*, no. 2, available at: https://www.cnil.fr/sites/default/files/typo/document/CNIL_CAHIERS_IP2_WEB.pdf, 2014.

[CNO 15] CONSEIL NATIONAL DE L'ORDRE DES MEDECINS, Santé connectée: De la e-santé à la santé connectée, White book, Paris, available at: www.conseil-national.medecin.fr/sites/default/files/medecins-sante-connectee.pdf, 2015.

[CSF 16] CSF SANTÉ, Créer les conditions d'un développement vertueux des objets connectés et des applications mobiles en santé, CSF/GT 28, Report, Conseil national de l'industrie, 2016.

[EUR 14] EUROPEAN COMMISSION, Green Paper on mobile health (mHealth), DG Communications Networks, Brussels, available at: https://ec.europa.eu/digital-single-market/en/news/green-paper-mobile-health-mhealth, 2014.

[FLI 95] FLICHY P., *L'innovation technique: Récents développements en sciences sociales. Vers une nouvelle théorie de l'innovation*, La Découverte, Paris, 1995.

[GRE 06] GREENFIELD A., *Everyware: The Dawning Age of Ubiquitous Computing*, New Riders Publishing, Berkeley, 2006.

[HAN 16] HANTOUCHE C., "Peut-on sécuriser l'Internet des Objets?", *Sécurité et stratégie*, vol. 22, pp. 31–38, 2016.

[HAU 16] HAUTE AUTORITÉ DE SANTÉ, Référentiel de bonnes pratiques sur les applications et les objets connectés en santé (Mobile Health ou mHealth), available at: www.has-sante.fr, 2016.

[HUC 15] HUCKVALE K., PRIETO J.T., TILNEY M. *et al.*, "Unaddressed privacy risks in accredited health and wellness apps: a cross - sectional systematic assessment", *BMC Medicine*, available at: https://bmcmedicine.biomedcentral.com/articles/10.1186/s12916-015-0444-y, 2015.

[IST 00] ISTEPANIAN R.S.H., LAXMINARYAN S., "UNWIRED, the next generation of wireless and internetable telemedicine systems-editorial paper", *IEEE Transactions on Information Technology in Biomedicine*, vol. 4, pp. 189–194, 2000.

[IST 04] ISTEPANIAN R.S.H., JOVANOV E., ZHANG Y.T., "Guest Editorial. Introduction to the special section on M-Health: beyond seamless mobility and global wireless health-care connectivity", *IEEE Transactions on Information Technology in Biomedicine*, vol. 8, no. 4, pp. 405–414, 2004.

[JOU 93] JOUET J., "Pratiques de communication: figures de la médiation", *Réseaux*, no. 60, pp. 99–120, 1993.

[JUA 09] JUANALS B., "La traçabilité dans les systèmes d'information : un questionnement politique sur la gouvernance des populations", *Communications & Langages*, vol. 160, pp. 49–61, 2009.

[JUA 10] JUANALS B., NOYER J.-M. (eds), *Technologies de l'information et intelligences collectives*, Hermès Science-Lavoisier, Paris, 2010.

[JUA 14] JUANALS B., "Protection des données personnelles et TIC au cœur des enjeux de société et de la mondialisation: les mécanismes d'un contrôle distribué", *TIC&Société*, vol. 8, nos 1–2, pp. 228–253, available at: http://ticetsociete.revues.org/1475, 2014.

[JUA 15] JUANALS B., "TIC en société: pour une approche info-communicationnelle de la culture numérique", in MASSELOT C., RASSE P. (eds), *Sciences, techniques et société. Recherches sur les technologies digitales*, L'Harmattan-SFSIC, Paris, 2015.

[LAT 89] LATOUR B., *La science en action*, La Découverte, Paris, 1989.

[LAT 93] LATOUR B., *Petites leçons de sociologie des sciences*, La Découverte, Paris, 1993.

[MED 17] MEDIAMETRIE, L'Audience Internet Mobile en France en décembre 2016, available at: http://www.mediametrie.fr/internet/communiques, 2017.

[PHA 13] PHARABOD A.-S., NIKOLSKI V., GRANJON F., "La mise en chiffres de soi: Une approche compréhensive des mesures personnelles", *Réseaux*, vol. 177, no. 1-2013, available at: http://ethsp.hypotheses.org/232, 2013.

[RES 16] RESEARCH 2 GUIDANCE, mHealth App Developer. Economics 2016. The current status and trends on the mHealth app market, Report, available at: http://research2guidance.com, 2016.

[THI 16] THIERACHE C., "L'agrégation des données ouvertes dans le cadre de plateformes: les objets connectés dans le domaine de la santé", LEGICOM, vol. 2016/1, no. 56, pp. 101–109, 2016.

[TRO 09] TROMPETTE P., VINCK D., "Retour sur la notion d'objet-frontière", *Revue d'anthropologie des connaissances*, vol. 3, no. 1, pp. 5–27, 2009.

[WHO 11] WORLD HEALTH ORGANIZATION, mHealth – New horizons for health through mobile technologies, Global Observatory for eHealth series, vol. 3, Geneva, available at: www.who.int/goe/publications/goe_mhealth_web.pdf, 2011.

[WHO 16] WORLD HEALTH ORGANIZATION, 139th Executive Board; mHealth: Use of Mobile Wireless Technologies for Public Health, Geneva, Switzerland, available at: http://apps.who.int/gb/ebwha/pdf_files/EB139/B139_8-en.pdf?ua=1, 2016.

[WHO 17] WORLD HEALTH ORGANIZATION, eHealth at WHO, available at: http://www.who.int/ehealth/about/en, 2017.

Modeling Power to Act for an Ethics of the Internet of Things

10.1. Introduction

The development of the Internet of Things has brought with it a redefinition of the boundaries of the digital technologies that are so impactful on our societies from technical, industrial, commercial, social and political perspectives [BOU 16]. The proliferation of connected objects can be seen in our everyday lives for more and more varied uses, in particular, our mobile phones, which have been transformed into platforms for exchange with our cars, our televisions and other domestic objects (refrigerator, oven, heater, etc.). The definition of these exchanges, the evaluation of their end purposes and our methods of controlling them raise numerous questions [SAL 17, NOY 17] which are not confined simply to technical issues [YAN 17, ALO 17], but which encompass the wider field of the sociosemantic usages of digital technology [ZAC 05, BAC 11, OMO 14] and, more broadly still, the domain of ethics [MOR 06, COL 16].

To contribute to current thinking[1] and open a democratic debate on the issues raised by this thinking, we propose a method of modeling of our "power to act" for the Internet of Things, with the objective of evaluating and comparing the ethics of these technologies. To do this, we are

---

Chapter written by Samuel SZONIECKY.

1 For example: https://www.inria.fr/actualite/actualites-inria/transalgo.

developing tools for the modeling of these connected objects in order to understand their impacts on our daily lives. The goal of this research project is to propose a simple signage system, indicating the ethical position of objects, much like the pictograms that inform consumers about the energy quality of electric household appliances. However, before achieving the expression of power to act in this simplified form, we must ask ourselves a series of questions about the theoretical and graphic principles of these diagrams, as well as their method of design.

After having established the theoretical framework of these questions by showing that the definition of ethical positioning includes the modeling of power to act in a knowledge ecosystem following four fundamental existential dimensions (physicalities, actors, concepts and relationships), we use these principles to define a visual grammar that will enable us to represent these powers to act in the form of diagrams. This grammar will then be practically applied to model the ecosystem of the connected object Google Chromecast[2]. Next, we address the question of the automatic processing of the raw data necessary for the design of these diagrams. To illustrate our proposal, we document the ethical positions of the European Parliament, beginning with the debates concerning the regulations prescribed by civil law for robotics. We conclude our remarks by examining the viability of an ethical signage system constructed dynamically using collective intelligence procedures.

In the face of the challenges posed by the Internet of Things, isn't it true that researchers, and particularly specialists in ergonomics and information and communication sciences, have the responsibility to supply as many people as possible with the means to understand and manage these ultra-complex knowledge ecosystems?

10.2. Principles of ethical modeling

We have, in several previous publications, discussed our method of modeling by applying it to issues having to do with research in the digital humanities [SZO 15a, SZO 15b, SZO 17]; therefore, we will not give a

---

2 Link to official website: https://www.google.com/intl/fr_fr/chromecast/tv/chromecast/.

detailed description of these principles here, and instead refer readers wishing more information to the aforementioned articles.

10.2.1. *Theoretical principles*

The theoretical principles we use are based on a desire to model information- and communication-based issues using the analogy of ecosystems in order to benefit from an approach that includes the complexity of living beings in a domain traditionally analyzed using fixed models, such as those employed in architecture. Moreover, ecosystems offer analogies such as that of the garden, which are easily understandable and make it possible for the general public to understand these models and, importantly, enable them to be designed for educational purposes.

Under this analogical framework, the work of modeling includes the definition of the entities which populate these ecosystems and the relationships these entities have with one another. In designing these existential models, we have referred to multiple sources[3], the principal ones of which are as follows:

With regard to existential modeling, we have drawn on the work of Gilles Deleuze on Spinoza's proposals for "an ontology that would be the correlate of an ethics" [DEL 80]. More particularly, we have made use of the principles of an existence composed of three dimensions (extensive parts, relations and essences) correlated to three types of knowledge (shocks, relations and intuitions). We would also cite Philippe Descola [DES 05] as an important source of insight; with his "ontological matrices", he offers a simple view of existence based on the cardinal importance of relations between physicalities and interiorities. Bruno Latour has contributed to a typology of the modes of existences [LAT 12] that place the actor at the heart of a network in which ecological principles [LAT 15] are used to understand the complex processes of influences.

---

3 http://www.samszo.univ-paris8.fr/spip.php?page=biblio.

To model the activity of existences and understand their limits, we would cite Pierre Rabardel, whose research on ergonomics has given us the concept of power to act [RAB 05], which is useful not only in explaining situations and defining an "ultimate end purpose" for these but also in modernizing Spinozist principles in light of recent research in activity analysis [BRU 17].

From the perspective of modeling complex systems, we have also build upon the research on complexity conducted by Edgard Morin [MOR 81], Jean-Louis Le Moigne [LEM 99] and Miora Mugur-Schächter [MUG 09] as well as from studies carried out on multi-agent systems and their applications to human and social sciences, and more particularly to spatialized phenomena [AMB 06, ABR 14]. This type of phenomenon is, of course, the principal field of study in geography, the contributions of which to the study of the environment [BER 10] and the representation of inhabited spaces [THI 17] have provided us with tools highly useful in the consideration of these issues.

These references have led us to propose a method of measuring the ethics of an ecosystem of connected objects by calculating the increase or reduction of this ecosystem's power to act. To do this, we begin by modeling the ecosystem's potential power to act and then measure how exchanges within this ecosystem increase or reduce the power to act of the participating existences.

10.2.2. *Graphic principles*

Our modeling processes rely on very simple graphic principles based on the use of four geometric figures (rectangles, hexagons, circles and lines), each representing one of the existential dimensions of the model (physicalities, actors, concepts and reports). Unlike models constructed with tools such as GEPHI, which uses a unique type of representation, that of a network composed of nodes and links, our graphic modeling principles lie in pretopology [THI 17], which employs a richer vocabulary, in order to superimpose existential dimensions without denaturing the characteristics proper to each of them, particularly in terms of metrics and consistency with the plant analogy used.

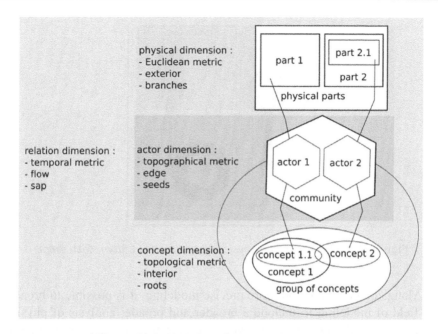

Figure 10.1. *Modeling of existential dimensions*

To illustrate the principles of graphic modeling, we use the Chromecast ecosystem, which is used to duplicate the screen of a smartphone or a tablet on a television equipped with an HDMI port, as an example.

10.2.2.1. *Physical dimensions*

The physical dimensions of the ecosystem correspond to Spinoza's "extensive parts" and to Descola's "physicalities". They are the material dimensions of existence such as the Chromecast housing, an AC adapter and an HDMI cable. They are subject to the basic laws of physics and can be measured using a classic Euclidean metric: dimensions, weight, colors, etc. They are represented by titled rectangles. These rectangles may overlap to define a tree diagram of parts, in order to specify the physical composition of an element. For example, Chromecast possesses a round part inside which is an electronic housing composed of several elements which can themselves be described in greater and greater detail, until the atomic composition of the entity itself is defined.

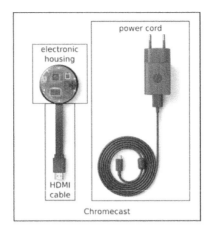

Figure 10.2. *Modeling of the physical dimensions of Chromecast: simple*

Alongside this more and more precise modeling, it is possible to broaden the field of modeling to include a broader and broader analysis of physical dimensions, including the room where the connected object is located, or even the residence or the neighborhood, when the object's connections increase its physical range. In the case of Chromecast, the WiFi range is a dozen meters, but because it is connected to the Internet via an ADSL box, its physical range is that of the telephone network and, even more broadly, of our planet. The same is true concerning the electrical connection that gives this object a range corresponding to that of the energy distribution network into which it is plugged. For the sake of exhaustiveness, we could also mention the mobile network via which the duplicated smartphone transmits and receives data.

The modeling of physical dimensions is thus conceivable by simultaneously taking into account scales outside the object and larger than it, but also scales natural to the object and smaller than it. The choice of these modeling scales is guided by the scope the analyst wishes to give to the ethical measurement, depending on whether he wishes to calculate localized or global power to act. We would also add that the physical modeling of a connected object is also dependent on the location of this object within worldwide communications and energy networks, since, depending on the politics of these places, the extent of these networks varies. To take into account its localization and specific topographical characteristics, physical dimensions are associated with the actors involved.

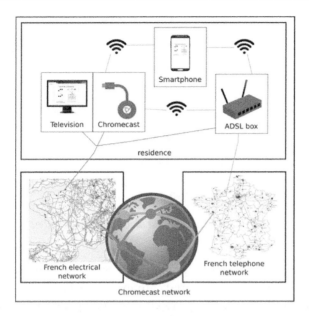

Figure 10.3. *Modeling of the physical dimensions of Chromecast: expanded.*
For a color version of this figure, see www.iste.co.uk/saleh/challenges.zip

10.2.2.2. *Actors*

Actors are the entities responsible for the creation of relations in a given space and time; they are represented by titled hexagons. In an ecosystem, multiple actors are present who can associate with one another in five set-theoretic types of relations defined by Serge Thibault as topotypes [THI 17]: place, community, cluster, link and heap. However, we have not fully duplicated the representation model proposed by this author, because it does not allow us to denote the belonging of one actor to multiple communities. We utilize the principle of differential semantics [BAC 07, p. 142] to indicate the community and the difference between a parent actor and child actors, representing them by the inclusion of one hexagon within another. Actors belonging to multiple communities are placed at the intersection of the hexagons representing them, as in Venn diagrams [THI 06]. For example, in the representation, the actor "Samuel" is part of two communities: that of the "C-S family" and that of the "Paragraphe Laboratory".

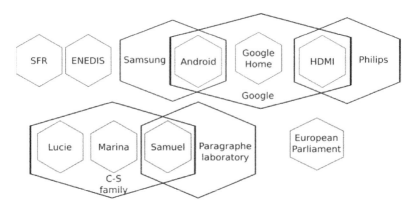

Figure 10.4. *Chromecast actors: without metrics*

Actors are not exclusively humans or communities of humans (institutions, businesses, industrial groups, associations, etc.); we also categorize algorithms, operating systems and computer programs as actors, since they are at the origin of specific relations between physical dimensions and other actors and thus create specific dynamics by imposing a logic of their own. For example, a telephone manufacturer like Samsung cannot bypass the rules imposed by Android that allow a user to install Google Home software on a Samsung mobile phone and thus share content between this mobile phone, another mobile phone or a connected chromecast device. The same is true concerning industry standards such as HDMI, with which the Chromecast ecosystem must comply in order to be viable; indeed, a television without HDMI will be excluded from the ecosystem if it does not possess this type of port. The HDMI port could be considered a physical dimension, but its existential impacts in terms of encryption and permissions management via digital locking generate particular relations that make this technical solution into an actor specific to the Chromecast ecosystem. The same is true for Google's compliance with laws issued by the European Parliament, particularly in terms of the sale of radio equipment[4].

---

4 See http://www.europarl.europa.eu/sides/getDoc.do?type=TA&reference=P7-TA-2014-0246&format=XML&language=EN.

The ecosystem's power to act is affected by such actors as we have just defined, hence, the importance of assessing the intensity of this power to act and of representing it. To do this, several metrics are possible, for example placing the actors in a list according to a scale ranging from the most specific actors down to the most general ones. Actors that are indispensable and necessary for the viability of the ecosystem are at the top of the list, and those whose role could be filled by individuals other than those mentioned are listed further down. A second metric might be the color given to an actor according to a colorimetric scale[5], taking into account, for example, the number of individuals this actor represents in the hypothetical case where power to act fluctuates according to the number of individuals. While it is easy to find out the number of people employed by Google or the number of researchers in the Paragraphe Laboratory, knowing which individuals are effectively involved in this particular ecosystem is a much more complex matter. Thus, the representation of this type of metric should be seen not as an index of reality but as the modeling of a potential, depending on the modelers' choices. At that point, it is the refutability of the metric that becomes fundamental. For example, to define the color of the actor "European Parliament", we have used an automatic modeling algorithm (see section 10.4) to count the number of individuals who participated in the legislative process[6] to which Google refers in its declaration of European conformity[7]. The calculation algorithm we are using is open[8], as is the source data[9], which enables others to dispute its relevance.

This initial modeling of actors gives only a partial overview of this dimension of the ecosystem. We could add as additional actors: sellers of products, publishers and sellers of content, etc. We could also multiply the metrics. However, we are not seeking exhaustivity; our objective is to model the actors necessary for the argumentation of the point of view we will explain in greater detail with the final two dimensions of the ecosystem: concepts and relations.

---

5 We have used this scale: https://github.com/d3/d3-scale#interpolateWarm.

6 See the record of the process: http://parltrack.euwiki.org/dossier/2012/0283(COD).

7 https://support.google.com/chromecast/answer/7477422?hl=fr&ref_topic=6178743.

8 https://github.com/samszo/jardindesconnaissances/blob/master/library/Flux/Eu.php#L81.

9 Data table with source: http://jardindesconnaissances.univ-paris8.fr/data/ice/Acteur ChromecastNbIndividu.csv. Diagram of positioning of colors: http://jardindesconnaissances. univ-paris8.fr/public/graph/posicolor.

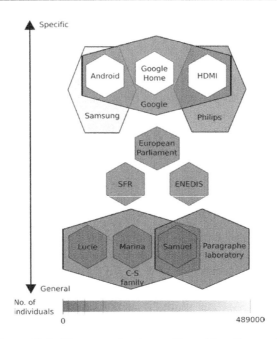

Figure 10.5. *Chromecast actors: with metrics. For a color version of this figure, see www.iste.co.uk/saleh/challenges.zip*

10.2.2.3. *Concepts*

Concepts correspond to the semantic dimensions of modeling, in the form of either a keyword or a phrase. Be aware that, a word in a physical dimension does not correspond to a concept whose meaning cannot be reduced to a representation and thus must necessarily and perpetually renegotiate with itself and others [RAS 08]. The result of this is that models are only supports for these negotiations in the end and do not represent a unique and absolute truth.

According to the principles defined by Philippe Descola, a circle is associated with an actor to signify this actor's interiority; concepts connected to each actor belong in these circles. They can combine to form groups in order to express a hierarchical dimension, or as a Venn diagram to indicate logical relations[10]. Ideally, these conceptual organizations are generated by an ontology, a thesaurus, or some other classification in order to render the model interoperable within the limits of semantic calculability [LEV 11,

10 https://en.wikipedia.org/wiki/Venn_diagram.

JUA 16, SZO 17]. The author of the model collects, in these conceptual organizations, elements corresponding to these analytical needs. For example, the diagram shows a conceptual model that uses both the IEML dictionary[11] to reference social actors and the ontology proposed by [VIN 11] to define protection of privacy.

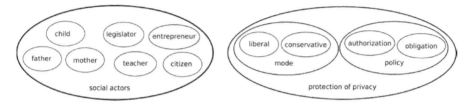

Figure 10.6. *Concepts of the Chromecast ecosystem*

The remarks of the previous chapter on the exhaustiveness of modeling are even more relevant in the case of concept modeling. This is because if we accept the theory of unlimited semiosis [PEI 68, ECO 94], it is always possible to create an interpretive route between concepts, even those that are extremely far removed from one another. We have thus chosen to limit the concepts in our ecosystem to only two sets that seem particularly important to us in reflecting on the ethics of the Internet of Objects. These choices will allow us to put forward the hypotheses of an argumentation that the modeling of relations will serve to clarify.

10.2.2.4. *Relations*

Relations represent the relationships between the physical and conceptual dimensions instantiated by an actor in a given space and time. They appear in the form of simple lines to represent a finalized state, or lines with arrows to represent a process.

Relations are characterized by a source, a destination and a predicate; they can be considered RDF triplets (subject, predicate, object) [GAN 08]. For example, we can model relations of belonging (predicate) of actors (source–subject) to categories (destination–object) using the diagram, in which the colors of the lines have no particular significance, merely serving to make the representation more legible.

---

11 Accessible online at: http://dictionary.ieml.io/#/dicEdit/IEML/FR/M%253AM%253A.a.-M%253AM%253A.a.-f.o.

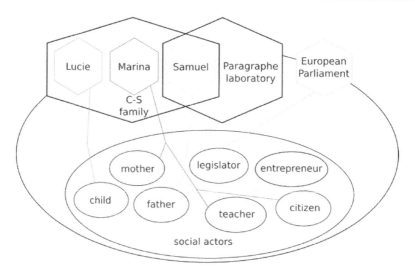

Figure 10.7. *Completion relations of belonging. For a color version of this figure, see www.iste.co.uk/saleh/challenges.zip*

In the case of the modeling of a process, relations have an origin and a destination corresponding to the completion of the process, the sequential stages of which can be followed using the square marking the source and the arrows present on the lines. For example, the reflexive process of the researcher can be divided into three stages:

– contact between a physical element and an actor;

– interpretation of this contact by the actor via a link with a concept;

– expression of this interpretation via a link between the concept, the actor and a physical element.

Other sequences are possible, however; they form communicational archetypes, the most singular of which Pierre Lévy has expressed in his research on "the language of folds" [LEV 11, p. 34]. The diagram gives an example of the use of these archetypes to model the process of validation of the launching on the market of the Chromecast ecosystem and its implications in privacy management for a user.

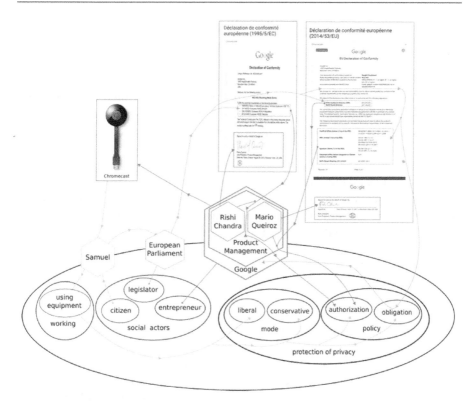

Figure 10.8. *Modeling of the process of launching on the market. For a color version of this figure, see www.iste.co.uk/saleh/challenges.zip*

The model above shows how processes can occur sequentially and repeat to form reflexive cycles that will cause relations to evolve in time and space between physical elements, actors and concepts until an "existential pulsation" is produced [BER 09, SZO 18], the traces of which will be the representation of the power to act of an ecosystem of knowledge. This power will therefore be unstable and dependent on the space-time context. Modeling allows us to show potentialities and to provide analysts with support for their studies and the formalization of their hypotheses. In particular, this dynamic conception of modeling makes it possible to express multiple interoperable points of view, for which the extent and complexity of power can then be calculated.

10.3. Calculating the complexity of an ecosystem

Based on these principles of modeling, it is possible to calculate the complexity of an ecosystem of the Internet of Things according to general rules that apply, no matter the objects involved. Comparison between objects becomes possible in terms of complexity and extent of the power to act and by the same expression of an ethical evaluation of these objects and of the ecosystem analyzed.

We must once again emphasize the relative character of these models and the measurements of power to act that result from them. It is irrational to defend the idea that modeling can be exhaustive; it is always affected by the subjectivity of the analysis, which chooses this or that element to integrate into the model. Still, what is important is that we are able to evaluate the complexity of the developed model and to create the conditions of its interoperability.

10.3.1. *Existential complexity*

The complexity of an informational existence is calculated from the sum of the elements composing the dimensions of its physicality, actors, concepts and relations. According to the fractal principle, complex informational existences are composed of informational existences that are simpler but constructed on the same model. For this reason, complexity increases when the dimensions are composed of subsections describing the detail of a dimension. Thus, to the simple addition of sections, we must add a fractal coefficient that multiplies the number of subsections by the level of detail. Calculation of the complexity of relations is a particular case; it is done based on the number of separate elements in the viable permutations of the four existential dimensions (physicalities, actors, concepts and relations) with three relational properties: non-empty source, non-empty destination and non-empty predicate[12]. To this element sum, we add the total sum of the relations of each permutation to calculate a complexity, which increases with the number of permutations and diminishes with the number of repetitions of a single element in a permutation.

12 A list of the 64 possible permutations can be downloaded at: http://jardindesconnaissances. univ-paris8.fr/data/ice/icePermutation.csv.

For example, let us again look at the model presented in Figure 10.2. Chromecast is considered a physical dimension composed of three subsections: an electronic housing, a power cord and an HDMI cable. This model does not take into account the actor, concept and relation dimensions. It has a complexity of 7, which we clarify in the table.

Dimensions	Level	Number of elements	Complexity
physicality	1	1	1
	2	3	6
	3	4	7
actor	0	0	0
	0	0	0
concept	0	0	0
	0	0	0
relation	0	0	0
	0	0	0
Total	3	4	7

Table 10.1. *Complexity of Figure 10.2*

The example mentioned above takes into account only the physical dimensions of the ecosystem. For greater complexity, let us take the example of Figure 10.7, which models the process of a market launch through the dimensions of actors, concepts and relations. The simplest method of calculation consists of counting the number of elements of each dimension in the diagram to fill out in the table, carrying out multiplication operations for each level and adding up the results.

Dimensions	Level	Number of elements	Complexity
Physicality	1	3	3
	2	5	10
	2	**8**	**13**
Actor	1	3	3
	2	1	2
	3	2	6
	3	**6**	**11**
Concept	1	3	3
	2	8	16
	2	**11**	**19**

No. of relations	No. of sources	Type of source	No. of destinations	Type of destination	No. of predicates	Type of predicate	Complexity
2	2	concept	5	Physicality	2	Actor	11
1	1	concept	1	Actor	1	Actor	4
3	4	Physicality	5	concept	2	Actor	14
1	1	Relation	1	concept	1	Actor	4
2	2	Relation	2	Actor	2	physicality	8
9	**10**		**14**		**8**		**41**

TOTAL: **1** | **8** | **9** | **34** | **41** | **84**

Table 10.2. *Complexity of Figure 10.7*

10.3.2. *Comparing the complexity of points of view*

Alongside the existential complexity of an ecosystem, we can calculate the complexity of an analyst's point of view on this ecosystem. The analysis of an ecosystem of knowledge cannot truly be exhaustive, as it is infinitely describable in each of the dimensions composing it. The analyst must therefore make choices and take into account only part of the ecosystem. If we use the example of Chromecast again, the analyst's point of view does not necessarily take into account all of the ecosystem's elements, but only some of them. Thus, the complexity of their point of view can be calculated and compared to other points of view on the same ecosystem. To do this, we propose that the number of elements common to both complexities for each dimension and their permutations be counted. For example, let us compare the complexity of Table 10.2 with the complexity of the modeling of the different uses of Chromecast between a father and his child.

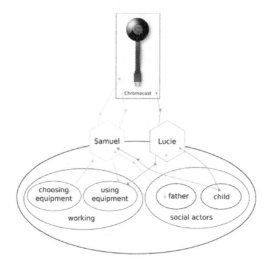

Figure 10.9. *Modeling of different uses of Chromecast. For a color version of this figure, see www.iste.co.uk/saleh/challenges.zip*

This very simple model expresses the differences in Chromecast usage by showing that the father chooses the equipment, while the child only uses it. The complexity of this model is 32, as detailed in the table.

Dimensions	Level	Number of elements	Complexity
Physicality	1	1	1
Actor	1	1	1
	1	2	2
Concept	1	2	2
	1	2	2
	2	4	8
	2	**6**	**10**

Relation	No. of relations	No. of sources	Type of source	No. of destinations	Type of destination	No. of predicates	Type of predicate	Complexity
Relation	1	1	Concept	1	Physicality	1	Actor	4
	2	1	Physicality	2	Concept	2	Actor	7
	2	2	Actor	2	Concept	2	Actor	8
	5	**4**		**5**		**5**		**19**
TOTAL	**1**	**5**		**14**		**19**		**32**

Table 10.3. *Complexity of Figure 10.9*

In order to compare the two complexities, we count, for the 15 possible resemblances, the percentage of common elements in relation to the total number of elements of each correspondence (see Table 10.4). We use a Venn diagram to represent, in the form of vectorial spaces, the 15 permutations possible between the four dimensions of the ecosystem (see Figure 10.10) The background color of each of these spaces is calculated with the same colorimetric scale as for Figure 10.5; it associates an array of colors ranging from purple (rgb(110, 64, 170)) to green (rgb(175, 240, 90)) with a number field going from 0 elements to the total number of separate elements composing the points of view to be compared (14+34=48). Beyond its overall view of the comparison of points of view (see Figure 10.11), this representation is interesting as a system of navigating complexity. We have already shown [SZO 18] how Venn diagrams are useful in exploring a complex situation, since the selection of a vectorial space enables us to display the corresponding data.

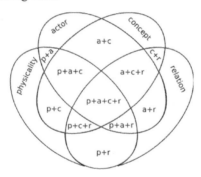

Figure 10.10. *15 neutral permutations*

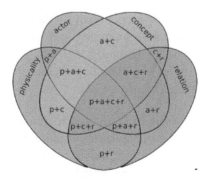

Figure 10.11. *Comparison of complexities. For a color version of this figure, see www.iste.co.uk/saleh/challenges.zip*

Common dimensions	No. of commonalities	Total no.	%
physicality	1	9	11.11
actor	1	8	12.50
physicality AND actor (p+a)	1	17	5.88
concept	3	17	17.65
physicality AND concept (p+c)	4	26	15.38
actor AND concept (a+c)	4	25	16.00
physicality AND actor AND concept (p+a+c)	5	34	14.71
relation	1	14	7.14
physicality AND relation (p+r)	1	23	4.35
actor AND relation (a+r)	1	22	4.55
physicality AND actor AND relation (p+a+r)	1	31	3.23
concept AND relation (c+r)	1	31	3.23
physicality AND concept AND relation (p+c+r)	1	40	2.50
actor AND concept AND relation (a+c+r)	1	39	2.56
physicality AND actor AND concept AND relation (p+a+c+r)	1	48	2.08

Table 10.4. *Comparison of the complexity between Figures 10.8 and 10.9*

We are working on a prototype platform for the exploration of knowledge ecosystems that should facilitate modeling and automate the calculation of existential complexities and the comparison of points of view. At the time of wirting, this tool was not yet operational, but here is a screenshot that gives an idea of the user interface (Figure 10.12).

The purpose of this tool is to facilitate the modeling of highly complex ecosystems for which manual calculation is much too difficult. It will also integrate functionalities of sharing and comparison of points of view to supply a recommendation engine based on an automatic controversy generator. We have used an initial version of this tool to automatically enrich the Chromecast ecosystem with European parliamentary debates on the ethics of robotics.

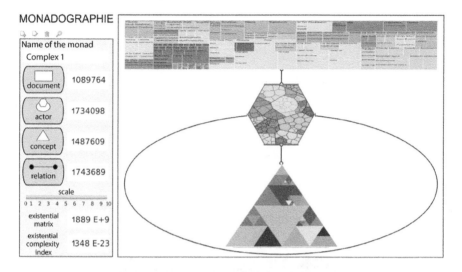

Figure 10.12. *Platform for modeling the complexity of an ecosystem. For a color version of this figure, see www.iste.co.uk/saleh/challenges.zip*

10.4. Automatic ecosystem enrichment

As part of a legislative initiative procedure, the European parliament spent more than two years (January 2015 to February 2017) on civil law concerning robotics. The reports, debates and recommendations resulting from this work are of particular interest to us due to their potential to enrich the Chromecast ecosystem with the European vision concerning the challenges posed by the Internet of Things.

10.4.1. Constitution of raw data corpus

To construct our model, we begin by describing the methods we have used to collect the corpus we have gathered. The corpus is initially made up of web documents we have found on the European Parliamentary website dedicated to the observation of legislative procedures.

Figure 10.13. *Unannotated web page*

Figure 10.14. *Diigo annotations*[13]*. For a color version of this figure, see www.iste.co.uk/saleh/challenges.zip*

13 Link to annotated page: https://diigo.com/09p0jf.

The documentary entry point of our corpus and the web page of the legislative observatory is dedicated to legislative initiative procedure concerning robotics[14] (Figure 10.13). Using this page, we can create a first model that represents the important information according to our rules of ethical modeling and thus structure the page by highlighting with Diigo[15] what stems from physical dimensions in green, actors in yellow, concepts in red and relations in blue (see Figure 10.14). The collection of these annotations can be consulted on the Diigo portal, which presents them in the form of lists with the highlighting color chosen (see Figure 10.15). To exploit this information and use it in a modeling process, we can take these lists manually and construct the diagram by copying them into a vectorial design tool such as Inkscape[16]. However, in the case of a highly complex ecosystem, this task becomes far too onerous, and even impossible.

Figure 10.15. *List of annotations on the Diigo portal*

Several scenarios are possible for the automatization, at least in part, of the modeling of this ecosystem, but regardless of the data used and the manipulation of it, the algorithm needed to do this work must carry out the following actions.

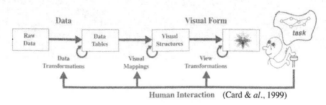

Figure 10.16. *Algorithm for data modeling [CAR 99]*

---

14 Link to web page describing the legislative process: http://www.europarl.europa. eu/oeil/popups/ficheprocedure.do?lang=fr&reference=2015/2103(INL).

15 Diigo is a tool for annotating, organizing and sharing Web resources: https://www. diigo.com/index.

16 Link to software website: https://inkscape.org/fr/.

10.4.2. *Transformation of raw data*

Diigo is a highly practical tool used to rapidly annotate Web documents as well as to collect raw data. Using the Diigo API[17] is not wholly effective, as it does not provide information concerning the color of annotations and thus the existential dimension to which we have linked them. An automatic content extraction algorithm (Web scraping) could be used to collect this information; however, in the case of the European Parliament legislative observatory, it is more effective to use tools such as ParlTrack[18], created by freelance developers to collect information on a legislative process in a form easily exploitable by an algorithm. The data supplied by this tool can be exploited to observe and analyze networks of influence among EU MEPs, for example.

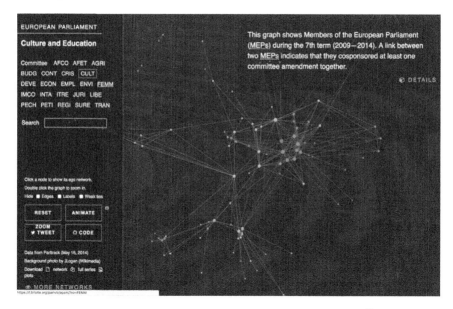

Figure 10.17. *Networks of influence among European MEPs[19]. For a color version of this figure, see www.iste.co.uk/saleh/challenges.zip*

17 Link to documentation API: https://www.diigo.com/api_dev.
18 Link to European parliament procedure observation API: http://parltrack.euwiki.org/.
19 Link to ParlViz application: https://f.briatte.org/parlviz/epam/?co=FEMM.

Dimensions	Level	Number of elements	Complexity
Physicality	1	1	1
	2	837	1,674
	3	11,816	35,448
	3	**12,654**	**37,123**
Actor	1	792	792
	1	**792**	**792**
Concept	1	1	1
	2	7	14
	3	40	120
	3	**48**	**135**

con't overleaf

Dimensions	Level			Number of elements			Complexity	
	No. of relations	**No. of sources**	**Type of source**	**No. of destinations**	**Type of destination**	**No. of predicates**	**Type of predicate**	**Complexity**
	1,330	132	actor	779	physicality	1	relation	**2,242**
	13	13	actor	8	actor	1	relation	**35**
	17,323	636	actor	547	relation	1	relation	**18,507**
Relation	756	9	actor	3	concept	28	physicality	**796**
	13	13	relation	3	concept	1	relation	**30**
	2	2	concept	1	physicality	1	relation	**6**
	17	5	concept	9	relation	1	relation	**32**
	7	7	concept	2	concept	1	relation	**17**
	19,461	**817**		**1,352**		**35**		**21,665**
		1		19,461			21,665	
TOTAL		8		32,955			59,715	

Table 10.5. *Complexity of the parliamentary process. Continued from previous page*

Using ParlTrack, we have developed an algorithm to collect, categorize and store information concerning European parliamentary debates for civil law on robotics, referenced by case no. 2015/2103(INL). This algorithm[20] uses the JSON file[21] supplied by the ParlTrack platform as a source to record information in a database dedicated to the modeling of ecosystems of knowledge. We have constructed the algorithm using the information architecture proposed by ParlTrack, developing three main importation procedures for activities, amendments and votes. For each of these procedures, we have created corresponding documents, actors, concepts and relations. This structured data serves as a basis for the automatic calculation of the complexity of the ecosystem, which we have summarized in Table 10.5.

Through this example of the automatic transformation of raw data, we have attempted to show that it is possible to model a highly complex ecosystem in order to evaluate its complexity. It now remains to develop tools that will enable us to easily explore this complexity and enrich it even further via the exchange of free and open resources.

10.5. Conclusion

This research is a first stage in the work of analyzing the ethics of ecosystems of the Internet of Things by modeling the power to act of these objects. We have specified the theoretical principles and graphic rules we have applied, using the ecosystem of Chromecast as an example. In this way, we have shown how to automatically collect a corpus of raw data and then transform it to enrich the ecosystem and calculate its power to act. It now remains for us to implement collective intelligence procedures to assess the ethics of this power to act.

To continue this research, we exploit the database we have created to enrich it by analyzing the documents it contains. For now, our modeling has to do with the structuring of raw data but not its content. It is now advisable to analyze, in the texts supplied by the various commissions, what stems from each existential dimension. For example, it would be of great interest to

---

20 Link to algorithm's PHP code: https://github.com/samszo/jardindesconnaissances/blob/ master/library/Flux/Eu.php#L81.

21 Link to JSON file: http://parltrack.euwiki.org/dossier/2015/2103(INL)?format=json.

know which elements come together or diverge in the 4,941 opinions that compose the 806 amendments of the debate.

Another point on which progress is yet to be made has to do with the automation of the representation of the model. Using a JavaScript library such as D3.js[22], we intend to automatically construct a diagram based on a selection of data in order to provide analysts with a basic model they could then develop according to the point of view they wish to defend. This automatic modeling would also make it possible to show the historic evolutions of relations according to the temporality of their instantiations. With these early models, our objective is to be able to standardize other models and thus achieve a modeling of the ecosystem of the Internet of Things in which different points of view will be represented and dynamically comparable to one another.

Using these tools of exploration and enrichment of the ecosystems of the Internet of Things, we are able to consider the question of the guidance of these ecosystems via collective interpretation games in which the intelligence of each player participates in the development of an ethics via assessment of the ecosystem's power to act and how this power is increased or reduced to that of the participants. The diagram shows these challenges by integrating into the data modeling algorithm (see Figure 10.18), a new retroactive loop making it possible to construct ethical models and simple diagrams that would be the result of collaborative, progressive work able to impact the ecosystem at its source.

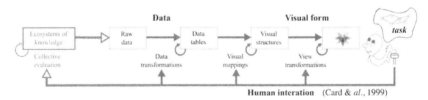

Figure 10.18. *Collective interpretation algorithm for ethical modeling. For a color version of this figure, see www.iste.co.uk/saleh/challenges.zip*

---

22 Link to the library website: https://d3js.org/.

10.6. References

[ABR 14] ABRAMI G., AMALRIC M., AMBLARD F. *et al.*, Modélisation multi-Agents appliquée aux Phénomènes Spatialisés, PhD thesis, 2014 UMR G-EAu, available at: https://halshs.archives-ouvertes.fr/cel-010906312014, 2014.

[ALO 17] ALOUACHE L., NGUYEN N., ALIOUAT M. *et al.*, "Nouveau protocole robuste pour les communications dans l'IoV", *Internet des objets*, no. 1. doi: 10.21494/ISTE.OP.2017.0139, 2017.

[AMB 06] AMBLARD F., PHAN D., *Modélisation et Simulation Multi-agents: Applications pour les Sciences de l'Homme et de la Société*, Hermes Science-Lavoisier, Paris, 2006.

[AND 16] ANDRO M., Digital libraries and crowdsourcing, PhD thesis, Université Paris 8 Vincennes Saint-Denis, available at: https://hal.archives-ouvertes.fr/tel-01384692, 2016.

[BAC 07] BACHIMONT B., *Ingénierie des connaissances et des contenus: le numérique entre ontologies et documents*, Hermes Science-Lavoisier, Paris, 2007.

[BAC 11] BACHIMONT B., GANDON F., POUPEAU G. *et al.*, "Enjeux et technologies: des données au sens", *Documentaliste-Sciences de l'Information*, vol. 48, no. 4, pp. 24–41, doi:10.3917/docsi.484.0024, 2011.

[BEA 16] BEAUGUITTE L., *L'analyse de réseaux en sciences sociales et en histoire*, Presses Universitaires de Louvain, available at: https://halshs.archives-ouvertes.fr/halshs-01476090/document, 2016.

[BER 09] BERQUE A., *Ecoumène: Introduction à l'étude des milieux humains*, Belin, Paris, 2009.

[BER 10] BERQUE A., *Milieu et identité humaine: notes pour un dépassement de la modernité*, Editions donner lieu, 2010.

[BOU 16] BOUHAÏ N., HACHOUR H., SALEH I., *Frontières numériques et artéfacts*, L'Harmattan, Paris, 2016.

[BRI 16] BRIATTE F., "Network patterns of legislative collaboration in twenty parliaments", *Network Science*, vol. 4, no. 2, pp. 266–271. doi: 10.1017/nws.2015.31, 2016.

[BRU 17] BRUN G., "Pouvoir d'agir, en analyse de l'activité", *Activités* vol. 14, no. 1, doi: 10.4000/activites.2957, 2017.

[CAR 99] CARD S.K., MACKINLAY J.D., SHNEIDERMAN B. (eds), *Readings in Information Visualization*, Morgan Kaufmann, 1999.

[CHE 04] CHEN H., PERICH F., FININ T. *et al.*, "SOUPA: standard ontology for ubiquitous and pervasive applications", *The First Annual International Conference on Mobile and Ubiquitous Systems: Networking and Services*, pp. 258–67. doi: 10.1109/MOBIQ.2004.1331732, 2004.

[COL 16] COLLOC J., "L'éthique des systèmes d'information autonomes vers une pensée artificielle", *Les Cahiers du numérique*, vol. 12, nos 1–2, pp. 187–212, 2016.

[COU 17] COUTAZ J., CROWLEY J.L., "Evaluation of programmable domestic eco-systems: 'Living in it' as an experimental method", *29ème conférence francophone sur l'Interaction Homme-Machine*, pp. 157–168, doi: 10.1145/3132129.3132138, Poitiers, France, August–September 2017.

[DEB 13] DEBRAY R., *Éloge des frontières*, Folio, Paris, 2013.

[DEL 80] DELEUZE G., Spinoza – Des vitesses de la pensée, La voix de Gilles Deleuze, Article, available at: http://www.univ-paris8.fr/deleuze/article.php3?id_article=91, 1980.

[DES 05] DESCOLA P., *Par-delà nature et culture*, NRF, Gallimard, Paris, 2005.

[ECO 94] ECO U., *Les limites de l'interprétation*, Le Livre de Poche, Paris, 1994.

[GAN 08] GANDON F., Graphes RDF et leur Manipulation pour la Gestion de Connaissances, PhD thesis, University of Nice – Sophia, Antipolis, available at: http://www-sop.inria.fr/members/Fabien.Gandon/docs/HDR_Fabien_Gandon.html, 2008.

[GHE 12] GHERNAOUTI-HELIE S., DUFOUR A., *Internet*, PuF, 2012.

[JUA 16] JUANALS B., MINEL J. L. "La construction d'un espace patrimonial partagé dans le Web de données ouvert", *Communication. Information médias théories pratiques*, vol. 34, no. 1, available at: https://communication.revues.org/6650, 2016.

[LAT 12] LATOUR B., *Enquêtes sur les modes d'existence: Une anthropologie des Modernes*, La Découverte, Paris, 2012.

[LAT 15] LATOUR B., *Face à Gaïa*, La Découverte, Paris, 2015.

[LEM 99] LE MOIGNE J.-L., *La modélisation des systèmes complexes*, Dunod, Paris, 1999.

[LET 16] LETRICOT R., CUXAC M., UZCATEGUI M. *et al.*, *Le Réseau: usages d'une notion polysémique en sciences humaines et sociales*, Presses universitaires de Louvain, Louvain-La-Neuve, 2016.

[LEV 11] LEVY P., *La sphère sémantique. Tome 1: computation, cognition, économie de l'information*, Hermes Science-Lavoisier, 2011.

[MOR 81] MORIN E., *La méthode: Tome 1*, Le Seuil, Paris, 1981.

[MOR 06] MORIN E., *La méthode: Tome 6*, Le Seuil, Paris, 2006.

[MUG 09] MUGUR-SCHÄCHTER M., *L'infra-mécanique quantique : Une révolution épistémologique révélée dans les descriptions de microétats*, Dianoia, 2009.

[NOY 17] NOYER J.-M., "L'Internet des Objets, l'Internet of 'Everything' quelques remarques sur l'intensification du plissement numérique du monde", *Internet des objets*, no. 1. doi: 10.21494/ISTE.OP.2017.0134, 2017.

[OMO 14] OMODEI E., Modeling the socio-semantic dynamics of scientific communities, PhD thesis, Ecole normale supérieure – ENS Paris, available at: https://tel.archives-ouvertes.fr/tel-01097702/document, 2014.

[PEI 68] PEIRCE C.S., "Some consequences of four incapacities", *Journal of Speculative Philosophy*, vol. 2, pp. 140–57, 1868.

[RAB 05] RABARDEL P., "Instrument subjectif et développement du pouvoir d'agir", in RABARDEL P., PASTRE P. (eds.), *Modèles du sujet pour la conception: dialectiques, activités, développement*, Octarès éditions, Toulouse, 2005.

[RAS 08] RASTIER F., "Sémantique du web vs semantic web ?", *Texto!*, vol. 18, no. 3, available at: http://www.revue-texto.net/index.php?id=1729, 2008.

[SAL 14] SALEH I., BOUHAI N., HACHOUR H., *Les frontières du numérique*, Editions L'Harmattan, Paris, 2014.

[SAL 17] SALEH I., "Les enjeux et les défis de l'Internet des Objets (IdO)", *Internet des objets*, no. 1. doi: 10.21494/ISTE.OP.2017.0133, 2017.

[SZO 15a] SZONIECKY S., "Interpréter la voix de Deleuze. Exemple de jardinage des connaissances", in BERT J.-L., RATCLIFF M. (eds), *Frontières d'archives Recherches, mémoires, savoirs*, Editions des archives contemporaines, Paris, 2015.

[SZO 15b] SZONIECKY S., LOUAPRE M., "Outillages numériques pour les humanités : cartographier des réseaux d'influences", *ISKO – Magreb 2015*, Hammamet, Tunisia, 2015.

[SZO 17] SZONIECKY S., BOUHAÏ N., (eds), *Collective Intelligence and Digital Archives: Towards Knowledge Ecosystems*, ISTE Ltd, London and John Wiley & Sons, New York, 2017.

[SZO 18] SZONIECKY S., *Ecosystems Knowledge: Modeling and Analysis Method for Information and Communication*, ISTE Ltd, London and John Wiley & Sons, New York, 2018.

[THI 06] THIEVRE J., Cartographies pour la Recherche et l'Exploration de données Documentaires, PhD thesis, Montpellier II University, 2006.

[THI 17] THIBAULT S., "Prétopologie et espaces habités, Revue électronique des sciences humaines et sociales", Article, EspaceTemps.net, available at: https://www.espacestemps.net/articles/pretopologie-espaces-habites/, 2017.

[VIN 11] VINCENT J., PORQUET C., BORSALI M. *et al.*, "Privacy protection for smartphones: an ontology-based firewall", *5th Workshop on Information Security Theory and Practices (WISTP)*, Heraklion, doi: 10.1007/978-3-642-21040-2_27, June 2011.

[YAN 17] YANG J., GELLER B., ARBI T., "Récepteur Multi-normes pour les Réseaux de Capteurs de l'IoT médical", *Internet des objets*, no. 1. doi: 10.21494/ISTE.OP.2017.0136, 2017.

[ZAC 05] ZACKLAD M., "Vers le Web Socio Sémantique : introduction aux ontologies sémiotiques", *Soumis à la conférence Ingénerie des connaissances, Nice*, available at: https://archivesic.ccsd.cnrs.fr/sic_00001347, 2005.

List of Authors

Makhlouf ALIOUAT
Laboratoire Réseaux et Systèmes
Distribuées
Setif University
Algeria

Lylia ALOUACHE
Laboratoire Quartz
ComUE Paris Seine, EISTI
France

Mehdi AMMI
LIMSI – CNRS
Paris-Sud University
Orsay
France

Hamdi AMROUN
LIMSI – CNRS
Paris-Sud University
Orsay
France

Margarita ANASTASSOVA
CEA – LIST
University of Paris-Saclay
France

Tarak ARBI
Laboratoire U2IS
ENSTA ParisTech
France

Maxence BOBIN
LIMSI – CNRS
University of Paris-Saclay
France

Stan BORKOWSKI
Grenoble Alpes University
Inria, CNRS,
Grenoble INP, LIG
France

Mehdi BOUKALLEL
CEA – LIST
University of Paris-Saclay
France

Rachid CHELOUAH
Laboratoire Quartz
ComUE Paris Seine, EISTI
France

Sabine COQUILLART
Grenoble Alpes University
Inria, CNRS,
Grenoble INP, LIG,
France

Sébastien CROUZY
Grenoble Alpes University
Inria, CNRS,
Grenoble INP, LIG,
France

Réjane DALCÉ
IRIT
INU Champollion
Toulouse
France

Georges GAGNERÉ
Laboratoire EA1673
Paris 8 University
France

Benoit GELLER
Laboratoire U2IS
ENSTA ParisTech
France

Brigitte JUANALS
Laboratoire AMU
Aix-Marseille University
France

Nga NGUYEN
Laboratoire Quartz
ComUE Paris Seine, EISTI
France

Cédric PLESSIET
INREV
Paris 8 University
France

Imad SALEH
Laboratoire Paragraphe
Paris 8 University
and
Cergy-Pontoise University
France

Rémy SOHIER
INREV
Paris 8 University
France

Samuel SZONIECKY
Laboratoire Paragraphe
Paris 8 University
and
Cergy-Pontoise University
France

M'Hamed (Hamy) TEMKIT
Mayo Clinic
Division of Health Sciences
Research
USA

Thierry VAL
IRIT
University of Toulouse
France

Adrien VAN DEN BOSSCHE
IRIT
University of Toulouse
France

Index

Other titles from

in

Information Systems, Web and Pervasive Computing

2018

ARDUIN Pierre-Emmanuel
Insider Threats
(Advances in Information Systems Set – Volume 10)

CHAMOUX Jean-Pierre
The Digital Era 1: Big Data Stakes

CARMÈS Maryse
Digital Organizations Manufacturing: Scripts, Performativity and
Semiopolitics
(Intellectual Technologies Set – Volume 5)

DOUAY Nicolas
Urban Planning in the Digital Age
(Intellectual Technologies Set – Volume 6)

FABRE Renaud, BENSOUSSAN Alain
The Digital Factory for Knowledge: Production and Validation of Scientific
Results

GAUDIN Thierry, LACROIX Dominique, MAUREL Marie-Christine, POMEROL
Jean-Charles
Life Sciences, Information Sciences

GAYARD Laurent
Darknet: Geopolitics and Uses
(Computing and Connected Society Set – Volume 2)

IAFRATE Fernando
Artificial Intelligence and Big Data: The Birth of a New Intelligence
(Advances in Information Systems Set – Volume 8)

LE DEUFF Olivier
Digital Humanities: History and Development
(Intellectual Technologies Set – Volume 4)

MANDRAN Nadine
Traceable Human Experiment Design Research: Theoretical Model and
Practical Guide
(Advances in Information Systems Set – Volume 9)

PIVERT Olivier
NoSQL Data Models: Trends and Challenges

ROCHET Claude
Smart Cities: Reality or Fiction

SEDKAOUI Soraya
Data Analytics and Big Data

SZONIECKY Samuel
Ecosystems Knowledge: Modeling and Analysis Method for Information and
Communication
(Digital Tools and Uses Set – Volume 6)

2017

BOUHAÏ Nasreddine, SALEH Imad
Internet of Things: Evolutions and Innovations
(Digital Tools and Uses Set – Volume 4)

DUONG Véronique
Baidu SEO: Challenges and Intricacies of Marketing in China

LESAS Anne-Marie, MIRANDA Serge
The Art and Science of NFC Programming
(Intellectual Technologies Set – Volume 3)

LIEM André
Prospective Ergonomics
(Human-Machine Interaction Set – Volume 4)

MARSAULT Xavier
Eco-generative Design for Early Stages of Architecture
(Architecture and Computer Science Set – Volume 1)

REYES-GARCIA Everardo
The Image-Interface: Graphical Supports for Visual Information
(Digital Tools and Uses Set – Volume 3)

REYES-GARCIA Everardo, BOUHAÏ Nasreddine
Designing Interactive Hypermedia Systems
(Digital Tools and Uses Set – Volume 2)

SAÏD Karim, BAHRI KORBI Fadia
Asymmetric Alliances and Information Systems:Issues and Prospects
(Advances in Information Systems Set – Volume 7)

SZONIECKY Samuel, BOUHAÏ Nasreddine
Collective Intelligence and Digital Archives: Towards Knowledge Ecosystems
(Digital Tools and Uses Set – Volume 1)

2016

BEN CHOUIKHA Mona
Organizational Design for Knowledge Management

BERTOLO David
Interactions on Digital Tablets in the Context of 3D Geometry Learning
(Human-Machine Interaction Set – Volume 2)

BOUVARD Patricia, SUZANNE Hervé
Collective Intelligence Development in Business

2015

ARDUIN Pierre-Emmanuel, GRUNDSTEIN Michel, ROSENTHAL-SABROUX Camille
Information and Knowledge System
(Advances in Information Systems Set – Volume 2)

BÉRANGER Jérôme
Medical Information Systems Ethics

BRONNER Gérald
Belief and Misbelief Asymmetry on the Internet

IAFRATE Fernando
From Big Data to Smart Data
(Advances in Information Systems Set – Volume 1)

KRICHEN Saoussen, BEN JOUIDA Sihem
Supply Chain Management and its Applications in Computer Science

NEGRE Elsa
Information and Recommender Systems
(Advances in Information Systems Set – Volume 4)

POMEROL Jean-Charles, EPELBOIN Yves, THOURY Claire
MOOCs

SALLES Maryse
Decision-Making and the Information System
(Advances in Information Systems Set – Volume 3)

SAMARA Tarek
ERP and Information Systems: Integration or Disintegration
(Advances in Information Systems Set – Volume 5)

2014

DINET Jérôme
Information Retrieval in Digital Environments

HÉNO Raphaële, CHANDELIER Laure
3D Modeling of Buildings: Outstanding Sites

KEMBELLEC Gérald, CHARTRON Ghislaine, SALEH Imad
Recommender Systems

MATHIAN Hélène, SANDERS Lena
Spatio-temporal Approaches: Geographic Objects and Change Process

PLANTIN Jean-Christophe
Participatory Mapping

VENTRE Daniel
Chinese Cybersecurity and Defense

2013

BERNIK Igor
Cybercrime and Cyberwarfare

CAPET Philippe, DELAVALLADE Thomas
Information Evaluation

LEBRATY Jean-Fabrice, LOBRE-LEBRATY Katia
Crowdsourcing: One Step Beyond

SALLABERRY Christian
Geographical Information Retrieval in Textual Corpora

2012

BUCHER Bénédicte, LE BER Florence
Innovative Software Development in GIS

GAUSSIER Eric, YVON François
Textual Information Access

STOCKINGER Peter
Audiovisual Archives: Digital Text and Discourse Analysis

VENTRE Daniel
Cyber Conflict

2011

BANOS Arnaud, THÉVENIN Thomas
Geographical Information and Urban Transport Systems

DAUPHINÉ André
Fractal Geography

LEMBERGER Pirmin, MOREL Mederic
Managing Complexity of Information Systems

STOCKINGER Peter
Introduction to Audiovisual Archives

STOCKINGER Peter
Digital Audiovisual Archives

VENTRE Daniel
Cyberwar and Information Warfare

2010

BONNET Pierre
Enterprise Data Governance

BRUNET Roger
Sustainable Geography

CARREGA Pierre
Geographical Information and Climatology

CAUVIN Colette, ESCOBAR Francisco, SERRADJ Aziz
Thematic Cartography – 3-volume series
Thematic Cartography and Transformations – Volume 1
Cartography and the Impact of the Quantitative Revolution – Volume 2
New Approaches in Thematic Cartography – Volume 3

LANGLOIS Patrice
Simulation of Complex Systems in GIS

MATHIS Philippe
Graphs and Networks – 2nd edition

THERIAULT Marius, DES ROSIERS François
Modeling Urban Dynamics

2009

BONNET Pierre, DETAVERNIER Jean-Michel, VAUQUIER Dominique
Sustainable IT Architecture: the Progressive Way of Overhauling Information Systems with SOA

PAPY Fabrice
Information Science

RIVARD François, ABOU HARB Georges, MERET Philippe
The Transverse Information System

ROCHE Stéphane, CARON Claude
Organizational Facets of GIS

2008

BRUGNOT Gérard
Spatial Management of Risks

FINKE Gerd
Operations Research and Networks

GUERMOND Yves
Modeling Process in Geography

KANEVSKI Michael
Advanced Mapping of Environmental Data

MANOUVRIER Bernard, LAURENT Ménard
Application Integration: EAI, B2B, BPM and SOA

PAPY Fabrice
Digital Libraries

2007

DOBESCH Hartwig, DUMOLARD Pierre, DYRAS Izabela
Spatial Interpolation for Climate Data

SANDERS Lena
Models in Spatial Analysis

2006

CLIQUET Gérard
Geomarketing

CORNIOU Jean-Pierre
Looking Back and Going Forward in IT

DEVILLERS Rodolphe, JEANSOULIN Robert
Fundamentals of Spatial Data Quality

Printed and bound by CPI Group (UK) Ltd, Croydon, CR0 4YY